Number Twenty-one:
The Centennial Series of
the Association of Former Students,
Texas A&M University

THIS I CAN LEAVE YOU

This I Can Leave You

A WOMAN'S DAYS ON THE PITCHFORK RANCH

By

Mamie Sypert Burns

Foreword by

David Murrah

TEXAS A&M UNIVERSITY PRESS

COLLEGE STATION

Library of Congress Cataloging-in-Publication Data

Burns, Mamie Sypert, 1896–1982.
  This I can leave you.

  (The Centennial series of the Association of
Former Students, Texas A&M University ; no 21)
  Includes index.
    1. Burns, Mamie Sypert, 1896–1982.   2. Pitchfork,
Ranch (Tex.)   3. Ranchers' wives—Texas—Biography.
4. Ranch life—Texas—History—20th century.   5. Texas—
Social life and customs.   I. Title.   II. Series.
F394.P53B87   1986   976.4'06'0924   86-5933
ISBN 0-89096-286-3

Manufactured in the United States of America
FIRST EDITION

Dedicated to
the Grands, Anne and Burns,
and
in simple tribute to
the Pitchfork Outfit

The Forks Forever

Some folks 'll try to tell ya
That th' West is fully tamed;
That th' broncs is all ben busted,
And th' final maverick claimed.

They say th' last bold rustler
Has ben sent to Kingdom Come,
But we know, down on th' Pitchfork,
There' still them as rustles some.

Ever' now an' then a waddy
Gets hisself all busted up
'Cause he's ben convinced a bronco
Is as gentle as a pup.

We still look out sharp fer rattlers,
An' th' songs some uf 'em sing
Make ya think they've ben Pitchforkin'
Since Dan Gardner waz th' King.

Some ol' dudes come out to tell us
Thet cow herdin's whut they crave,
But an hour in th' saddle
Always proves they ain't so brave.

Yessir, ranch life's kinda rugged,
Even in these modern days;
And you'd think we'd gladly trade it off
Fer city life 'n ways.

But we'll all be at the Pitchfork,
Jist as shore as you were born
'Til we trade our saddle leather
Fer a toot on Gabriel's horn.

Author unknown

Contents

List of Illustrations

Foreword

Mamie Burns's experience—reigning as First Lady of a vast West Texas ranch—was a dream come true. For twenty-three years, she was in charge of the Big House, making a home for her manager-husband and her grandchildren, entertaining distinguished visitors, and adding her own special charm to the historic Pitchfork Ranch. Her story begins with her account of how she and D Burns came to the Pitchfork and of her first meeting with the Williams family of Saint Louis, owners of the ranch. As her anecdotes show, she views those first, hectic wartime years through romantic eyes, for she was a true romantic, a lovely, gracious lady who appreciated the simple beauties of West Texas and the tender moments of life.

Her story also gives us an intimate glimpse of D Burns, her husband of fifty-three years. Known to most only as D, the Pitchfork manager became legendary because of his hard work, his loyalty to his employers, and his expectations of hard work and loyalty from those he supervised. One of West Texas' finest individuals, D Burns served as manager of the Pitchfork Ranch from 1942 until 1965. Following his retirement at age seventy, he served the ranch as an active director until his death in 1977.

It was not until 1976 that I became well acquainted with D and Mamie Burns. D had always had an interest in history, and, as the Pitchfork approached its centennial year, he sought someone to write the ranch's history. To my delight, he chose me. Later that year, I drove Mamie the eighty miles from Lubbock to the ranch to attend a cowboy reunion. She had with her in the car a black notebook, and during the three-hour round-trip, she introduced me to her stories.

The first one she read was about the Hefflebower dance; it was a well-written, delightfully funny story. I was amazed to learn that she had written hundreds of pages of such accounts. Like Emily Dickinson, she recorded observations on any piece of scrap paper available, capturing a special saying, a funny event, a family memory.

I certainly was not the first to discover this aspiring author. She had labored over her stories for many years and had drawn upon the expertise of practically every experienced writer in the Lubbock area. Those who helped her critique her writing knew that she frequently made use of literary license. In fact, her stories were a point of contention with D, who once threw one in the fireplace with the exclamation, "Do you want to get me fired?" In her introduction Mamie recalls D's frequent expressions of chagrin. When anyone would ask her if her stories told the truth, D would interrupt to say, "And a whole lot more!" While they are romanticized, Mamie's reminiscences describe real people and therefore make an important contribution to West Texas literature.

The Burnses moved from town to the country at a time when most Americans were doing the opposite. America's entry into World War II made days on an isolated ranch an even more out-of-the-ordinary experience. Although Mamie's romantic nature allowed her to give us only the positive side, she also lived with hot, dry summers, power failures, loneliness, and, for a couple of years, downright unfriendliness. Although she grew up in Texas, it was East Texas. Her refined East Texas ways made her seem different in the eyes of the 1942 ranch folk, and they were slow to accept her. In fact, the Burnses' first Christmas was much harder on her than she admits in her story about it. An unhappy employee, pased over for promotion prior to the Burnses' arrival on the ranch, aggravated the situation. But toward the end of the war, as manpower shortages ended, D was able to build a loyal work force, and life on the Pitchfork became the lovely adventure she had dreamed it would be.

One should visit the Pitchfork country in order to place Mamie's stories in proper perspective. Located in the heart of the Rolling Plains of West Texas, the big ranch covers a fourteen-by-twenty-mile block in Dickens and King counties. Its gentle hills and sheltered river valley make it ideal for a cow and calf operation. Although the ranch was easily reached by highway—U.S. 82 splits the Pitchfork in half—its isolation from towns was magnified by wartime restrictions. The nearest towns were mere villages; Guthrie was thirteen miles to the east, Dickens seventeen to the west. Their combined populations numbered less than six hundred. Lubbock, the nearest trade center, was a two-hour drive. Phone service was primitive at its best. There were plenty of people on the ranch, but those with families lived in the ranch's "camps," all located several miles from headquarters. Most of the cowboys who lived in the bunkhouse were single. For day-to-day company Mamie had the chuck-house cook, her own family, and her servants.

And most of her servants did not last very long. Meticulous to a fault, she expected untrained black West Texans to assume overnight the serving skills of New England butlers and maids. Several of her stories illustrate the sometimes comic results of her unrealistic expectations of her household help.

After D's death in 1977, Mamie seemed to live for her stories. Although her friends begged her to surrender them for publication, she continued to work on them as long as her health would permit. In 1982, within weeks of turning them over to her favorite group, the Ranching Heritage Association, she died, at age eighty-seven. But, thanks to her love of life and her habit of expressing that zest on paper, she left for us a wonderful account of that romance, with the loves of her life—her husband, D Burns, her two grandchildren, and the Pitchfork Ranch.

David Murrah

Preface

These stories are Mamie Burns's legacy to her grandchildren (the Grands), to the people past, present, and future who have made and will make good hands on the Pitchfork Ranch, and to those unfortunates who never have lived on a ranch. These are Mamie's words, thoughts, and views. These are the memories of almost a quarter-century on the Pitchfork Ranch during the years of war and years of rapid growth of the ranch under D Burns's skillful guidance. Through her memories you will come to know Mamie Burns along with a host of other Pitchfork hands.

The Pitchfork has long been known for its working cowboys riding gray quarter horses and for Hereford cattle wearing the distinctive Pitchfork brand, itself much older than the ranch. It was D Burns who began breeding the gray quarter horses in 1946 when he bought Joe Bailey's King from the 6666 Ranch.

The operation began in 1881 when Daniel Baldwin Gardner and another man bought 80,000 acres of land, including what was then and is now headquarters, and cattle wearing the Pitchfork brand. In 1882 Gardner's partner withdrew, and Eugene F. Williams of Saint Louis, Missouri, put money into the ranch. In 1883 it was incorporated as the Pitchfork Land and Cattle Company. Williams remained the financial backer and Gardner the manager. William F. Williams III, the founder Williams's grandson, today serves as chairman of the board of seven directors.

Following Gardner's death in 1928, O. A. Redmud Lambert served as interim manager until Virgil V. Parr was selected in 1931. Rudolph Swenson became manager in 1940 but was killed in an auto-train accident in 1942. D Burns managed the ranch from 1942 until 1965. When D left the ranch, the young man D had taken on as an assistant manager some eighteen years earlier assumed the manager's job. D said of Jim Humphreys, "I've been grooming him for the job from the first month he came. That's the reason we hired him, and it will be no compliment to me if he doesn't make a good one. He's the best-liked, the most interested, the most conscientious and capable young man to my way of thinking in the livestock business in this state." And Mamie added, "And like Armando, he throws in a *pilón* of kindness, consideration, the sweetness of a great and gentle nature, politeness, and perfect honesty." After twenty years as manager Jim Humphreys is training his assistant manager Bob Moorhouse to step into his boots.

By the time of the Pitchfork's 100th birthday in 1983, the ranch had more than doubled its Texas acreage to 165,000 acres and added a 35,000-acre steer ranch in Wyoming and a 4,000-acre summer pasture in Kansas.

Mamie's notes reveal that she used "some literary license in telling certain of the incidents, used a few fictitious names, too, but in the main my stories are true. Three of the characters are products of my imagination, and yet no character is wholly fictitious. Names have been changed to protect the guilty. I have simply tried to tell the things as they happened, attempting to give you an idea of what goes on when a bunch of men and boys work and live together on a ranch infested with women."

She goes on to say, "I would scant no detail of our life there on the ranch, and most particularly I want nothing to obscure D's part in this cast of characters. He is my hero and the star of the production. Every once in awhile, his distinctive voice rings out memorably, 'God a'mighty, Mayme!' The summons might come during a wild search for a bit of equipment, his hat, or his spurs which 'were right here on this bed a minute ago.' Or perhaps as a challenge to my driving when he was an unwilling passenger returning home from his gallstone operation."

Later Mamie informs us, "This volume is in no sense a biography of Mamie and D Burns. It might be called 'a record of our lives on the Pitchfork Ranch' or 'a quarter-century on the Pitchfork.' Assembling these stories has been the pinning down, once and for all, of the great experience of our lives, living on the Forks." The title she chose reflects her view of the record of life there as a legacy for her grandchildren.

As a crown to her ranching years, in 1981 Mamie was honored by the Western Heritage Center, Hereford, Texas, when she was inducted into its National Cowgirl Hall of Fame. The tribute said:

"The National Cowgirl Hall of Fame and Western Heritage Center is honoring Mamie for the life that she has led in the West. Her background and training led her to have the courage and determination to bring a lifestyle to the Pitchfork that gave it new dimension and notoriety."

To aid in identifying some of the characters who are not given fictitious names, the editor offers here a bit of help:

Douglas Burns, better known as D and the other half of Mamie; known as Baba to the Grands.

Frances is Mamie's only child, married, and the mother of—

Anne (often called Cuppie because of her love of cupcakes when she was a child) and—

Burns, the two Grands who were raised by Mamie and D.

Willie or Aunt Willie is Mamie's younger sister and the mother of—

Anne McGuire, who rode for the ranch in the Stamford Cowboy Reunion story.

Dickie Austin is the son of the Austins, who were the cooks for the chuck house.

Dugan Adams, another playmate of the Grands, is the daughter of ranch hand Harve Adams.

Any other characters, fictitious or otherwise, are sufficiently identified in the stories.

Since the day Mamie began her notes and journals for "The Book," as she called it, Mamie wanted to have it published. However, for several reasons this was not possible. A few months before she died in 1982, Mamie gave her manuscripts, notes, and journals to the Ranching Heritage Association in Lubbock, Texas, confident that at last her wish would be fulfilled. It is our hope that Mamie reached the Pearly Gates she chose so long ago and looks down on us from there, joyful with all of us who have had the pleasure of working with her stories and with all of those who will laugh and cry with the reading of Mamie's legacy.

Mrs. Cathryn Buesseler
Volume Editor for the Ranching Heritage Association, Lubbock

Mamie's Introduction

I've always thought when I break my leg I'm going to write a book. At first, of course, I'd write from my bed, the sweet old four-poster that Mother Burns had given us. I'd use that lovely wicker tray with the paper racks at either end. Its soft ivory color would be perfect with old rose bed jackets. I'd wear the gray chiffon when callers came. Then, when I was stronger, I'd move to the chaise, pulled up by the window. The Whig-rose coverlet that Grandmother Shelton wove in 1824 would be across my knees. Perhaps I'd write pen portraits, brittle and delicately humorous.

But, on a ranch if one breaks a leg, they shoot you. And we'd been on the Pitchfork for five years when Dan Casement said, "Mamie, you must write a book."

D brought a bunch of men home from a Cattle Raiser's Association meeting, among them Jack Turner, Dan Casement, R. J. Kenzer, and Dan Thornton. Dan Casement was one of the Pitchfork's most charming guests. Many we have enjoyed greatly; some we can never forget for one reason or another. As long as I live I shall remember Mr. Casement's hilarious, salty stories told with a Princetonian flavor. He was highly articulate. Without our quite realizing what was taking place, he had, with tact and finesse, drawn from D and me several stories of ranch happenings and of how one manages a ranch like the Pitchfork with less than half enough help.

He turned to me and said, "Mamie, are you keeping a record of these incidents?"

"Heavens, no," I answered, "my personal correspondence drives me wild, besides I don't know how to write."

"Rubbish! Tell it like you talk. Do set these things down. You think now that you will remember them, but you won't."

"But I have no time. What would I write about?"

"Write about the things you know, those on which you are an authority."

How could a person with such a limited outlook as mine be an authority on anything? Well, it may be true, as D says, though I know little of mathematics and business, I should know everything about a woman's work on a ranch.

Mr. Casement continued, "You two are sharing a way of life that is vanishing, even in Texas. This is history that will never be repeated. When this war is over everything will be changed."

Mr. Casement's suggestion to write it all down took deep root in my mind, although there seemed little I could do about it at the time. I was too busy. I reached for my Levi's rather than a pencil, but the idea of "The Book" began with his enthusiasm. In the weeks that followed his visit, the notion of writing it all down returned constantly to my thoughts.

But how does one start a book? What should the first words be, the opening lines? Many friends said, "Tell where the Pitchfork Ranch is located."

Well, let's see, that shouldn't be too hard. The Pitchfork Ranch is in Texas, the big pasture part of the state in the short-grass country, two hundred miles south of Amarillo, eighty-three miles east of Lubbock, one hundred miles north of Abilene, and two hundred and forty-five miles due west of Neiman-Marcus.

I read it to D, but D, not given to flippancy, objected to the very first paragraph. Before I could say "one if by land," D had the floor. "If you are going to write about the Forks, let your first words be 'Dan Gardner.' He's the man who put the outfit together." So, if I should take D's advice, "The Book" would begin:

Daniel Balwin Gardner was born February 25, 1851, at Carrollton, Alabama. (But what a dull way to start a book!) His father was of English ancestry. In 1871 Dan Gardner and two friends, lured by adventure, traveled to Texas in wagons. He secured employment near Fort Griffin in Shackleford County. He worked on ranches in various ways long enough to fall in love with Texas and with the ranching business and to adopt it as his life's calling. He went "up the trail" to Colorado as an employee of Judge Lynch, a well-known rancher of that section. Later he accepted a job as a surveyor with the Land Department of the Texas and Pacific Railroad. During this time, Dan Gardner assisted in some important surveys made on the Brazos, Col-

orado, and Red rivers and on their tributaries. This gave him an opportunity to find and to study the best grazing areas in the Southwest.
When he decided to locate permanently, he picked a spot which later
comprised parts of Dickens and King counties, on the headwaters of
the Brazos and Red rivers, now the Pitchfork Ranch, known affectionately as the Forks.

The spirit of Dan Gardner will inevitably walk through these
pages, but Mr. Eugene Williams said, "Write about Dan Gardner
and D Burns. They are the two men who have done the most for the
Pitchfork." I started making inquiries of those who had known Mr.
Gardner and whose memories of the early days had been handed
down by word of mouth. I would scribble down every scrap of information, hoping some day to tack the fragments together. When
people who still remembered Mr. Gardner spoke of him, they
would always smile, and then they'd repeat some remark of his,
prefaced invariably with his, "I say, I say—".

Although D felt he had started my book, I did not. If I could
decide on those first few words, the rest would be easy. Words do
not flow from my pen; they stumble with great difficulty from my
stubby pencil, which always needs sharpening.

"Is it the ranch on a silver platter?" someone asked.

"Not exactly," I'd answer.

"Have you told the truth?"

"And a lot more," D would jump in before I could reply, "with
exaggeration and embellishment."

I finally made my own decision. I'm going to try to stick to
facts. But the total lack of understanding of my situation as a
would-be author seems contained in the deadly serious suggestion of
one little Englishwoman, who said, "Mrs. Burns, what you need to
do is assemble some notes." I wonder what she'd make of the tons of
material I've accumulated, the filing cabinets, the whole way of life
evolved in my effort to write "The Book."

I kept the glove compartment of my car and the pockets of
every coat stuffed with notebooks and pencils ready for the random
thought. The night table beside my bed had paper ready, a pencil
and scissors tied to my bedpost so night thoughts couldn't vanish.
There was writing equipment on the kitchen window above the

sink at the ranch house. Composition books were hooked on the trees behind the rock benches. A twine string with a pencil on one end, an eraser on the other, was the necklace I wore. I had to take notes surreptitiously because the boys would clam up at the sight of a pencil and paper. Often I'd have a notebook beside me on the car seat. Jolting along in the Jeep with D, I found it hard to write or think connectedly. Many times I have stopped the car when I was alone and clumsily made notes with a mittened hand. (The boys say that I didn't always stop the car all the way off the road!)

Now in 1973, facing the awesome task of organizing the accumulated bits and pieces of our twenty-five years into an orderly chronicle, I fight my tendency to dawdle and dream over each precious scrap of paper I pick up as memories come flooding back, as I remember when and where a particular note was made.

Many, particularly men, have said, "Give the history of the Pitchfork." I did not set out to write a history of the Pitchfork Ranch, nor a chronicle of the cowboy. At least, not a history as it comes down from books, but rather history as it lingers in the memories of old-timers: the Deatons, Uncle George Watson, Pee Wee, Ed Nolan, and scores of others who have lived and worked in this section and who recalled the stories told them by their elders. Frank Dobie and many others have written eloquently of the longhorns and the history of the cattle industry. This is a Texas story, but frankly it could have taken place anywhere. Anywhere on a ranch, that is. Ours has been an exciting, but not an historically important existence. My book is about the ranch people more than it is about the ranch's history, or its skunks and rattlesnakes. It is about those who lived here before us and those who have lived here with us. Forgive me for making it so personal. I would like to tell this without self-pity or self-approbation.

To write each page, I am drawing upon recollections and upon the notes taken through a quarter-century. When a friend of mine commented, "It is a leisurely book," my granddaughter Anne said, "It should be. It's been twenty-five years in the writing." All through the years, writing on "The Book" has been my hobby, my vocation, my lifesaver. I have worked on my notes at the ranch, at the cabin, in Wyoming, at Little House, and at The Trees.

When we moved into Lubbock from the Pitchfork in 1965 I thought, now at last I have the leisure that retirement and advancing years bring and I can get those stories together. But I soon discovered that my memory and concentration were not what they had been. The moment I pick up a pen my mind goes blotto. Luckily, during the first hectic decade on the ranch I somehow managed to write several complete stories, my best (while the iron was hot)—"Old Man Hinch," "The Big Jump," parts of "Jake and Slim and Others," and especially "The Forks, Now and Then." D said, "Don't ever publish those riproaring, ribald things." But everyone else shouted, "Print 'em without fail!"

Confronted with a ton of material—scraps of paper, file cards, a mass of trivia—I wish that I had dated more of them, that I had kept a tidier journal, but time was so precious, and I was so weary at the end of the day that I had barely the energy to jot down a few brief words to help me remember the incidents. I'd tuck the fragments into any drawer or pigeonhole around. Some I have found in hat boxes or suitcases, pockets of coats or in purses unused for months. Some pieces are meaningless now; others fall into place at once.

There were weeks, even months, when I had no time for a line in my narrative, but then I might pull from a smock pocket some soiled, folded bits of a paper napkin on which I had jotted conversation I'd heard at the chuck-house table, and I was off again. Now these yellowed and crumbling scraps recall that lively group of cowboys joking and hoo-hawing.

It is a strange experience reading entries in your own journal so many years after you have lived them. I did not realize when these notes were being made that they would give us so many moments to treasure. Whole segments of our lives would have vanished without my memory-joggers that bring back a person or a scene to D's recollection all these years after the event. My fragile, disintegrating bits of paper help us to recall small, tender, private things. Characters keep appearing whose very existence we had forgotten, yet there they are. We read these pages and recall the circumstances, the crisscross lines, at which our lives intersected theirs. Nothing in this jumble of memories and images that I find in these notes about

the people and our first experiences on the ranch surprise me now.
They show me how little I knew, how much I had to learn.

Mamie Burns

Lubbock, Texas
1973

THIS I CAN LEAVE YOU

1

The Pitchfork Ranch

"There she is, Mayme," D exclaimed as we topped I Spy Hill. We didn't know then that hill would be called I Spy or that one of the pleasant-looking, red-roofed houses that we could glimpse almost five miles away across Little Wichita Creek was going to be ours. We did know that it was the Pitchfork, one of Texas' largest ranches, and we were going there in high hopes that D would be the new manager, a job he had been wanting for twenty years. We were getting close to the ranch. D had assured me that I'd like the Williams brothers—"darned nice people." But would they like me? I simply had to say something silly to break the tension.

"You'd better be nice to me. You know, I could queer this thing. After all, they did say, didn't they, that the little woman had to be satisfactory? Believe I'll call Mr. Neiman and tell him I'll take that suit and those blue Staffordshire cups, and—"

"You've got the ax, baby," D laughed. "There's something a lot more important to me than these men hiring me for this job, and that's if my girl likes it." I knew and he knew that he'd hang me to the highest mesquite if any word or action of mine kept him from landing that job, but it listened good. That's the way he'd kept me happy, wearing the same old clothes year after year. "Isn't that a new suit, Mayme?" It always worked.

"Of course I'll like the ranch; I'll love it," I said.

The highway had carried us out of sight of the ranch buildings for several miles. We saw low-rolling hills. Cattle were grazing alongside the fence with their red coats gleaming in the bright sun. I must remember to tell Cuppy that Herefords wore red coats and white vests. "I think Herefords are the prettiest breed of cattle," I happily babbled to D. "I love their dark red—"

"I like the yellow ones better," D said. "Their hides are so mellow." (I never saw a yellow cow, I never hope to see one, my mind raced off giddily.) The whole concept of a mellow hide was new. I searched my mind for synonyms. I must give a thought to everything regarding cattle now, for if D got this job, I had much to learn.

The car almost stopped as D carefully looked over some cows. "There's two that want to go to town," he commented. I started to ask why, but instead turned around in my seat and craned back at the two tired-looking creatures. I wouldn't get D wild by starting out asking fool questions, but if ever two cows looked as if they belonged in the country, those two did to me. I know now that going to town with a cow means taking it to the slaughter house, but I wasn't reared on a ranch (though my father was a stock farmer), and a good many expressions of the cowman were still new to me. I had yet to learn that Arbuckle was coffee, a punk was a green hand, axle grease meant butter, son-of-a-gun was stew, and that a nipple—I wonder if you know what else a nipple is?

"I hate to ask you to give up that house, Mayme. I know how crazy you are about it, how hard you've worked to get it just the way you want it. You won't get in much bridge out here. It's a long way in the country. I'm afraid you'll be lonely."

"Why, D Burns, I've never been lonely in my life. I don't care about bridge as I used to, and as for the house, why, what's a house?" But the words stuck in my throat; I shut my eyes tightly and prayed—we were almost there—prayed that D could put over his deal, that I could be sport enough never to let him know just how much I did care about that house, and hoped he'd think the way my eyes were watering was caused by the early morning West Texas wind. Suddenly, a bluebird flew ahead of us, and then another, darting, circling, swirling. They were the unfailing sing of happiness; it was answer enough.

"Bluebirds, my dear," I called D's attention. "Congratulations on your new job. With such an omen of happiness, luck—"

"Ummm," from D, who added in a wistful tone, "I've always heard that a 'bird in the hand—'"

Of course, I wouldn't be lonely. D would be at home all the time. We'd sit under the trees and read books. At dusk, we'd—. Dusk was such a lovely time when D was home. I always hated to turn on the lights and shut it out. It would be such fun if we got this job. We'd ride together over the ranch on horseback, just like we had planned before we were married. I'd go everywhere he went. It wasn't our fault that those plans had not materialized. The last twenty years had been lean ones. I was having all the dreams and wonderings to be expected of one going into a new situation. It would be wonderful to have nothing on my mind for a while. No committee meetings or even bridge. Oh, there were many lovely things that we could do. It would be pure joy doing just what we wanted to do, and doing it together.

The houses disappeared but emerged again in the bright sunlight. We passed the creek bridge and climbed a sharp hill. Near the top, on the right, was the entrance gate, two cement pillars with an iron brace overhead bearing the words, Pitchfork Ranch, a swastika-like symbol between them. "What is that sign, D," I asked?

"That's the Pitchfork brand." I made a mental reservation to change that ugly sign. I'd replace it with a recognizable pitchfork, which was after all, a graceful implement. This thing wasn't the least bit graceful and I didn't think it would be cute on stationery.

A rough stretch of road lay ahead of us. To Jeet, it would have been a first omen of bad luck, a symbolic moment. Mandy would have said, "Have a care not to drop into them ruts." But you don't know Mandy and Jeet, and we didn't know them either then.

As we headed down the lane from the gate the headquarters seemed a small village within itself, a red-roofed village. But presently, immediately to my left, an enormous house gained my horrified attention. I had passed the Pitchfork many times and had never noticed this house before. Now that it might be my home, it completely filled the landscape, not a tree, not a shrub near it, only a big cement porch that stood for all the world like a fortification, fatal to the hospitality I had envisioned. This couldn't be the house! But, of course, the manager's place would be the largest. D had said so little about the house when I questioned him, except, "Oh, I know there'll be a lot of changes you'll want to make. You always do."

I'll say I would, I thought to myself. But how in the world could one change this monstrosity to make it homelike and livable? Paint it white, green shutters, of course, and scads of trees and shrubs.

"Boys' bunkhouse," explained D with a wave of his hand as we drove past. "Oh, is it?" said I with a wave of relief. Then, right in the middle of a grove of trees I saw the colonial house—white it was with green shutters, and columns, too. I had time for one quick delighted glance before I saw two tall tweedy men coming toward us. D was out of the car. I was conscious of well-bred voices full of charm and sincerity, and D was introducing me to the Williams brothers of Saint Louis, owners of the Pitchfork.

I could hear my Aunt Fannie's voice across thirty years, "Mamie, you speak too harshly. Softer now, and deeper." So in my deepest, very best Southern voice, I said, "How do you do?" And Mr. Gates Williams, all solicitude, asked, "Do you have a cold, Mrs. Burns?" (Why hadn't I thought of my mother's oft-repeated advice, "Just be yourself, daughter.")

"Be careful what you say, Mayme," D hissed in my ear. Later he said he just crossed his fingers and hoped for the best.

Mr. Eugene Williams led the way to the house, past a row of Chinese elms that threw long morning shadows across the walk and made dapplings of sunshine at our feet. Yes, I would love it. I had never chosen any place because of the house. It was always the spot of ground or a clump of trees that took my fancy, but this house had charm and dignity. Well, perhaps it was not dignity at all but a comfortable weather-beaten shabbiness that gave me at once the feeling of home. It needed a coat of paint. That was part of its charm. Well, it should never be painted a glary white-white; it would definitely be an off-white, a sort of grayish, purplish white, say one part gray to two parts white. I almost forgot to preface all this with "if we get this job."

My eyes were darting here and there, trying to take in everything at once—past the white-columned house to the creek. It was only a few hundred yards away and so beautiful. Unfortunately, the long part of the house was toward the west, bad Texas planning. It would be hot in the afternoons. But the long porch was wide and welcoming, the columns supported a balcony. We stepped into its shadowy depth—but delightfully cool in the mornings, went my thoughts. And here was that symbol again, in red cement this time, spang in front of the entrance door. *That* would be a little harder to change. The door with its dulled brass knocker stood hospitably open. If only the inside is sweet, I prayed.

We stepped into a large and gracious living room of truly beautiful proportions with massive beams and two-storied windows. The heat was shut out, but so was the brightness of the Texas sun. The room was dark and earth-dull because of brown oatmeal paper and Venetian blinds. Golden oak woodwork didn't help. I took a look, a very calculating look, at that room. Those Venetian blinds could come down. As for the two simply enormous radiators that sat glaring under the windows, they weren't needed in this climate. Why, with a few hundred dollars and a deft touch one could—.

Mr. Williams interrupted my calculations. "We thought you were coming last evening; we expected you for dinner." D had not told me we were expected the evening before, and, of course, they had waited dinner for us. We'd come as far as Lubbock and spent the night so as to be at the ranch early. They'd think us boors. We hadn't even called. This was a bad start. Lack of consideration, no regard for the social niceties. I opened my mouth to say something, I didn't know what, but this was D's business. He was less apt to say the wrong thing anyway. D can be utterly charming in such situations, and it isn't the thing he says so much as the thing he doesn't say, and the nice way in which he doesn't say it. He had the look of serious, sweet concern now, that he saves for these occasions. He said, "I'm sorry. I didn't understand."

"How about breakfast?"

"We had breakfast in Lubbock."

"Perhaps a cup of coffee then." Bessie served us nicely. I saw a pitchfork etched on the water pitcher and glasses, a pitchfork, too, on the matches that lay on the coffee table, also on the cigarette box and ash trays. No, it wasn't like a swastika, it was a stylized sort of pitchfork. It would be smart looking in brown on a soft yellow paper—brown ink, too. The room had an atmosphere of solidity and comfort; the furnishing were good, not exciting, but livable. When D sat down on one of the deep sofas and stretched out his long legs, he had the look of belonging to the place.

"Shall we show Mrs. Burns something of the ranch before lunch?" Gates inquired. The men started looking for dark glasses and guns. One seldom goes out on a ranch without a .410 or a .30-30. One is likely to see a rattlesnake, a coyote, or a skunk.

Walking ahead to the edge of the bank on which the house sat, I saw the creek not two hundred feet below. It was so beautiful, an unexpected delight D had failed to mention.

A big flowering willow tree leaned precariously from the slop-
ing bank with its roots exposed. A strong wind might finish it.
Obviously the first thing to do was to save this tree. I'd prop it up,
then on another level build a retaining wall. I had always wanted a
garden on different levels. I could drag up some big rocks— So
absorbed was I with the idea of saving that tree I almost missed
hearing Gates say, "Let's show them some country D hasn't seen."
Turning back toward the car I beheld an ugly sight. The south wing
of the house was supported by exposed brick piers. The creek had
washed this part of the bank away. Chickens and dogs had claimed
it as their domain. Why, that was an eyesore. Besides, we'd have
fleas, mites, mice, even rats.

"Come on," D shouted and we were off. My first excursion on
the Pitchfork.

A few saddle horses stood tied to the trees in the circle just in
front of the iron gate. Our departure was briefly delayed by a vener-
able character who dismounted and ambled over to the car to greet
the Williamses. It was Uncle George Watson, an old and well-
loved Pitchfork hand who had come back to help with the spring
branding. As we drove off, Mr. Eugene told us how they had tried
to pension Uncle George, but he would have none of it. The old
fellow had strenuously objected, saying "I want no charity. I've
been paid for every month I ever worked here."

"And that was for forty-five years," Mr. Williams added.

2

The Lay of the Land

Gates Williams was at the wheel, D beside him except when he was climbing out to open the wire gaps. (The visitor always opens the gate. It's an old ranch custom.) Mr. Eugene and I were on the back seat. I remember that he warned me several times about mesquite thorns. I answered reassuringly that I'd been raised among mesquite.

We saw the commercial cattle, the purebred herd, the thoroughbred horses, and the cow ponies. Everywhere I saw that brand, the Pitchfork—on the left rib of the cattle, on the rump of the horses, painted on trucks, on the men's hats, and on the gates as we drove from pasture to pasture.

D was a man transported. This was what he loved, pure country as far as the eye could see, and cattle everywhere. He was asking many questions, was all eyes and ears for the livestock. "We run about 8,000 . . . the grass, an unusually fine season." He was especially interested in the watering places. "Some seventy windmills."

D was noticing landmarks and directions. My thoughts were full of the details of house and family life that they'd mentioned. What it was like to have been a woman on the Forks almost a hundred years ago, trying to picture Dan Gardner, the first manager of the ranch in 1883. "This is Shinnery Pasture," Gates Williams said, and brought the car to a stop before the gate.

"Shinnery." The word had a pleasant euphonious sound. And "filaree." I leaned back and thought about the names I was hearing for the first time. Some, like Stinking Creek, were easily understandable. East Long Canyon and Red Hills revealed their meaning by their shape and color. "Brushy" was so descriptive of the pasture that lies just south of the house that even the veriest "greener" could not mistake its significance.

But "shinnery" and "filaree"? I asked about them right then. D told me filaree, correctly called *alfilaria*, was a winter weed highly thought of for fattening cattle; that shinnery, really shin-oak, was not so highly thought of because of its deadly effect on cattle in the early spring, particularly if it has been frozen back at the time of budding. Then he turned, smiling, to Mr. Eugene and me: "The cowboys would tell you that filaree is a little bitty weed about this high"—he measured a half-inch between his thumb and forefinger—"needin' rain." I wish I had a dollar for every time I've heard the cowboys say it since. The next time the car stopped D brought one of the plants for us to examine.

"What's that little yellow flower called? The one right by your feet?" Mr. Williams asked. "Little yellow flower," D answered seriously. And so it is.

But I was hearing other names—Devil's Playground, Get Away— and I wondered how they had come to be. I guessed correctly that many reasons had mingled in the naming of these places, that little incidents and jokes had been commemorated by these names. In a short time I would know that a canyon or pasture without a name is hardly a canyon or pasture at all, that a name is necessary for identifying a place or thing. How else would the boys know what the foreman meant when he said "We'll start at Willow"?

We listened to the story of the Pitchfork beginnings. We were rolling on hallowed ground. Our tires were following in the tracks made by the iron rims of Dan Gardner's frontier wagon wheels. This was the road the first settlers had built in the wilderness, the road Dan Gardner had used to make his monthly forty-six-mile treks to Paducah for provisions. The narrow road twisted and turned, dropped and rose, as we dodged the thorny mesquite limbs and prairie dog holes, avoiding the high centers where the road had washed. We crossed red-earthed canyons, the dust rising in rosy clouds behind us.

At a distance we saw a herd of cattle resting in a patch of shade and they saw us. Some of them raised their heads, sniffed the air, and headed for the thickest brush they could find. Some, mostly bulls, resenting our intrusion, pawed the earth, snorted and otherwise acted as if they might do something about it. But a few of the critters, and these were mostly cows, stopped in the middle of the road to stand and chew and stare. We had almost to shove them out of our way. Many were lying down, resting, but they regarded us with curious interest.

"Why are some of them so much gentler than others?" I asked. "Been fed," D answered.

Gates cut off the engine. "These are some of our younger commercial cattle."

Just then D leaned out of the car and made the most unearthly sound. It came from somewhere way down deep inside him, a sort of groan or moan. It sounded as if he were going to be sick. He made the noise again. No, it sounded like a train coming out of a hollow, a lonesome *whooo . . . whooo*. He was doing it intentionally. I had never seen D act in this manner before. What on earth would the Williamses think of such peculiarities? And of all times, while hoping to get a job. This wasn't like D. I gave an uneasy glance in their direction. There was surprise, but also respect and admiration on their countenances. The cattle that were lying down got up slowly, cow fashion, back end first; a horse gets up with a surge. I had not noticed this difference before. Those that were on their feet started coming toward the car. Even from a distance of a quarter-mile those bovines drifted our way. They had recognized the familiar feed call, and before long had completely surrounded the car. I was tremendously proud of D. Imagine having all that knowledge and talent hidden behind an office desk. I'm not as hopelessly infatuated with cows as D, but I did right then and there fall a little bit in love with their wistful faces.

We had not yet made the whole tour of that section of the ranch. After lunch we started out again. Gates noticed some shell jackets, smelled them. They were newly shot. It infuriated him to know that poachers had been on the ranch. We learned right then how emotional he could become about quail. Gates was concerned about their survival on the ranch, especially the bobwhite, a species already severely endangered. He said, "The blues can pretty well take care of themselves."

I didn't think the names of the camps showed much originality, North, South, East, and West Camp indeed! I had expected something unique in ranch nomenclature. From North Camp field we went into Dripping Springs across from the Roosevelt Mill (Mr. Eugene said to *change that name* and we learned what he thought of Roosevelt), then through the east portion of South Shinnery into the steer pasture, and on to South Camp. When we were on the T 41

divide we were overlooking the Croton Brakes country belonging to
the Matador Ranch. D said, "Mayme, that's the country your father
is always talking about. That's where he worked in the '80s. From
his report and all I've heard of it, it must be a great piece of cow
country with a lot of natural protection." Mr. Eugene said, "The
Matador offered to sell us that country during the drouth in the '30s
but we thought it was priced too high." D remarked, "Yes, it should
fit in well with this operation." My silent reaction to the big rough
country beneath us was that there were plenty of rocks there for
building purposes and landscaping.

Coming home in the late afternoon with the west streaked
with red, we rounded a turn, and I was overcome by a fresh view
that sent me into ecstasies. The roadway was busy with the sound of
cattle lowing, field larks bursting their throats in song, and the stac-
cato notes of the crow. I leaned forward so that I could see through
the open car window the beasts they were discussing. At that celes-
tial moment a mesquite limb slapped me, the old hand at mesquite,
across the face.

3

Requirements

We talked long that evening with the Williamses about the things that were most important to them in a manager. Mr. Eugene locked his fingers together and set his hands down squarely on the table; it was his peculiarity and distinction that he gave even the smallest matter due consideration, and we were to see him like this many times.

The Williams brothers gave us a brief history of the Pitchfork and its environs. They were proud of the ranch's reputation, of the principles that Mr. Gardner had established. The Pitchfork had the rare distinction of never having been in debt or mortgaged despite drouths, depressions, and cheap cattle. They said from its beginning the Pitchfork had served good food at the Big House, the chuck house, and the wagon; that they kept a well-stocked commissary for the camp families. They wanted the Pitchfork to remain as nearly as possible as it was in those early days; they felt a deep responsibility to Dan Gardner's memory. The Williamses were not selfish with the ranch and made it plain that any manager's family and friends were welcome and emphasized their wish that special courtesies be extended to former employees.

They let me know how valuable a manager's wife could be and what would be expected of her. They enthusiastically recounted the many ways in which the earlier one, Mrs. Parr, had been outstanding: energetic, capable, and saving. I knew the frugality of Northern women in housekeeping; I knew my own extravagance in that direction. I hoped, if given the chance, I could keep the place functioning as well as she had.

We finally said goodnight, knowing full well that with this job we'd have a responsibility to live up to the letter of the law of Dan Gardner's ranch. We took the Pitchfork's past record as a good omen. The spell of the past and a desire to fulfill all the great things Mr. Gardner envisioned for the Pitchfork came over me.

As we walked to our bedroom, my gaze took in that brown oatmeal-papered hall with its five doors and general ugliness. Always acute about discovering my feelings and thoughts, D divined my intentions. The first minute we were alone he ventured, "It's in good condition, the house I mean." This was not the time to get D upset so I'd not mention my plans right then. "Not a partition to be knocked out," I said amiably and truthfully. The rooms were of noble size. D nodded appreciatively at my good sense. The very thought of remodeling, tearing into a wall throws him into panic. "The whole house looks all right to me. There is certainly enough of it, warm and dry."

"I expect it keeps out weather in fine fashion," I returned. To the average man a house is only shelter, but as Ink would say, "It don't pleasure you none." I didn't have that bit of philosophy then, however.

As he closed the door of our bedroom, D said, "This is a great ranch, Mayme, I hope I get a chance at running it." "We've seen a lot of country," I remarked. It must have looked the same to Mr. Dan Gardner when he first saw it in the 1870's, I thought. D had seen a lot more than country: fences and roads in bad condition, mesquite taking over the ranch. "They need that Croton country. The ranch needs a lot more windmills." As D undressed, his thoughts were on the ranch, mine were indoor musings.

"The telephone worries *me* more than anything else, it hasn't worked since we've been here, and with the children and Mother and Pops so far away—" "That's the first thing I'm going to take care of," D promised. "*if* we get the job."

As I remember, we talked about the Williamses. "They're nice people," D said. And indeed they were, terribly nice, but entirely different. I tried to analyze that difference; it was as much in their voices and laughter as anything. Gates had a hearty guffaw, Mr. Eugene, a soft chuckle.

"Oh, different as hell," D agreed. "Gates is so outgoing and enthusiastic, Mr. Eugene's thoughtful and reserved." But both the Wiliamses had equal charm and sincerity, we thought.

After D had gone to sleep I lay thinking about the things the Williamses had told us about the many facets of the job. I had naively supposed it was only a cattle ranch—why, my responsibilities would be tremendous. I became aware of all the noises one hears in a strange place as I lay listening to the creaking of the windmill not a hundred feet from my bed. The house, too, was full of noises, eerie and unaccountable (strange noises then, but friendly now): the scraping of a branch against the screen, the wind pushing through a torn gutter-pipe, a loose shingle fluttering, a venetian blind's click-click-click against the window facing, the sharp yelp of coyotes, the call of a whippoorwill— But suppose, the thought struck suddenly as I startled awake at 2 A.M., suppose we should not get the job?

Next morning we were off again. Exploring the vast reaches of the ranch could not be accomplished in the three days we spent with the Williamses, but we'd hit the high places. Hour after hour we followed the maze of roads, roads that made no sense to me, roads made, no doubt, by cows. D said, "Cattle are trail makers, their cleft hooves cut the sod and they walk in Indian file." I fancifully wondered if they'd marched two abreast to make many of these parallel ruts we bounced over.

"There is history in this rocky strip of road, too," Mr. Eugene said as we drove to the farm camp. "Mr. Gardner told me the last skirmish with the Comanches happened around here." It intrigued me to realize that while Pops was cowboying on the Matador in the '80s, Dan Gardner was pioneering on the Pitchfork not forty miles away.

Sometimes the road plunged straight down or leaped straight up. The Williamses said that most of the ranch roads were passable in all weather, but some should be avoided after a rain. D was making mental notes on all the dirt work that was needed on the ranch roads. I simply enjoyed all the trips wholeheartedly from the moment the car started—smelling the growing things, planning future gardens.

I was also sizing up what part would be my job if the Pitchfork became our job. Sitting quietly while the three men talked ranch, my mind was busy weaving my own country memories into this possible new life. This, I smugly assured myself, would be living! We would have the help of a well-trained couple; there were four bathrooms; and the place just looked restful (which only goes to show how far off the mark a first impression can be).

Came our last night on the ranch, and everything seemed rosy to me. The Williamses obviously liked D, and I knew how desperately D wanted this job. As we dressed for dinner I asked confidently, "D, how do you think it's going?"

"Mayme, there's something I haven't told them or even you. You know I have a chance to sell my ranch (the Cross C), and that capital can best be invested in a ranch where I'm manager. I know ranching and trust that I've sold myself to the Williamses, but if they are unwilling to let me have stock in the company . . . somewhere in the United States there's the right setup for me." I froze, numb with shock. I'd thought everything hinged on their accepting *us*, and now this.

We were barely seated at the table when Mr. Eugene said, "Well, Mr. Burns, you seem to like our ranch, and we are delighted with the two of you. How do you feel about becoming our manager?"

"Gentlemen," D said. "I want this job more than I've ever wanted anything in my life, but I have one condition. I own a small ranch, the Cross C below Lamesa. I've had a good offer and plan to sell, and I want to put my money wherever I may be working. Probably I should have mentioned this earlier, and I guess I'm sorry I didn't, but I felt a few days with you would convince you I'm the right man for the job. Will you consider letting me have stock in the Pitchfork Land and Cattle Company?"

I've never heard D's voice more earnest or sincere than when he tried to make the Williamses understand his position regarding his wish to own stock in the company. They understood D's position exactly, but they had their own interests to consider.

Equally grave, Mr. Williams replied, "I'm sorry that this is your prerequisite, because our company policy prevents us from selling stock to anyone outside the corporation." My heart nearly stopped beating.

"I feel now that I should have told you this at the outset," D went on. "It has not been my intention to mislead you by not mentioning it before."

The Williamses made many counterproposals—they did not want to lose D—but he stood his ground. My hopes rose somewhat when Mr. Eugene said, "Surely we should be able to work out something." The men turned to ranch talk, Gates and Mr. Eugene continued to pump and probe for advice and counsel in the running of the Pitchfork, in the same vein they had used all afternoon, as though D were already their manager.

As I finally dropped asleep, my last thought was, if it hurts me so much to give up this job, how must D be feeling? I crawled out of my bed to give D a consoling kiss, but he was already sound asleep.

4

It's Ours!

We got in the car to leave, two disappointed, sick-at-heart people. Bidding the Williamses adieu, we tried to let them know how much we appreciated their consideration of D for the job, how disappointed we were that we couldn't accept it, and how we had loved knowing them and seeing the ranch. They were so charming. D started the car engine. But the last word had not been said. Mr. Eugene reached into the car, put his hand on D's arm, and said, "Mr. Burns, take this job for five years. If you still want to be our manager, and if we're satisfied with you, I'll sell you some of my own stock in the ranch."

D's decision was the matter of a moment. "What are we waiting on?" he asked, turning off the key and getting out of the car.

My heart was doing flip-flops. We'd been so achingly unhappy at leaving without the job, what seemed the perfect setup to D. He'd never again find anything so much to his liking, and now, presto, the job was ours. All was supremely well.

From that moment on, the Pitchfork became D's, the ranch and everything on it—"my horses, my cattle, my boys, my organization, my roads, my men"; he put his very soul into it. The Williamses loved D for his total identification with the Forks, and for his complete dedication.

Gates Williams turned to me. "Mrs. Burns, we will have several hours of talking. Would you like to come with us or rest inside the house?" Flushed with happiness I answered, "I think I'll go and take a look at my new home." This was my time to inspect the house in detail, to draw a floor plan, and to take measurements.

What glorious closets and storage drawers I found upstairs. And the basement! Its entrance was built under the stairway. It was a housewife's dream come true, two giant rooms, storage to spare. Now we could keep Christmas wrappings, those divine boxes that we'd never had room for and hated so much to throw away. Space, I thought, coming up from the basement, is man's greatest luxury.

But there was no spot in all that huge living room for our chest-on-chest. The room cried aloud for wall space, but how could it be arranged with five big doors, six enormous windows, a fireplace, and a coat closet covering everything but a few strips of wallpaper between openings? There was hardly enough room for the small pictures, good pictures they were too. It would not be long until I would know of Gates's passion for pictures. Old print shops all over the country knew him well. Somehow with all this floor space I'd find room for that chest-on-chest, even if I had to cover up a window.

Although I had enjoyed going over the ranch with the Williamses and was interested in everything they had to say, now I was impatient to see my domain, the house and the buildings surrounding the headquarters. Which of the small buildings could be used as servants' quarters? And which of the rundown shacks would the Williamses be willing to have moved or torn down to make the place less cluttered and more attractive? But I had to wait for the proper moment to start plying them with questions about such things.

My first real find was a shed full of lumber—pine in assorted lengths, widths, and patterns; a lot of center match; dozens of two-by-fours; and, would you believe it, some siding, exactly like that on the house? What couldn't one do with all that beautiful, well-seasoned material? "Mamie Burns," I said ecstatical, "You've been living right!" Then immediately, to nip such nonsense in the bud, I said, "Mamie, you sill!"

May I interrupt myself here to say that for the last three days, I'd been cherishing a secret hope that I'd find a place and a way for a sitting room—bedroom of our own, a place to which I could retire when D had business friends in the house, where I could sit by my own fireplace and have my own old furniture and books around me. It would make the difference between a house and a home.

But I have carried you a long way from the lumber shed with my thoughts. Breaking the news to D and the Williamses that I wanted such a room was going to be difficult, if indeed I could bring myself to do so at all. Suppose when I told D, he said, "What the hell for?" or "We've got more room now than we know what to do with." I'd just die. How could I make them understand my need for a little privacy? But I couldn't stand there rhapsodizing, transported by something as unlikely as getting to use all this lumber. I might as well forget it, but I was in utter despair at having to give up the one thing— Disgusted at my self-pity, abruptly I decided to give my attention to our job and to something I knew I could do. And here was a windfall, right at hand!

The three-roomed, former schoolhouse would serve nicely for my help. Its location was perfect, about fifty yards from the Big House. Some old desks and blackboards needed to be taken out. With a bit of fixing up, a call-bell—

Memories of my childhood enveloped me as I went about the ranch to the chicken yard, the cowpen, and the smokehouse, empty save for some tins of rancid lard, dirty jars, and a few bars of lye soap. It brought back every detail of my father's smokehouse with its unforgettable odor of salt and lye soap, its rows of hams, sides of bacon hanging, and sausages smoked, sacked, and in casings. I could picture Mrs. Garner, Mrs. Goshack, and Aunt Nannie Snead, all the kindly, friendly women who had helped my mother at one time or another many years ago. Everything everywhere touched a chord of memory: the smokehouse, the big barrel on wheels to take away the garbage, the buckets of foaming milk brought up from the cow pen.

I remembered listening to Mother's instructions to her helpers and running my legs off fetching and toting for both of them. I had always been delighted to help as long as the errands kept me out of doors. Pure joy went with feeding chickens, gathering eggs, hanging out or taking in clothes; the clean, beautiful odor that wind and sun gave the freshly washed garments I still remember. I loved going to the orchard and the garden. I'd climb the trees to get the peaches from the highest branches so they would not be bruised by falling. The ripest, very largest ones would be saved for Mother. But I loathed having Aunt Nannie call me indoors to help and saying, "Pick this chicken. An' you ain't gonna larn to cut one up no younger." Churning was the most onerous task. The churn was waist-high, and the dasher came up to my head. I could hear Aunt Nannie: "Come down here, chile, an' git anuthuh can o' lye an' brang me a chicken feathuh. Heah, stuh this soap till it's thick." I remember how proud I was when Aunt Nannie let me test the lye soap and bring the feather out clean to the spine. I was soon to find at the Pitchfork that being an apprentice and having complete responsibility were entirely different things.

After my long ramble over the place, I went into my bedroom to lie down, to rest, to plan, to take a look at my thoughts. There was more work to be done here than would appear to an arriving guest. But wasn't I my mother's daughter? When I had a good couple that I myself had trained, I would get things straightened out and running smoothly. It would be shipshape in no time with certain jobs for each day in the week as I had always managed my household. As Mother always said, "A place for everything and everything in its place." I'd have my hour of solitude, I'd never let a day go by without slipping away to a quiet haven to bind my scattered thoughts, to close my eyes, to drift into space, to bring peace and serenity into my life. No helter-skeltery, unorganized life for me.

Five years later, I am remembering those blithe resolutions, now when I have so many things to do and scarcely anyone to help me do them. With help that is almost worse than no help. It's hard to find a minute to lie down or even sit down, what with the telephone ringing, or someone at the back door wanting D, or questions coming from the kitchen, if I had anyone in kitchen.

"This heah stuff ain't congeelin'." (I knew in the first place I should have made that mayonnaise.) "Whut'm I gonna do with it, thow it out?" or "This heah da way you wants these heah spargusses?" She'd thrown away the wrong end of the asparagus.

Aggravations of every kind bedeviled me. Bind my scattered thoughts indeed! Mine were galloping, racing around in my head: water shrubs, turn brooder down at two o'clock, get those onion sets out, air blankets, spray storage drawers (out of spray, put it on list). Oh my goodness! the laundry—must gather that laundry and list it right now! They'll be leaving for Spur in a few minutes. Don't forget to order lemons and red ant killer. *Where is that list?* The telephone rang—guests were coming! This was the *coup de grace*. It mattered not how charming and entertaining the expected guests might be; they could be family or dear friends we were hungry to see; or our ranch family from Saint Louis, who were always enchanting; or just business acquaintances. Without help, the arrival of anyone was the worst sort of news. We could not make them comfortable, and we would have to stop everything we were doing to show them around, to take care of their needs, and to feed them.

After a short rest, I walked back into the cubicle that Mr. Swenson had used for his office. Originally a tiny bedroom, it was connected by a bath to the larger bedroom, the one we were occupying. If this office were larger, I speculated, it would be splendid, but it covered every foot of ground there was to spare on that side of the house and therefore could not be extended. In fact, the east door that opened to the outside had only a narrow walk between it and a fifteen-foot drop. The creek had washed away the bank right up to the house on the south and east sides. A somnambulist or the inebriated would do well to avoid this path. The bank needed to be built out, such terrain was not suited to one who is absent-minded like me. Why, that was the answer! The bank should be built out! We'd seen scads of the most wonderful rock, right here on the ranch, and we surely had plenty of soil. But what was I thinking about? That office would be D's office. Wild horses could not drag D away from an established situation. D was not one to change the location of an office or anything else once it was placed, established, and in good condition. So this was out.

What a surprise to hear D say, as the men came in for lunch, "I'd like to take that little house for my office."

"But what would we do with the polo equipment?"

D's answer was typical. "Mr. Williams, they won't be playing polo while I'm manager." And sure enough, they weren't. So D would not be using that little room after all! I was so excited and delighted, I could hardly contain myself.

Gates had a request. He enthusiastically described to D his need for having an ungrazed area as coverage for his doves and quail. "Come on, D, let's go up to the North Camp, and I'll show you where I want it." Before their return they'd chosen four spots to be fenced in.

Their departure left me alone with Mr. Eugene. "Mrs. Burns, you tell me you were reared in the country and that you would not be lonely out here. Yet several times I've seen a faraway look in your eyes. Is there something troubling you?" His unexpected words overwhelmed me with joy and gratitude. He was both kind and understanding. I looked into his earnest face. Yes, one might speak freely to Mr. Williams, and this was the time, for he had asked. D was not going to be happy about this. He'd think I should have discussed it first with him, and I had intended to. He'd feel I had taken advantage of the situation, Tact, he had pointed out to me, was of the greatest importance. Well, I'd let that bad moment take care of itself. I had so little time.

"Mr. Williams, I guess I'm worrying about my furniture. I have an eight-room house filled with antiques, and this place is already completely furnished. I'm afraid I couldn't be entirely happy without some of my own things."

"Why, Mrs. Burns, store our things. Put all this in the lumber shed. There is no sentiment attached to any of it. Mr. and Mrs. Parr bought it all in one day in Saint Louis. Naturally, you'd want your own things. Is that all, Mrs. Burns, or is there something else?" I took that as a small hope.

"That is the point, Mr. Williams. My pieces are not scaled to your house, especially your two-storied living room." I told him about the lumber I'd seen, and about some beams at an old oil well "try." We walked back to the small office-bedroom. Falteringly, I said, "If I could add twenty feet to this, put in a fireplace, and make a sitting room—bedroom for D and me, a private place—"

Just then Gates and D returned. Mr. Eugene said, "Mrs. Burns would like to do some remodeling." D just stood there looking stricken. He looked serious, quite darkly serious.

"I'd like to do this room at my expense," I interjected.

"No, Mrs. Burns, we would not consider your putting your money into our house."

"Well, if you don't like the addition when it's finished I'll put everything back the way it was at the outset at my expense."

"Do anything you can that the $500 wartime regulations will allow."

What a cozy, warm feeling it was to know we'd have that room. The Williamses were wonderful about it, and D was pleased about it too. I took one last look around the huge room, as we were leaving. "I wish we could do something about those radiators," I moaned. They would spoil any amount of planning. "Well, we just can't," D said hurriedly, and with finality. I wondered why we just couldn't.

5

Ending and Beginning Again

Let's get going," D said. There was a new and surprising note of authority. It was disconcerting to have D say, "Let's get going," instead of his usual "Ready, Mayme?"

We said a warm goodbye to the Williamses, and D promised to be back on Monday to help deliver the cattle. I told them that I'd return the minute I could sell my house. As we drove away, I thought contentedly that it would be impossible to find a more courtly and cordial pair than the Williams brothers. All the appeal of the Pitchfork was not its romantic ruggedness. We felt a sense of life well lived, of continuity, of life going on. We would be a part of all this; we felt humility.

"I was afraid you were going to lose the job the way you made me look like some kind of invalid," I remarked sarcastically.

"You thought I was going to lose it? What do you suppose I thought when I came in to find you planning a remodeling job, and moving all their furniture to the meat house?" Life had never seemed more wonderful. We giggled like kids.

"And I was afraid that was going to be our house," I confessed, pointing to the bunkhouse.

"You must have been wild!" D roared. "It's called Parr's Folly. It won't be long now before you'll be hearing about Burns's Boners or Burns's Busts. I hope that I have nothing more serious to answer for." As we drove through the gate, D teased, "And you don't like our brand."

"Don't like it?" Suddenly I knew that I loved that brand. I was never to see it again, especially when out of the state, without a feeling of pride, a quickening of the pulse, our brand! And I had thought to change that brand. I'd not tell D of this presumption, he'd consider it blasphemy.

We sat for a moment in silence at the wonder of our new-found prospects before turning onto the highway. D spoke of the marvelous opportunity that we held in our hands. "But it's not going to be easy, Mayme. We're going into the worst man shortage in history. An old ranch in new hands is a dangerous thing unless it is handled just right; unless the new manager brings his own organization with him. In ordinary times they'd have fired every man on the job, and had him hire to me, but war is not ordinary time, and anyway I don't have an organization of my own to bring in.

"There is going to be lots to do, but hard work won't hurt me. Everything is work that is worth doing, if you are conscientious, and you might just as well like it. It will be like play to me. I'm going to enjoy every hour of every day that rolls over my head."

Part of my mind was on D's words, part of it on packing, and part of it racing ahead on what I thought my own job would be. Selling our home in San Angelo—I wouldn't let myself think of this part of it just now.

"Our first job will be making friends of these people." Optimistic Mamie responded, "I'm going to love these people, and I believe they will love us." This was an incautious and extravagant hope, but I was recalling the relationship our family had always had with the people on Pop's places in McLennan County.

In the ten years D had traveled the United States for the Texas Cottonseed Crushers Association, he'd been on most of the big ranches and could make valid comparisons. "I'll take the Pitchfork! As far as I'm concerned, Mr. D. B. Gardner took the heart of this country, Mayme, when he put the ranch together. Its location makes it top mother-cow country; it has water and protection; it's well diversified, farming and livestock; it has accessibility to market and good roads. The owners are willing to put something back into it every year instead of bleeding it white." I understood. D loved ranching and ranches, and he was in love with the Pitchfork.

He stopped the car on the same hill where we'd paused four days before and sat for a time looking back at the ranch. Happiness, pride, and a sense of satisfaction shone on his face, but also a new humility. "I hope I'm big enough for this job, Mayme." There was a certain wistfulness about the way he said it. That was the only evidence of self-doubt I ever heard him voice.

"Big enough?" I couldn't believe my ears. For twenty years he'd been telling me that he could run this ranch with one hand tied behind him. Now he hoped that he was big enough. "Of course you are big enough, D," I said reassuringly. "What's to keep you from—"

"People resent changes, and I'll have to make a lot of them. We'll be starting from scratch, a new manager in an old organization. We don't know a man on the ranch."

I would have no part in D's gloomy predictions. "I'm going to love every one of those people and they are going to love us," I repeated. I knew all about cowboys, their soft hearts and hard shells.

We were twenty miles from the ranch, past Dickens, before it occurred to me to ask. "What is your salary?" D actually turned pale. "I'm afraid you'll think me unbusinesslike. I didn't ask them, but I won't worry about that. I have all confidence in those men. They'll do the right thing."

It did seem perhaps unbusinesslike, unbelievable, and hilarious to me, but I loved him for his eagerness and enthusiasm and his trust in the Williamses. I recognized the ranch had taken precedence over self. And that was only half the story! Mamie had a huge rival who was fascinating and all-absorbing.

"This ranch has been in operation since the early '80s," D said reverently.

"How did it get its name?" My friends would be wanting to know. "What is the story behind it?" I secretly hoped the story was as exciting as the tale about the 6666 and the poker game.

"Living-making places are rarely christened, Mayme. That is a distinction"—he said the word as if it were not a distinction at all—"reserved for gentlemen ranchers and dude outfits. The facts are rather prosaic, not at all tailored to your romantic requirements." I was somewhat nettled and changed the subject at once.

"Do you like the men you will be working with, the ones you have met so far?" I had not thought to ask before.

"I have been introduced to a few of them, casually as they passed by, but not as a prospective manager. Mr. Williams says Harve Adams and John Murd both are hopeful of getting this job and have applied for it. Harve came here with Rudolph from the Swensons as the wagon boss. He has made a good one and is a hard worker, but he lacks the education and acquaintance to be manager. Murd has been here only a short while, he is not well liked, but has been doing a fair job as assistant. They both have very high tempers, and Mr. Williams fears if they know the job has been filled they might walk off and leave the ranch without anyone to make decisions or to deliver the many hundreds of cattle due to be shipped within the next few days."

I had listened to all D was saying, but the kind of joy I felt was impossible to keep bottled up, the pride I felt in D, getting the job in spite of me, the happy plans I had for the house (I hadn't had a minute to explain it all to him). I'd tell him now that I was looking to Fredda, my antique dealer, for help. He anticipated my scheming. "Even with all that lumber, the remodeling can't possibly be done with $500," he said.

"But D couldn't we put in $500 also? It isn't right that the Williamses should bear the expense of this remodeling. Our living room—bedroom addition is entirely for our private use and pleasure. I'll talk with Fredda. She will gladly buy any antiques I want to sell."

D thought my plan was fine, as far as the carpet, slipcovers, and draperies went. They should definitely come out of our purse. He especially approved the idea of my getting rid of some of the junk I'd collected (my priceless antiques), as we didn't need half of it and I'd never get much of anything for it. I'd heard all this before, but I silently held to the conviction that I was riding a rising market.

D had misgivings about the expensive wallpaper he knew I'd use, and the moldings, the hardware, strap hinges, batten doors, and the cabinet work would greatly add to the labor cost. "Even if we paid for every extra dollar of expenditure," said D, "I'm not sure it's entirely honest."

"How can it be dishonest to want to save them money, D? I want our rooms to be unusual and lovely, but I don't want them to have to pick up the tab. If we don't do it now, we will never get it done."

"What are you going to say when they ask you what it cost?"

"D Burns, you are the only person alive who would ask me that. The Williamses wouldn't dream of it. They are too gallant, too gentlemanly, too well-bred."

"Mayme, these men think of this ranch as a four-legged bank roll. They will ask me about every dollar you are spending."

"Well, we can put down a nominal sum, like $1.50 per single roll for wallpaper, and labor as one-fifth the actual amount. I'll tell them, D, in a few months. Please help me."

"This doesn't seem the time to be remodeling, making changes of any kind, especially such extensive ones unless they are absolutely necessary." D didn't say yes, but he did say, "I suppose you're right about it. If we're ever going to do it, now is the time. Remind me to stop in Lubbock and call Ray Grisham. I need to see if he can get some pipe and a dozen windmills for us."

"And I'll order those trees for the driveway."

"Not so fast, Mayme," exclaimed D. "We have got to do first things first. Our first job will be making friends of these people."

I had my priorities, too. The first things I'd tackle were the ones I'd promised the Williamses: plant trees along the driveway to the gate, get rid of the dilapidated no-longer-used windmill that kept the Williamses awake, and move that clothes line. Gates had said they'd had men's drawers flapping in their faces for twenty years.

Folks were going around in Lubbock just like they always had; this was just an ordinary day to some people. D dropped me off at Fredda's Studio. Fredda was crafty, too. She lent her mind to my problem, saw nothing wrong about my suggestions. She said I could get anything I wanted practically at cost and pay for it as I liked: dangerous words, but beautiful to me. Furthermore, she'd be glad to take any of the antiques that I would have no use for on the ranch as part payment. What could be finer? What could be fairer? This arrangement would allow me to re-cover the divan, those two big chairs, and have a bed-spread and pillows made to complement them.

As we headed for San Angelo, D said, "We have a lot to learn, of course." I had a distinct feeling that he meant I had a lot to learn. The uncertainties of a new job did not in the least disturb me. The things I didn't know I could learn.

Every so often we'd fall into quiet, as one will when making a long trip, thinking our own thoughts. I, too, had plans, such rosy plans. Life would be as rural, as pleasant as a picnic, well ordered, I'd be efficient, big ash trays everywhere, flowering shrubs all over the place, blossoms in the house the year round. There'd be guests, house parties, I'd plan ahead, have an emergency shelf, great pots of black bean soup, hush puppies, huge platters of ham, beef tenders. I loved the country, had always liked its people. I knew it wouldn't all be fun, there'd be difficult times. My mind went back to our life on the farm. Mother played a vigorous role. Could I show the resilience and character that she had shown?

One of the most agreeable aspects of country living would be having our own milk, cream, butter, chickens, eggs, garden vegetables, beef, pork. Why, we'd hardly have to buy a thing for the table. We'd have our own lard, bacon, hams, dried beans, potatoes, black-eyed peas, sauerkraut from the cabbage. It would be easy for me, just remember how Mother and Pops had fed our people. We'd have to make up our minds at the start how to take advantage of everything the ranch had to offer.

Even though it had been thirty years since I'd been on the farm, it would all come back to me quickly. I saw myself testing the sausage to see that it had the right amount of pepper, sage, and salt; using a feather to see if the lye was strong enough for the soap; making hominy—

"Will we raise corn, D?"

"Yes, some. Why?"

"I just wondered," I fibbed. D didn't know I could make hominy. I'd make up a batch, yes, that was the word, it was all coming back. I'd have to find a kiln. I contemplated the Pitchfork picture with calmness and confidence. D had everything it took to fill that job, and I didn't intend giving a sleazy performance myself. What terrors could a ranch hold for us? I soon found out.

But right then I started thinking in terms of remodeling and rearranging. Nothing was crumbling. The buildings were too staunch to be knocked down. I was thinking also of something pretty husky in the way of food. Mass production, of course: red beans, big roasts, steaks.

D asked me what I thought about hiring Bessie and Tony to stay on and work for us. At every opportunity I had been watching them very closely with the same idea in view. I did not believe that

I would want them as permament help, however; their food was not exceptionally good, and they were not clean in housekeeping or in the kitchen. They had fallen into slovenly habits since Mr. Swenson's passing. With no supervision, they did little work. They would not likely want to crack down to such hard work as we'd be in for, a general housecleaning with the moving and placing of furniture to follow. On the other hand, they were familiar with the place, and it might be well to ask them to stay for one month, at least, until we could get things in better shape.

D promised to talk with them when he got back to the Pitchfork. He'd tell them we would try each other out for a while; if they did not prove satisfactory, we'd give them a month's salary and let them go. Surely with my supervision of the window washing, floor polishing, and all, I could get the house in good condition while we were scouting for better help.

We turned into our driveway at San Angelo. D was out of the car like a shot. He generally came around to open the door for me, but he didn't this time. He reached for our bags in the back seat. "I'll bring the rest," I said, but I don't think he even heard me. He was halfway to the steps.

A little sigh of contentment escaped my lips. The best part of a trip was getting home. But this wasn't home any more. A lump that I could not swallow rose in my throat. I wanted that job, of course, and was so glad and proud for D. I liked the Williamses, too; they were so kind, they'd understood at once about my wanting to remodel the house. It can be made attractive, too, and in time I'll have flowers. Then why this unaccountable sadness? That was it! I knew! I knew! It was my garden! If only I could take my garden with me. The lilac was in full bloom. D had stopped the car right against the bush. A limb of its purple panicles came into the car window, breaking my heart with its sweetness. I caught a bunch in my hand, buried my face in it, and sobbed, "It was because of you that I bought this house."

"Mayme," D yelled, "where's a box or bag that I can put my papers into? I want to take them with me." For Pete's sake! He was already packing!

There's something about leaving a place where you've been for a while, especially if you've loved it and have been happy there. I realized more clearly than ever before how deep was my affection for this place. Though I was not unhappy at the prospect of country life, I was filled with nostalgia for the things we were leaving, our house, the river, my garden. From my seat at the telephone, I could see the terrace and the pathway that led to it, with the grass, crocus, and daffodils growing up between the bricks. I'd laid that walk myself only last fall. I'd tucked the bulbs into the warm sand between the widely spaced bricks. It looked now as if it had been there forever. How quickly bermuda grass takes hold—and takes over! One's own roots take hold quickly, too, when you put so much of yourself into it.

"I must call my brother," D said eagerly and vanished into the hall. "John!" I heard him say jubilantly. "I'm going to be your neighbor over in King County. I landed that Pitchfork job today!" D's exultation was so great, so contagious, in no time at all I was sharing his luscious anticipations. We'd work with pride and purpose. We could hardly wait to begin.

I'm sure John answered, "The devil you did!" He was pleased, naturally. That placed two of the state's important ranches under the management of Arthur Burns's sons, John on the 6666 Ranch and now D on the Pitchfork. I knew the pride they felt in their pioneer cattle-raising father, and the cowboy know-how they'd learned at his side.

"Any advice you'd like to give me?" D asked.

John's sound and salty advice was: "Work like hell and pray for rain, boy." (D's brother was ten years older, and when he didn't call D "Pete," he called him "boy.")

It was a time of beginnings and endings, the transition from something old to something new. Such shifts are not made without a wrench to someone. D didn't seem to have a pang. He said that if the ranch became part of us, we were bound to become part of it. I went to sleep remembering Maristan Chapman's immortal words: "Seems a man's bound to buy whatever he gets with the price of some other thing he loses."

That night I admitted to D that I was a bit uneasy about all the things I had professed to being so knowledgeable about to the Williamses. I hoped I had been honest, but I'm afraid I forgot to say that my milking experience was witnessed from the top rail of the cow pen, that my soap making was observed from the smokehouse roof (a favorite perch of mine), and that all the chickens I'd dealt with most intimately had been cooked. D said he thought he had detected a false note in some of my assertions. He added, "I thought you laid the butter on a little thick." Surely though, I rationalized, I'd learned something from so much watching and from listening to Mother's instructions.

I had drawn a floor plan of the Big House at the Pitchfork and had brought it home with me. Every second I had to spare from showing the place, I used for poring over those drawings. Starting with the living room—bedroom that was yet to be built, I placed every piece of furniture and drew a divine country fireplace to scale. I'd use old soft red brick for the hearth and sides, and I'd use the beveled pine in that lumber shed above it and perhaps on the entire south wall. The mantlepiece could easily be fashioned from a long timber I'd seen there too. I planned grandly, push-button service, bells everywhere. I wished that I'd had the time to measure the furniture space in the big living room. I could have mentally placed everything we had and would have known beforehand the pieces of Pitchfork furniture we'd like to use.

6

The Welcome

I wondered if I should wear a dress or a pair of the new Levi's. I wanted to wear the Levi's, to start right out being a ranch woman. I know now those new unwashed Levi's would have been a mistake. When I did wear them Cuppie said, "Mamie, your Levi's are not the right color." She seemed to have a natural feeling for all that pertained to ranch life.

But my decision to wear the dress stemmed from the fact that I thought it might be more appropriate for the manager's wife to wear a dress just that first morning when I was being introduced.

I was glad to be going over to the chuck house for breakfast; I felt an excited glow of warmth at the sound of the chuck-house bell. It wasn't a harsh, clanging bell. It was deep toned, it had a kindly mellow sound, why it almost sang. I was eager to know my new neighbors, the Pitchfork people, and I hoped they would know how happy we were to be here, to be one of them.

"We'll have to hurry, Cuppie," Baba said. (Our grandchildren called D "Baba.") "We must be ready when the next bell sounds."

"Try to show the cooks every consideration," D had said, "They've got a heavy job and a great burden. Their little girl is afflicted; some nights they don't get three hours' sleep."

Cuppie said, "That next bell rings in fifteen minutes, Mamie, Dickie told me." Her eyes were wide with importance. I buttoned her dress, pinned the damp curls back with a comb, and we were ready. "Dickie don't wear shoes," she told me, looking down at her sandaled feet. "Dickie wear boots. Dickie wear Levi's, too."

I could see the men and boys streaming in from every direction as we left the Big House door, coming from the shop, the corral, the bunkhouse; a picture to remember, their broad shoulders, their slender hips, their Stetson hats, the blue of their skin-tight Levi's, and their gay neckerchiefs.

I sensed an intense thrill. I felt as if Uncle Sam's boys were marching by. And it is given to us, I thought, to be a part of it. The tears had started in my eyes. I couldn't have told you why. I stood there thinking, How foolish, and yet how nice to feel this way. The second bell gave out its friendly clang. We were just in time.

We had stopped where the walks came together to let the men pass. In an awed whisper Cuppie said, "Those fings that make that muserick are spurs, Dickie told me." Spurs are the badge of the riding man, I'd heard my father say it many times.

The men gave no sign of knowing we were there. I'd heard they were terribly shy of women. This was my only firsthand acquaintance with them. Though born and reared in Texas, I came from sections far removed from the pasture country. My ideas of ranches and cowboys had been built entirely by Pops, D Burns, and the movies, but the foundation had been solid. My father had told stories of the big Matador Ranch, where he had worked for a year when he was only a boy. I had thrilled to those stories as a little girl, and they had left an abiding memory. Cowmen were the salt of the earth, men of wit and brawn and daring. D Burns had finished the structure. He had lived on a ranch until about the time we were married, and every hour of those twenty bootless years he was aching to be back on one. D had peopled his stories with figures of the range, stalwart, brave and kind, real and alive.

They hadn't said much about women on the ranches except Pops had said calicoes were scarce. They had called women calicoes, bunnies, and sage hens then, he told me. D's stories were all of men, too, but of course there were women on ranches—look at the movies—and cowboys had all the respect and reverence in the world for a good woman. They'd lay down their lives for her, and often did, in the movies.

And today's crop was as colorful as those Pops pictured in the '80's. If there was a finer looking bunch of boys than these anywhere, I'd not care to see them. All our tomorrows would be spent in this world of motion and color; our yesterdays, though serene and happy, were picayune in comparison. That was sweet, our tomorrows and yesterdays, I'd read that somewhere no doubt, but I'd remember to use it.

The men took long drags on their cigarettes, stamped the butts into the ground with their boot heels, and filed into the screened porch of the chuck house.

We were close behind them, savoring every minute of this first morning of our new life. This would be a different breakfast from any we had eaten before. I was sorry D wasn't there to share the excitement of it with us. Everything was more fun for sharing it with D, and a thing as once-in-a-lifetime as this— But I'd make a little ceremony of it in my heart and try to impress it on Cuppie, who was three and a half. It was all so perfect, and I wanted her to remember it that way. "Cuppie, darling," I said, "Try to remember today, our very first day on the Pitchfork."

I knew that I was being sentimental, but Cuppie wasn't. "Let's go eat," she said practically. "Let's go eat," I echoed. I knew that once inside there would be much joking, laughter, and kindly talk. Such was my naive belief.

No one except the Austins answered my good morning when we were inside the chuck house. "Good Morning, Miz Burns," they managed busily. There were no introductions. No one said, "Fellers, this here's the new boss's wife," as they do in the movies. No one waited for the other person to be seated, no one was expected to wait. They crawled over the pine benches that flanked the long table, reached for the biscuits, forked great slabs of ham onto their plates, slid a few eggs on beside it, and fell to. Momentarily conversation ceased.

Surely, I thought, I should have been introduced, and the men at least could have spoken. They were bound to be aware of a stranger in their midst. They must have seen me standing outside, must have seen me come in, heard my greetings to the Austins, yet they ignored me as completely as if I weren't sitting at the table. They pretended to be unaware of my presence.

The big platters of food were not passed. The policy seemed to be every man for himself. There was enough food on that table for an army in the field, I thought, yet Mr. Austin was bringing in more ham and biscuits before I had touched a bite. The men stabbed their biscuits with their forks. This range etiquette was not lost on Cuppie. Next meal she speared one. She had to raise herself up from the bench on one knee, but she did it expertly.

Cups sat solemnly looking from one to another of the men, "I fink it's a race," she whispered. Pops had said a cowboy never hurried, that he had ample time. Well, these men were hurrying for some reason this morning, and the hurry was in definite contrast to their leisurely entrance. Maybe they had just decided to have a roundup or branding or something.

Cuppie and I had found a vacant place on the bench and had managed to squeeze in between an elderly man and a very fat one. A bit of talk started up. Someone mentioned a big auger and a steel windmill. This started the elderly man excitedly discussing windmills.

"I wouldn't give one wooden mill for a dozen of them steel ones," he said. There was anger in his words.

I wondered why, and was glad I knew what augers and windmills were just in case I was included in the conversation. I could have saved myself that thought. I didn't and I wasn't, for D was the big auger as I found out later, and windmills—I was to hear more about windmills in the next few months than I'd ever heard before or would ever care to hear again.

"Got any more of that brown gargle?" one of the boys asked, starting toward the kitchen.

"'At's Marvin Lee," Cuppie confided. Dickie again.

I had a grand throat swab and was about to offer to go back to the house and get it when I noticed the cup in Marvin's hand and the beeline he was making for the big range. The men ate hurriedly and drank their coffee noisily. I knew why they called it brown gargle now and was glad I hadn't made the mistake of saying anything. It was the only mistake I didn't make for the next two years.

Between bites, I took inventory of the crowd. To me they were an exciting lot, but I made the humbling discovery that I didn't register with them at all. The men seemed cautious and on guard. It was hard to catch the eye of one of them, but, when I did, I nodded and smiled. They simply looked the other way as quickly as possible. Their actions did not indicate shyness or timidity. You couldn't call them unsociable; they were sociable enough themselves. My presence did not seem to cramp their style. They didn't seem to know that I was there. They laughed and joked. "That was the year I lost twenty thousand dollars in wheat," I was surprised to hear Marvin Lee say to something they were discussing. I hadn't known cowboys had that kind of money. If he had large holdings, farms of his own, what was he doing here, I wondered. The answer to my wonderings was not long in coming. "How'd you lose it?" a sandy-haired, dour-looking man, who was sitting across the table from me, asked. "Wheat went to two dollars a bushel that year, and I never had air'n," Marvin answered, his black eyes dancing. I joined in the roar of laughter, for everyone laughed except the man who had snared the bait. He sat in red-faced silence, motionless as the sphinx and twice as glum. A purple flush spread slowly over his face and down his thick neck. Something told me the men enjoyed the joke, especially because this fellow had been taken in by it. I didn't think they liked him any too well. I wasn't sure I was going to like him either.

He was of medium height but powerfully built. The flat twang of his voice was grating on the ear and his eyes were mirthless. That night when I told D about the incident, hoping he could identify the crusty, fortyish individual, Cuppie chirrupped, "That was Jake, Mamie, he is the fightingist man on this ranch." Behind her back, D shut one brown eye at me, moved his head slowly up and down, confirming Dickie's relayed report that Jake was tough beyond description. "But a darned good hand," D said.

I sat on the bench, studying the rest of the crowd. I had a few of the group sorted out now. Not all the men wore Levi's and spurs. There were a few in clothes of an entirely different breed, their bibbed and shapeless overalls that made them look more like mechanics rather than cowboys. The cowboys were slender, but most of these men were as solidly built as their shoes. My glance fixed on a strapping fellow with reddish hair and three-day whiskers who was sitting across the table from me. He was almost hidden behind a mound of hot biscuits, and he kept right on eating. There was grease clear up on his bald spot. He had never said a word, but I had a feeling that he was a kindly man. He was the only one who seemed interested in my impressions of this hoorah. The men called him Floyd.

One of the boys had finished his breakfast, and, following ranch custom, he crawled over the bench and carried his plate, cup, and saucer to the kitchen. Two others were taking their dishes in when he put on his hat and dropped a letter in the mailbox that hung beside the door. Cuppie's eyes followed his every movement, "Jack Cook winned," she clapped her hands in ecstasy, "Jack Cook winned the race, I like Jack Cook," she confided. "Do you like Jack Cook, Mamie?" she whispered. This must be Jack Cook, I thought. "Of course," I whispered back and knew that I meant it. He was the sweetest-looking boy I had ever seen and the handsomest. I have to smile now, remembering, because every female between the ages of three and eighty-three thought the same thing.

The crowd was watching Jack as he sifted through the big stack of Pitchfork mail, fishing out his own letters. It was plain that he was a favorite. "Jest five?" one of them asked incredulously. "Mail's falling off, ain't it?" from another. "Mail ain't his specialty, the telephone is his real dish," Mr. Austin said. "It's got to where I can't get nothing done for answering that phone." "Is Jack Cook there?" Veto mimicked in a high falsetto. Jack's even, white teeth flashed, but his answer was lost in the hoorah of the men. So little did he himself think of those letters that he piled them on the table's end and took an unconcerned step toward the door. A long arm flashed across three plates and the letters were almost in the grasp of some long fingers when Jack Cook, without haste and without loss of dignity, slipped them from under the hand and into his pocket. He turned around and grinned as he opened the door to the outside and, for a moment, his clear blue eyes looked straight at me. Of course, I grinned too. Jack Cook frowned slightly. He was not to be taken in by smiles from strangers, he left no flicker of doubt about that. He pulled his hat down tight on his forehead and, without a backward glance, was gone.

I felt suddenly tired. All the excitement of the hour before had gone, that pleasant glow of warmth and anticipation, and in its place a vague feeling of disappointment. I went back to the house slowly, arguing inwardly. They didn't like me. Nonsense, they couldn't not like me, they didn't know me. They hadn't even spoken. Well, there was nothing unusual about that, I reassured myself. They were shy. Hadn't I heard Pops tell always the story of the timid cowboy of the Matador, who had backed into the campfire and a pot of boiling beans rather than face a female visitor? I smiled in memory of that story. But the ones Pops told about were kind of characters, witty, taciturn codgers with hearts of gold, and D had said that cowmen were the friendliest on earth. Well, Pops and D Burns to the contrary, they were anything but chummy.

When we reached the house, Cuppie pointed to the big, red pitchfork on the porch with her toe. "Look, Mamie, that's the way they monogram their cows," she said, then mounted her tricycle and rode away to adventure with Dickie.

Let me go ahead here a little and say that's the way it has been every day that we have spent on this ranch. No matter how low or discouraged we were, how bleak our outlook for the day, something of beauty, of fun, of wit or interest would claim our attention. A skunk, nose to the ground, will mosey by, a jackrabbit, big-eared and curious, will raise his head in interest, and if you are lucky, a coyote, a coon or badger will show. Sometimes it's the sight of a flowering bush abloom on the creek, white, pink, yellow or lavender, that wasn't there yesterday, or the turkeys gone to roose in the dead cottonwoods, the sunset behind them. Artists and writers say our sunsets are the most beautiful they have seen. They try to capture them with brush and pen.

Later the men at the chuck-house table could always lift our spirits, but only little Cuppie's blithe words, "That's the way they monogram their cows," cheered me now. I thought of D happier than I had ever seen him. It was worth a lot just to see that look on his face. And little Cuppie beside herself with joy in the things she was doing and learning with Dickie. A voice accused me of being selfish. How could it possibly matter that those people had not noticed me? Or what difference could it make to our job what they thought of me? I'd put such immature thoughts out of my mind. The ranch was all that mattered, the ranch and our job. I'd get to work, that's what I'd do, that's what I always did when I was disturbed or unhappy. There was something I could do, I could clean those dusty closets, the walls and the shelves, and take stock of the linen room. Going around back through the kitchen, I picked up a stepladder, broom, mop, and dustcloths and put myself to the task of cleaning. Yes, work was a panacea, but my thoughts spiraled. Each time I remembered our sweet old clock, broken beyond repair in the move from San Angelo, I found myself shedding unwilling tears. All that day the happenings at the chuck house kept passing through my mind: feelings of mingled excitement and apprehension, Marvin Lee's subtle baiting, Veto's droll comments, and Jack Cook, what a charmer! It was all there, the fun, the wit, the spar-

kle; I just hadn't been included in it. I remembered the old gentleman in the blue bibbed overalls who spoke most emphatically about
windmills. Why was he so disgruntled? And the Austins hadn't
introduced me. Veto's explanation was simple two years later, once
I got around to suggesting that a new comer be introduced at the
chuck-house table, at least to the person sitting next to him. They'd
feel so much more comfortable. I thought the chuck house should be
a place where a new boy, a visitor, or a new manager's wife could plug
in. Veto never missed a point, nor was he ever caught without a
plausible answer. "Aw, Miz Burns, they'll find out who one another
is if they stay around here any length of time, and if they don't, why
it don't make no difference." But of Veto's classic remark and this
attitude, I knew nothing then. I kept feeling, and trying not to feel,
that something was terribly amiss only eighty-five miles from Lubbock, a place we had once lived for five years, yet I felt like a
stranger in a foreign land. And I'd worried about what I should wear!
The one or two glances given me had not merited my concern.

I tried but could not recapture the happiness of the morning.
I'd gone over all eagerness to shake everybody by the hand, to talk
about our plans, to let them know at once that D wanted more than
anything else to be friends and to make the Pitchfork the most wonderful place in the world to live, where every man would feel he had
a home, not just a job. It had not turned out that way. I could not
throw off the blue mood that had descended upon me. I didn't
know what was the matter or what I could do about it, but of one
thing I was sure: if there had been, subconsciously, any "lady of the
manor" feeling lurking about, it had all been knocked out of me.

The chuck-house bell tolled the noon meal, but I didn't go
over for lunch. I just wasn't hungry. Cuppie went over to eat with
Dickie. "My Mama says it's all right," he told me shyly.

When she returned for her nap, I inquired, "Did you have a
good lunch? What did you eat?" D had said the Austins served well-
balanced meals. "Uh huh!" She emphasized both syllables. "I ate
two pieces of pie and some ice cream." The Austins' pies and
cakes—in fact, their whole dessert table—have caused strong men
and determined women to forget calories and well-balanced meals,
to weaken and go back for seconds. "Do I have to take off my sandals, Mamie?" She was crawling onto the bed. She yawned, closed

her eyes, and was gone. When I removed the sandals and socks, dirt, grass, and sand poured out. We'd have to get stouter, less open foot gear for our little girl, boots maybe.

About the middle of the afternoon, D walked in. "How did you come out?" he asked. I guessed that he meant at breakfast, and I told him that I had occasioned no noticeable flurry among the Pitchfork crew. This gave D a chuckle. "Likely didn't know you were there," he pointed out. I thought I detected a relish of the situation, for his eyes held a gleam of amusement, as he dialed his radio. D knew that something had set me back on my heels, and he suspected what that something was. I felt a quick resentment. He was actually enjoying my discomfiture. I was somewhat miffed, too, that he could read me so easily. I'd as soon live with a ouija board as D Burns. Well, if those men were as happily oblivious of the boss's presence as they were of his wife's, he was going to have a sweet time running this ranch. But the thought was cold comfort. With a look in his eye and a solemnity that commanded my attention, D said, "They give their regard and friendship to no one, Mayme. Those who have it have earned it." Well, if that was all, I knew boys; one had only to feed them. I'd use charm if I had it. Sincere good will, a few tricks picked up from *How to Win Friends and Influence People,* and a few from my mother (cookies, cakes, candy), they'd come on the double. One had only to feed them. My spirits lengthened. Things would take a more genial turn. I said as much to D. He warned me not to expect an overnight turning. He was a long way from believing that cookies and pleasant words would bring them around. I went to bed that night wondering how I might contribute to a finer, fuller life.

7

Old Man Hinch

Chokie and Urina had come and gone. They were anything but loathe to leave us. "We ain't nevah wukked nowheres that Chokie ain't had his drinkin'," Urina informed me. Chokie had had his drinking here too, so they had gone.

"Ten days on the ranch and we are without help," I grieved. "Ten days on the ranch *without* help, you mean," D grumbled. "We've got to get an ad in the paper." We got ads in several papers. I hoped we'd get an answer soon. Every way I looked, things were crying to be done. Weeds were window-high, trying to get into the house. We'd spent all our time so far unpacking dishes, arranging furniture, cleaning.

"Could you spare a boy to cut these weeds?" I asked as D started to the chuck house for breakfast next morning. D looked as though he had been stabbed by his best friend. This look, blood brother to the ones I was to get each time I asked for a man the next five years.

He pulled on his chin and assented reluctantly, "I guess you can have Old Man Hinch; he isn't any good for anything else." I was to learn that if a man was any good for anything else, he'd never be turned over to me. "I'll send him over right after breakfast."

Later, quite a bit later, I saw the old man saunter into the yard carrying a hoe. He examined the iron gate carefully, studied its design, rubbed his hand over it, swung it back and forth, scrutinized the hinges, seemed to find its latch satisfactory after opening and closing it a few times, leaned his hoe against the fence, and rolled a cigarette. He gazed into the newly leafed Chinese elms, blew some smoke heavenward, and sighed. He was finding life dull. In a little while he parted the weeds, walked through them to a bench, and sat down. Every gesture of his relieved body seemed to say, "This is more like it."

This wasn't Mr. Hinch, I reasoned, perhaps only someone who carried the hoe for Mr. Hinch. But I was wrong. In less than half an hour he walked to that hoe, picked it up, held it out in one hand, raised and lowered his arm as if judging its weight, felt the handle, slid his hand up and down it a few times, laid the hoe down, and ambled to the shop.

Presently he returned with a ball of black tape, wrapped that hoe handle for about eighteen inches midship, and then, with the ball of tape dangling, reached into his pocket. He pulled his hand out with a puzzled, worried look, felt in all his other pockets, leaned the hoe against the tree (tape still dangling), and started off again. He passed the office and the shop; I saw him take the path to the bunkhouse. After a distressing lapse of time he was back with a pocket knife. He cut the tape and pressed it down tightly, put the knife in his pocket, the ball of tape in the fork of a tree, and gave his attention once more to the hoe. He placed his hands a few inches apart on the bandaged portion of the handle and made several experimental swings, careful not to strike a weed. He seemed pleased with the grip.

Now we're set, I thought, but he changed ends with the hoe, ran a finger along its edge, and found it dull. He took himself and the hoe slowly to the office. Soon I saw the Pitchfork's new manager, file in hand, down on his knees by the office steps sharpening the hoe. I wondered if D were the executive type after all.

At exactly eight-thirty the first weed fell, and only two hours after breakfast. But, I wondered, why didn't he start at the gate? He had walked to the middle of the yard and chopped down a careless weed; maybe he was the type who liked to cut his way out of a situation.

He had a long, sad face, but a lot of ideas, I'd found. He took six more steps and attacked another careless weed, then the third. Maybe he had hay fever. I watched this procedure with interest. He cut only careless weeds and only the big ones! Perhaps a dozen weeds had been cut; their pattern of falling formed a perfect X. A plane was circling over the house. Could this be some signal he was giving? Was he a spy? What kind of a name was Hinch, German? I thought not. Certainly not Japanese.

He went to the hydrant, turned on the water, followed the hose to the nozzle and got a drink, walked to the back steps, sat down, took off his hat, fanned himself for a while, and rolled another cigarette. The weeds were knee-high. It was evident he wasn't afraid of rattlesnakes and equally apparent that he was afraid of work! Finally, still sitting on the steps, he raised the hoe and started cutting the weeds within arm's reach, but only the big ones. At last I understood his "working" methods. He was cutting the big weeds to cover up the smaller ones.

This was the worst sort of hoeing. My rural senses were outraged. Surely this man had not been long in the country. No one had ever taught him to cut weeds. I'd go and show him!

"Mr. Hinch, may I show you how to cut weeds?" I asked sweetly, remembering D's warning. "For God's sake, be careful what you say, Mayme." I was being very careful. He looked at me with no sign of comprehension. Hinch, Hinch, English, that's what he is. I felt sure now of his nationality.

I took the hoe from his hand. He looked positively amazed. "There's an art in cutting weeds," I explained brightly, "You start right at your feet." I snapped off the first few expertly, scraping the earth, getting the roots. He was looking straight at me, not at my art, giving me his complete attention, but he did not seem impressed. "You cut weeds as you come to them, sort of pull them back like this," I went on with the lesson. I handed him the hoe and smiled. "Not everyone can cut weeds properly," I prattled on.

He stood there stolid as stone. Then I caught his expression. His eyes, hostile, granite hard, bored me through. He took the hoe deliberately, set it firmly beside the door, and walked toward the office. What was the matter? I wondered. Was he offended? It occurred to me that he'd not said a word during the instructions. I felt terrible. I had the uneasy feeling that the man had gone to the office to get his time; I was sorry I'd said anything to him. And yet, one didn't want that kind of work. He was drawing pay, but he was slacking on the job; he wasn't halfway doing it.

Maybe he hadn't been offended after all. Maybe he'd gone after the file again and would be back in a minute. I went inside, but watched out the kitchen window, wishing I knew. In a little while I saw him leave the office. He did not turn toward the house. Oh well, I certainly hadn't done or said anything I shouldn't. It would work out all right, and I felt that I had righteousness on my side. But I was sorry.

I could see D coming to the house, his mouth set in a grim line.

Yes, the man had quit. I wondered what D's reaction would be. Would he be angry with me? "We've got some sick horses, Mayme, over in the Shinnery. The vet is here and I'm going over with him. We won't be back for lunch." His words sounded flat and discouraged, and the look in his eyes— Reproach in D's voice and eyes shrivels me inside.

Well, if he wouldn't mention Mr. Hinch, I would. "What did the old man want when he went to the office, D?"

"His check."

"Did he get it? Is he gone?"

"Certainly. He said he didn't intend to take orders from a woman."

"I wasn't giving him orders, D. I was only showing him how to cut weeds."

"Mayme, nobody likes to cut weeds. Nobody wants to be on the blister end of a hoe, especially a ranch hand. Mr. Hinch was a ranch hand. These people aren't used to having a woman here. There has been a bachelor managing this ranch for two years. Most of these men have never taken an order from a woman, it isn't customary on a ranch. You will have to remember that."

Trying to justify myself, I burst out rebelliously, "But D, what else could I have done? Did you see how he was cutting those weeds?"

"No, but I can imagine, just about like he did everything else. Now Mayme, when you have a couple here for this yard and house, they will be under your jurisdiction, but until that time, where that fence ends," he pointed through the window at the fence enclosing the yard, "your authority on the Pitchfork ends."

8

Why I Am As I Am

I think the two people who most influenced my early life were Aunt Fannie and Aunt Lizzie. One was my father's sister, one my mother's.

Uncle Tom Padgit and Uncle Ed Castleman were considered the wealthy men of their separate communities. Therefore, Aunt Fannie and Aunt Lizzie were the affluent members of our family. They lavished on me things my father considered unimportant. Their generosity took different forms. His sister, Fannie, thought my quality of life was enriched by lessons in dancing, riding, painting, bridge, and homemaking. Aunt Lizzie gave me gifts of the spirit, frivolous gifts of joy.

When I longed for anything, Aunt Fannie wondered if I truly needed it, if it would be of lasting value. Aunt Lizzie need only know that I wanted it. Because of Aunt Fannie and what she considered the amenities of life, I studied piano and art, but with indifferent results, and was allowed to drop them. Dancing and bridge, however, became sources of lifelong pleasure.

Pops would often remark to Mother: "Sister Fannie and Lizzie are going to make a dang fool out of Mamie. She doesn't think of anything now except playacting. She needs to stay home with us, and learn something worthwhile." He felt, in short, that the aunts were putting ideas into my head, and not very practical ones. I do not deny that he had a point there. I had the grain, tiny as a mustard seed, of an actress in me. Waking or sleeping, my dreams were all of the stage, and, nursing such ambitions, I begged Aunt Fannie not to enroll me in the homemaking courses. "I may never have a home or house to look after (picturing a glamorous life as a star in New York, Paris, and London), and I shall never marry a man who cannot afford help."

Aunt Fannie did not ridicule or deride my remark. She simply said, "Every woman must learn household skills. You must know how to do everything well in order to direct others." Subsequently, my Aunt Fannie had me take five years of homemaking courses at the high school on Saturday mornings when the rest of my friends were out horseback riding, bicycling, and playing tennis. I despised every minute of it, but I have been eternally grateful for everything I learned. Certainly not one acquired talent was left buried during the testing Pitchfork years. Though theater was not to become my medium of expression, Mother vowed I had been on stage, front and center, all my life.

While I was being indulged by the doting aunts, Pops was busily buying up all the land adjoining his and trying to meet the notes he'd made for the purchases. Late in the night I heard conversations not meant for my ears. Pops would say, "Dear, I've got a note due on the first, and I don't see how I'm going to raise the money. It keeps my head hot." Mother would reply, "I know, dear, it bothers me for you to be so worried, and I don't think it's necessary at all. Why don't you sell some of those places and clear the ones that mean the most to you? It would relieve us both. Being a big landowner doesn't mean a thing except more responsibility for you." Pops had no intention of selling anything, and he never lost a piece of land either. My family, by birth and inclination, has belonged to the soil.

Sometimes I hear my aunts' voices in my heart. Such different voices, expressing such different philosophies, such different people. Aunt Fannie had a flair for the grand manner, the lovely gesture. There was a quality of magnificence about her. Nine months of each year I spent with her, yet I never absorbed her graces or her charm. I think I remember best her voice, low and vibrant. The sound of it is never quite out of my memory, sometimes dim, sometimes clear, but never quite forgotten. Her voice was never raised in mirth or anger, a low chuckle when she was amused, a biting silence when she was displeased.

Her ways were those of dignity and tradition. She hadn't the slightest idea of changing them. Though rooted in the past, she prided herself on keeping abreast of the times. She read everything, knew and enjoyed artists, actresses, people in every walk of life. She could forgive anything except dullness, but for herself and her family she demanded the straight, the narrow path. I remember some of the things she tried to hammer into me in my childhood. With all her charm and dignity, Aunt Fannie was firm.

She thought the knowledge of words was essential. Being able to express one's thoughts precisely was important. One must possess the words. They were the tools. Reading with a dictionary beside you, looking up every doubtful word, digging out its meaning, tasting it, smelling it, feeling it. This was Aunt Fannie's method of improving one's mind and vocabulary.

"Learning makes a man fit company for himself," she quoted so often. She had a quotation for every occasion, and an apt one, too. I recall another favorite, "Her voice was ever soft and low, an excellent thing in woman," and a profound thought she liked to repeat, "Loneliness is not to be alone, but to expect no one." Her love for learning did not detract from her practicality. Aunt Fannie could be stern if sternness was required, and she was always frank. She made it plain to me that I was no beauty, that I would have to put something into my head and heart or go in for good works, a disheartening alternative for which I felt small interest.

Aunt Fannie thought the home you graced, the kind of clothes you wore, the stationery you used, your choice of words, your tone of voice, the way you spent your leisure hours, the way you liked to live, the way you dealt with those less fortunate or with those who served you, these things, she said, you are.

Money gave one no status with Aunt Fannie, but family was of the greatest importance. "Ector?" echoed Aunt Fannie, "I don't know the Ectors. Where are they from?" Though I'd met the Ector boy at a dance at the home of one of her friends, I was not allowed to accept his invitations until Aunt Fannie had shaken down his family tree.

Her brother did not share these attitudes. There was no dwelling on achievements of dead ancestors with Pops. You must amount to something yourself, and that something did not have to be reckoned in dollars and cents. Every tub sits on its own bottom. It's true, if your father and grandfather paid their bills and were true to their word, you were likely to do the same—a fine inheritance. But more power to the man who did not have this heritage yet who could lift himself by his own bootstraps, above parental reputation, and become known as a gentleman.

When I was seventeen, Aunt Fannie tried to explain the male segment of the species *Homo sapiens*. Men, she said, were a push-

over for a pretty face. Of course, she didn't express it that way or
put it so baldly. Men, she thought, were important. I sat up, intrigued. Here was something worthy of a girl's interests. It called for
a subtle bit of doing, but Aunt Fannie thought they were worth it. I
thought so too! She said men were susceptible to flattery and soft
glances, of course. She thought camraderie was more my line,
however.

I must be different. A lot could be done by dress. If others were
going formal, why not appear in sweater and skirt? But Aunt Fannie
made it clear that sweater and skirt must be elegant beyond words.
My thoughts cut through her refined phrases. "But *what* a sweater
and skirt" was what she meant. Why didn't she just say so? That
was the only trouble with Aunt Fannie. She had taken all morning
to tell me a few simple facts. It all simmered down to the premise
that men were simple souls and no match for a clever girl, with or
without beauty. They could be had! I thought she meant I must develop a technique and that I should go to work on it right away. I
knew just where I'd start.

In the first days of June before school was out in Houston, I'd
begin dreaming of going to Aunt Lizzie's farm near Waco, of wading
through meadow grass as high as my waist, cool and green under my
bare feet. I'd think of the marvelous congregation of animals she
always saved for me to name, and all the fascinating details she
would tell me of their stories and the circumstances under which
they'd come to her. Usually a hired hand would bring an orphan or
a cripple for her to minister to. She fed them buttermilk. "Never
sweet milk," she'd say. "That gives them the scours." I believe today
infectious scours (calf diarrhea) is blamed on a complex of bacterial
agents and viruses. Aunt Lizzie managed on sour milk to feed her
starving babies into butterballs. After she had nursed them back to
health and they had outgrown her nursery, she would give them to
some child on the place for a pet. Aunt Lizzie loved animals. She
talked to and treated them like human beings. She would teach
them tricks according to their abilities so that they would not feel
inferior to a stronger competitor at the trough.

Frequently there was a baby pig underfoot, the runt of a litter
who could not scrounge for itself. Always there was a lamb or two.
The story of one lamb she rescued was so sad. A sheep is a clumsy

animal, and if for any reason it is thrown on its back in a furrow or trench, it is unable to right itself. One ewe with a baby lamb got out of her pen into a cotton field, where she stumbled into such a position between the rows that she could not get up, and she lay writhing and scrambling in the summer heat until she died. Her baby was found alive, trying to nurse a mother who must have been dead for hours. This heartbreaking tale brought tears to my eyes, and the first religious doubts of my young life. How could a just God let this happen?

Aunt Lizzie's pets lay around the dooryard waiting for her to appear. They jumped up and ran to her with such vigor they would almost knock her off her feet as they vied for her attention, making their individual sounds—a pigeon lighting on her shoulder cooing, the soft nudge of a sheep, the bark of a dog as he leapt upon her, a calf butting away at the others, and, most noisy and demanding of all, a pig squealing at the top of his unpleasant voice and grabbing at her clothes. Aunt Lizzie fondled them, called them by name, and fed them fruit or grain from her pockets. "There, Squealer, there, aren't you a noisy boy?" "Come here, Lambie." She'd carry the crippled baby in her arms.

Aunt Lizzie was a born researcher. She must always know the why of all she saw and experienced. When she came upon something unusual, she asked questions of all who might enlighten her on the object or subject. She would search book stalls for material pertaining to it.

It was the same with people, especially young ones whom she found striving for knowledge or expertise in some field. She immediately set about trying to help, buying books or tools or furnishing a quiet place for them to study, a desk and a good light in her garage or unused servant's quarters. She would make it possible, somehow, for them to realize their dreams.

Aunt Lizzie liked to help people to help themselves. She did not believe in giving money. "It impoverishes one," she said. "It robs one of dignity." She took pleasure from the pleasure she gave and found only those who had something to give interesting.

I remember the instance of a hot tamale man in Waco who passed Aunt Lizzie's home on the way to a nearby park where he set up his wares. His tamales were delicious, as were the pralines he sold. One day I remarked that he had a new cart. With great pride he told me that my aunt had bought it for him.

Aunt Lizzie did not like her charitable deeds to be known. "Honey," she said, almost apologetically, "the old rig was too small and worn out. The canister he used to keep his tamales hot would no longer hold water. He'd have to walk back to his home to replenish his supplies and hot water. He lives in a hut on the other side of Cameron Park—it's miles from here." (How did she know where he lived unless she'd picked him up and taken him home?) "He works so hard and does his job so well. He is very deserving."

Aunt Lizzie believed in the unfailing power of herbs. She explained their properties. In her garden grew rosemary, sweet basil, thyme, dill, mint, oregano, lavender, balm, verbena, chives, parsley, and others I have forgotten. "If we knew how to use prayer and herbs properly," she declared, "We'd seldom have need of doctors."

One was amazed at the range and vigor of her conversation, at her exact knowledge, and even more amazed when she stepped out of her car (one of the first in McLennan County), wearing a tweed suit purchased in England, a velvet picture hat complete with egret that she had seen in a Parisian shop window and found too beautiful to resist, and a pair of tennis shoes for comfort. That was during a time when comfort in foot gear was a dirty word. One saw at once that with all her travels and the studies she had mastered, dress was the one thing that concerned her least.

I asked Mother, who was born with impeccable taste, a quiet sense of clothes, and what went with what, "Why don't you help Aunt Lizzie to coordinate her wardrobe?" "Why, daughter," she reproved, "Aunt Lizzie is above clothes. Her mind is on more important things. I thought you recognized and appreciated that quality in her." "Yes, of course I do, Mother," I answered. "Her indifference to clothes is part of her charm." Thereafter I would see her in that light, always proud that on every and any occasion Aunt Lizzie had the upper hand of her clothes.

Aunt Lizzie knew all there was to know about nature and the out-of-doors. Her philosophy was that the wise gardener learns to work with nature. As nearly as he can, he finds out what her laws are and obeys them. Nature will then help and work with him. For example, when I was an impatient little girl attempting to force a wisteria frond to wind Mamie's way, she said: "Honey, as a general rule most twining plants twist only in one direction, to its left or to its right. Honeysuckle, for instance, always twines clockwise, to its right, while jasmine always twines counterclockwise, to its left. Efforts to make them go the other way have always failed." I think I got my great love of plants and flowers from her. She taught me the small knowledge that I have of them. She not only knew their habits, she knew their families, their names and different parts. I was fascinated by the words she used. "A panicle is a pyramidal, loosely branched flower cluster," she told me.

I remember to this day the exact words of the definitions she used. "Lilac, *Syringa vulgaris*," Aunt Lizzie would tell me, as she held one in her hand. Then she'd add the something that would make it easy for a little girl to remember. "Its stem was in use as pipe stems long ago." She made learning fun. "Rhizomes"—we were dividing iris. Aunt Lizzie called everything by its botanical name. She could not abide an iris being called a flag or vinca called periwinkle.

So many times sitting under a tree here on the ranch, gazing over the rolling hills, the creek beyond, surrounded by blooming flowers and shrubs, listening to the birds—all those things Aunt Lizzie loved and lived for—I'd think of her and wish she could be here beside me. How she would have loved this place, the hop toads, the turtles, wild turkeys, baby pigs, baby calves, baby colts. She loved the young of every living thing and wanted to be sure before we killed anything that it did more harm than good and that it was an enemy to man. She created in me the love of nature. She taught me a reverence for life.

I feel I must insert a letter, written to my mother in 1945, which, twenty years later when my letters were returned to me and today, almost thirty years later, seems to sum up my continuing and eternal love for Aunt Lizzie and Mother and gardens.

May 5, 1945

Dearest Mother,

I wish you were here with me today. All the trees are in leaf and flowers are everywhere. I've just brought in an armload of lilac branches, put them in our old black pitcher. Their scent fills the room, and me, with nostalgia, remembering how you, Pearl and I tended those two big lilacs at the old home place, cultivating, fertilizing and watering. How we delighted in their blossoms, but what an onerous task it was removing them after they were spent. This seems always to have been my job, snipping, snipping, snipping those dried clusters. The big scissors left blisters on my fingers. Of course I complained. I can still hear you and Aunt Lizzie trying to encourage me, "Why, Honey, that's the way you prune lilac. It won't be as pretty another year unless you cut everyone of those old panicles off the bush."

This is a confession it shames me to make, but I had to be a woman grown before I came fully to appreciate my parents. Their life there on the farm seemed so prosaic compared with the enchanted goings-on at Aunt Fannie's and Aunt Lizzie's. Aunt Fannie's homes in Waco, Boerne, and Houston were near-mansions with four or five servants slithering about. She dressed from the great houses, but with the utmost simplicity. She used little jewelry; pearls were her preference. Her at-homes on Thursday afternoons in Houston were justly famous. What dimensions were added to my life by encountering on an intimate basis such renowned people as Teddy Roosevelt, David Warfield (*The Music Master*), Helen Keller, Thomas Dixon (*The Klansman*), Anne Morgan, Dr. George W. Truett, the Tom Connallys, the Morris Shepherds, Ruth Bryan Owens, and even Elwell, the world's bridge authority. It was from him that I learned to call a spade a spade at the age of ten, and I have never been the same since. Aunt Fannie's years as dean of women at Baylor University had enabled her to meet many of the famous, but it was her charm and elegance and erudition that served as a magnet for the exceptional personalities who thronged her home and life.

In Waco, the aunts lived just two blocks apart. One had to look for Aunt Lizzie's Georgian colonial behind the noble trees and flowering shrubs. In the verdant summertime when the coral vine and clematis were blooming and climbing clean up the columns, Aunt Lizzie's visitors met under the trees or around the kitchen table rather than in the drawing room with its cherrywood Tennessee antiques. You'd come upon a group of friends, with baskets and trowels, who had dropped by to get a fan from a new variety of iris, or a fresh start of mint or thrift (*Armeria maritima*), or perhaps a cutting from a prize rose bush that was rooting under a fruit jar just ready to transplant to a neighbor's garden.

I was too young to comprehend the feudal nature of my parents' relationships with the people on our place. There were families of Mexicans, Bohemians, Negroes, Germans, and Anglos who all looked to my parents for their every need. Perhaps the larger part of my alienation stemmed from the stark surprise of a brand new baby sister, Willie, firmly ensconced in the center of the family when I returned from a triumphant year in Houston of living at Aunt Fannie's and attending school. No warning, no modern psychological sibling preparation—there she was! Loving surprises as few people do, Pops suggested this one for me, keeping the new baby a secret. Willie was the delight of the family from an early age. The delight of everyone but me, that is.

I was not the queen bee at home. I was the middle child. Pearl, a foster daughter older by seven years, was the young lady of the household, so naturally the prettiest clothes and other considerations were reserved for her. Willie was seven years younger and as the baby was entitled to the best. At the family table she expected and got "the liddy, the giddy, and the heart of the chicken," although before her coming the gizzard had my name on it. If she wanted to maul my favorite prize doll, the baby must be served. So, I had boundless devotion to offer to someone, and those someones were Aunt Lizzie and Aunt Fannie.

It was only when my twin, Skeeter, was there that I felt important. He was not really my twin, of course, but his father and mine were the closest of friends. Skeeter and I were born in the same week, and the Shelton's black maid said, "Lawd hep us, them two woulda been twinses ef he hadn't been born to the Sheltons and her to the Sypertses." In him I had an admiring audience, a friend and champion in all I suggested and did. We played in the tree house, which was the "castle on yon hill." We raced old Runey and Beauty, our gallant steeds (plough horses to the pragmatic). These activities acted as a safety valve for the energies of two highly imaginative youngsters.

We wrote stories together. He produced the chapters of derring-do, and I supplied the romantic settings and details of life in the castle. Each of us wholly approved the talents of the other. "You are the only girl I know who can climb as high or run as fast as a boy." Such praise filled me with pride, and Skeeter showed great admiration for the stories I put into the mouths of my pet dog and horse. One, I remember, my dog Dandy composed. Mother saved these gems for me.

> "I hate cats," Dandy told me.
> "I hate them because they can climb a tree.
> When they are high on a limb,
> They smirk down at me.
> I hate them because they can climb a tree."

Runey, my horse also wrote a poem, but it was in prose:

> "I am a horse and I am supposed to be a dumb animal, but I see her coming and I hear her calling: 'Runey, Runey, here Runey.' I know she has an apple or some sugar or an ear of corn in her hand. But sometimes she has a bridle in the other hand that she is holding be-hind her back. Sometimes I just kick up my heels and run away but most times I get caught."

One rainy afternoon when I was thirteen, I made my first divinity, and of course, Skeeter was there to help beat it, and said it was good and that he really liked divinity you had to eat with a spoon. My first compliment bestowed by the opposite sex was Skeeter's admiring comment, "Mamie, your hair is so long you can sit on it."

I was out of the country when Skeeter went away, and I did not know of his death until my return. These are my flowers, Skeeter. No mention of my childhood would be complete without you.

But going back to my parents, and go back to them I did in every crisis in my life. Mother and Pops were stalwart parents, strong, brave, and resolute. The standards they set for me seemed at that time impossible of achievement. But I know now they were not, and that they were also practical.

Annie Ophelia Shelton married James Lee Sypert on February 25, 1891. I've often wondered why, for a more temperamentally opposite pair would be hard to find. If Mother was sugar and spice and everything nice, the personification of quiet love, Pops was salt and pepper and quite a bit of ginger, and High Boss by his own admission. D always said, "Miss Annie should have taken a wet rope to Mr. Jimmie a long time ago." If Mother ever considered trying to control Pops, it was before I knew them.

Pops had a fiery temper and was a great cusser. He'd almost unhinge the front door slamming it after an argument. Like a stream, his temper was soon up, soon down. He'd cool immediately and circle the house whistling a tune peculiarly his own. No one could ever identify it. It went like this:

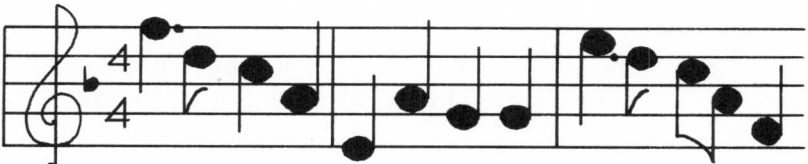

Coming in the back door he'd say to Mother, "Dear, Jim Sypert lost his head that time."

"Yes, he did." Mother always took the martyr's tone and manner with her "I'm hurt, not angry" attitude.

His constant profanity was tempered by his blue eyes twinkling with excitement. "He's the best damn preacher I ever heard" meant only how much he liked that minister. "Hell, by God, dear," he swore with every breath. But somehow it didn't sound like swearing when he'd rip out "he's not worth a barrel of hell" or "that's a damn fine baby" or "dear, where in hell is my hat?" He'd preface any search for anything with "Where in hell is—?" When I asked Mother how she had managed to put up with his profanity all those years, she said, "Honey, I can't be angry with Papa. He always calls me 'dear.'"

Mother lived so near the kernel of life as it should be that one never doubted her rightness. One never felt irritated with or critical of her, nor did one resent her counsel, which was seldom given unless asked for. Not so with Pops. Most typically, Pops was plainspoken, frank to the point of bluntness. "I'll tell you what I think," he'd say, and then he'd tell you without mincing words. He gave me some fairly ruddy convictions, all of which still echo through my ears, and I cannot desert them.

Loyalty was Pops' credo. He'd fight a circle saw in defense of a friend. He never forgot a kindness and had short memory for slights or injustices. "Dear," he'd ask Mother, "what was I upset with Judge Garland about last fall?" "The election, of course," she retorted. On that occasion Pops had told Judge Garland, with considerable zest, that he was the best man he had ever known to be on the wrong side of every damn question that came up.

I have not tried to smooth Pops up. As Aunt Fannie said, "He's a rough piece of cloth, but all wool and a yard wide." And furthermore, she added, "Jeems was born a farmer in the way that a prince is born a prince." Pops liked the feel of loamy earth sifting through his fingers. Tenderly he would pick up a handful and press it together. "Look here, honey, this is a sign of good land. It'll grow things."

Her being so close to my heart makes any attempt to describe my mother embarrassing to me. She was a peacemaker. This was her special gift. Coming from a large and sensitive, not to say tetchy, family, she had much practice smoothing things over. Mother had a definite set of values, and she lived up to them unflinchingly and unswervingly, but she had tolerance and compassion for those less strong. "That poor girl!" she'd say of a maiden betrayed by a moment of moonlight madness. More than anyone I have known, Mother practiced what she preached.

My aunts had given me a rare and unique adventure in my childhood, but in my maturity I came to know the true worth of my parents, and Willie—that little interloper, that little scene-stealer —came to be one of the dearest and most necessary things in my life. It is said that naming is a form of possessing. I named her William years ago, and though she is known as Billie or Willie to most, she is William to Sister.

9

First Christmas, 1942

Christmas! We got the feel of it early, and hope and dreams began to bubble as soon as Thanksgiving was behind us. Following the pleasant custom of the ranch, Christmas dinner was planned at the chuck-house for the evening of the 22nd with a dance to follow at the bunkhouse. The boys who wished to go home for Christmas would have time to do so.

The Pitchfork was a small community within itself. When we drew names, there were eighty-seven in the box for the gift exchange, as each man had the privilege of bringing his family or a friend to the festivities.

Enormous preparations were necessary, with most of the work falling to the couple at the chuck house, but many hands were involved in executing what Veto pictured as "putting the big pot in the little one and stewing the dishrag." I offered to furnish a fruit cake for each family, and these went under the tree. The day before the party I was astir long before dawn to prepare eight makings of my mother's eggnog recipe, which was more than ample as I found some disapproved of eggnog. Vanilla was there to wash up after me.

As D and I were dressing for dinner, Vanilla came into my bedroom. I said, "Vanilla, you're not dressed!" "Is we goin'?" she asked. "Of course, you're going." "Lawd God," Vanilla exclaimed, the eternal woman coming through, "What is I goin' to wear?" She exited on the run.

D spoke to me of his gratitude to the Williamses for breaking precedent and allowing him to give bonus checks to the men. "They can surely use them, especially the married ones. With Uncle Sam freezing salaries for the duration, this may help us keep our hands and build up some loyalty." He had thought of making a little talk to say a few words to express his appreciation for their help, let them know what he was trying to do, and how badly every pair of hands were needed to get the job done. "Mayme, it might not be the best thing, but I think I'll do it."

He had made up his mind, and we started for the Christmas tree and dinner. As we left the Big House we could hear the laughter from the dining room, it was a good sound. We hurried to join them, but when we opened the door and walked in, the laughter stopped. D and I headed for the big stove; we needed the warmth.

The food was ready and waiting on the long tables, and most of the people on the ranch had assembled with a few stragglers still coming in. Frances, Lefty, and Cuppy arrived with a beaming Vanilla carrying five-month-old Burns. Vanilla's voice called out, "Miz Burns, this baby is sho pretty since his hair done tuk effect." Vanilla was an ice-breaker on any occasion. The hungry crowd began loading their plates. The Austins and the ranch women had outdone themselves.

After the feast, the gifts from the tree were passed out by the small fry, and everyone was milling around visiting. Frances mingled happily with the crowd. My child never met a stranger, she didn't know of our concern; but I felt as alone in all the hubbub and gaiety as I had felt seven months before on that first morning at the chuck house. I watched these people greeting each other with enthusiasm and affection. It showed that when they wanted to they could be wholly charming or engagingly friendly, but they didn't want to where we were concerned.

It was time to distribute the bonus checks. D had told Harve Adams to have the boys stay for that part of the program. D rapped on a glass to get their attention. It was the first time in so long that I had seen D out of western clothes. I had not noticed how thin he had become. His coat hung so loosely on his shoulders. He must have lost twenty pounds.

Though the night was cold, D blotted the perspiration from his face and neck with his handkerchief. I guess he had already planned what he was going to say, though I doubt it. In all those speeches D had given for a dozen organizations all over the country, he'd never written down a word he was going to use. Those poor faltering speeches, I always wondered why he accepted or why they kept on asking. Tonight his words came easily. It seemed more like a prayer than just a talk.

I can see the laden table and remember the faces of the people who circled it that evening. I prayed that He who gave us Christmas would give us also a better understanding of each other. I searched those faces to see if D's words and his feelings were being understood. As I looked from one to another, fear arose in my breast, sharp and sure, shutting out the hope of the moment before, shutting out the talk and the laughter. I could read only hostility in their honest faces. I wanted to cry out, "You are good people! We know you are! So are we. Give us a chance!"

D's words came slowly. Never one for flowery speeches, he was pouring his whole heart into every word. He spoke of the cattle, of the responsibility each man had toward the ranch. He told them that in giving their best in producing food, meat, and grain, they were actually giving essential service to our country. We were all pledged to the utmost of our abilities so all honorable men could consider their job vital to the war effort. We must do our part, however small, D continued, and every man is important in his role. He asked them to remember that war wasn't fun, freedom not cheaply bought, that working long hours, wearing old clothes, not having everything we'd like to have to eat, and a few inconveniences were small sacrifices compared to these our boys on the firing line were making.

As D stood speaking so earnestly, pride stirred my heart; my ears were ringing with his words. They'd know now how he felt. They'd recognize his honesty, his sincerity. He'd touch their hearts, I just knew he would. It was then I observed the younger men exchanging amused and skeptical glances. I had to leave my place beside Frances to walk down to him, to stand near him. He seemed to me so incredibly alone.

"As in war, so on the home-front, unity is essential," D went on. He reminded them of the solemn fact that our soldiers and allies must have beef, and he hoped that every one of us would do our duty, though we were far from the bands and the flags and decorated heroes. He tried to make them realize that a man who was sending food to a soldier was also soldiering. The burden of his talk was cooperation, a plea to get more done.

The anticipated climax came when D took out the checks and called out: "Roy Bradford." From the far corner of the crowded room a small serious-faced man made his way toward us. I had most of the ranch group sorted out now, and as D spoke the name, my mind telegraphed, "Farm Camp, nice smile, gold teeth, tobacco." I could see him in his setting as manager of the Farm Camp, with the barns back of him, the pig pens, the fields of maize, and his overalls. But this clean-shaven man in the blue serge suit elbowing his way to D's side wasn't fitting my picture. Then our glances crossed, and his shy smile revealed the gold I was expecting. It was the dress-up clothes and the absence of the chew of tobacco that had momentarily thrown me. I had not seen him before without that lump of Star Navy in his jaw. I would never mistake Roy Bradford again. I would remember him for the thing he did, and the words he said as he took the check from D's hand: "Thank you, Mr. Burns. I never worked under a man who has helped me more with my job, or one I like better. You are my boss, and I want you to call on me anytime I can help you. Day or night."

D had called out the next name, "Robert Koonce," before he realized that Roy was going to speak, and Robert made his way across the room as Roy said his memorable words, loud and clear, and in plain sight and hearing of everyone on the ranch. Handsome Robert stood at Roy's elbow and said, "That goes for me too, Mr. Burns." Then Robert turned toward me and said, "Thank you also, Mrs. Burns." I had no words, just blinked back the tears.

The incident throbbed with significance for us. D had two known friends, Roy Bradford and Robert Koonce. Except for these two, it seemed none other quite dared to show themselves friendly.

You are thinking now, as I was at that moment, that this is the beginning of better days. Cooperation, however, did not come easily or all at once. Of course it was heartening for D to know that when he gave an order to Roy or Robert that it would be carried out to the letter. Roy could do this without interference from anyone, as he was responsible only to D, but Robert, who was under the wagon-boss and the assistant manager, would be helpless when Murd slyly but bluntly countermanded D's orders.

There were other men and women on the ranch who were our

friends, but we did not have the good fortune at that time to know it. As far as I know this was the only evidence of goodwill or support D had received, but we lacked, and there is no doubt about it, the friendship of the ranch in general, and without their friendship and help D could achieve nothing. D was cheered by the words of Roy and Robert, however, and as we were going back to the house he thought aloud, "If a man has two friends—" As we walked home from that dinner, not a word was said about those hostile glances. I, too, was cheered by the fact that Babe Oliver had smiled, wished me a Merry Christmas, and introduced me to his mother and dad. In a short time, Babe would be leaving us for the armed forces.

The long-awaited, traditional Christmas square dance of the Pitchfork was about to begin, old hat to most of the people to be there, but a brand new experience to us. For weeks the ranch children had been swinging their partners, do-si-doing and sashaying all over the place. Cars were beginning to arrive from neighboring ranches. Frances, Cuppie, and I hurried to the house to dress for the ball. I wore a cotton squaw dress, the blouse buttoned from chin to waist over a voluminous skirt, and donned one ring set with an enormous turquoise worn on the forefinger.

Frances had on a triple-tiered affair of yards and yards of calico, and yards and yards of turqoise and silver jewelry. She looked like a southern dream. Little Cuppie said with delight, "Oh Momee, you are lovely!" She was lovely herself in a stiff starched organdy pinafore with curls tied high on her head, very swish indeed. D wore his usual western attire, whipcord of the finest quality. People were always saying D looked exactly like Gary Cooper. But just between you and me, D was handsomer. After giving mutual approval to each other's attire, we drove up to the bunkhouse, site of the shindig.

Music and voices washed out over us as we pulled to a stop. We could see lights of more cars coming through the big gate on the highway. The sharp, merry sound of Veto's fiddle came to us in bouncing rhythm. There were lanterns and luminarias lighting up the yard around the bunkhouse.

The enormous hall was filled with music, dancing people laughing and talking, and the smell of sweat, horses, and bay rum. The ranch hands turned up not newly booted and spurred, as we expected, but with hair slicked down and boots polished. They too had raced to the bunkhouse from the Christmas festivity to shower and don their dress-up clothes. Even when freshly bathed and shaved, a cowboy exudes a persistent odor of horses. A cow hand is never entirely at ease out of his Levi's. He assumes a stiff starched manner, seems awkward and embarrassed, and loses half his charm.

Everyone was there, parents and toddlers, teenagers, grandmas, and babies. The walls were lined with oldsters holding babies and canes. Young children danced together around the edges of the floor. The boards shook as Veto called out a popular square and boots and slippers alike stomped to the music. Young Dick, Cuppie, and their friends tried out the steps.

It was a celebrity-studded affair, for there was George Humphrey, foreman of the 6666 Ranch, high sheriff of King County, and idol of every budding cowhand in the country. Nine-tenths of the boys at the dance wore their hats in a George Humphrey crush. Then there was Scan'lous John Selman. If you lived anywhere around this part of the country, you would have heard of him. He is one of the Swenson, or SMS (Spur Ranch), immortals. "Scan'lous"—the reason for the compelling nickname is a story well known in our section and told many times, but I shall tell it once more, for I heard it right from the horse's mouth that night.

It seems that John Selman was widely regarded as a bronc buster, or "peeler," in those parts. There was an unruly, unridable bronc that many a brave cowboy had come to grief trying to gentle. The day John and that bronc got together, John was pitched not once, but three times. Trying to regain his dignity, John got up, dusted off his pants, and, walking away from his own defeat, said, "Don't he pitch *scan'lous?*" With a whoop the assembled cowboys adopted John's new nickname, Scan'lous John Selman.

Then there were Al and Rachel Bingham. Al had the lofty grace of a prince. He was filled with chivalrous old-time courtesy. He was given the impressive title of Cornwallis by a visitor because of his elegant and courtly ways. Al could dance every square known and call it, too. In a manner almost forgotten now, Al Bingham bowed before me. "Mrs. Burns, may I have this dance?" Thanks to Pops, I did not have to learn to do-si-do. And away we went, heel and toe and a-one-two-three, Al's silk handkerchief protecting my dress from his immaculately clean hand. This was quite a contrast to the other cowboys, who mopped their foreheads and dried their hands with their cambric handkerchiefs and bandanas.

Jigs, reels, and square dances, dances as old as America herself. And round dances, which had been considered bold in my mother's day, the polka, and the waltz. They were daring because they permitted a gent who was not married or otherwise committed to a woman to put his arm about her waist.

Al Bingham had taken over Veto's fiddle and Veto approached me. "Mrs. Burns, I'll bet you can waltz." I said, "I'll sure try, Veto." So to the tune "Over the Waves," we circled the hall. Veto kept perfect time.

"Miz Burns, I'd shore admire to dance with ya." This was Scan'lous John Selman. I remarked to Mr. Selman, "We are pleased and surprised that so many have come so far on a bitter night to be with us. Stamford must be sixty miles or more." Scan'lous answered, "Miz Burns, to keep one of our men from this shindig it would have been necessary to cut off his legs."

Far gone in spirits, a young soldier came toward me. I accepted his invitation to dance. What he lacked in grace, he made up in vigor. After a few steps, he said in a loud voice, "Say, you can dance!" He danced in an abandoned way, sometimes kicking out to one side but more often kicking his partner on the shins. Overcome with Christmas and good cheer, he reeled over to Frances. "Wanna dance?" Now Frances was the best dancer this side of the Follies, but I wouldn't have taken anything for the remark I overhead, "Ain't danced much have you, girlie?"

I sank down gratefully on a chair and eased my bruised foot out of my shoe. Scan'lous John hurried over to me, "Want me to put him out, Miz Burns? I'd admire to do it." "Never mind, Scan'lous," I replied. "He's one of our soldier boys and it's Christmas. He means no harm."

Past midnight our family headed for the house. D had been ready to go since he got there. He said he'd never seen anything to dance about unless he had had a few drinks, but then "Mayme would be mad at me." Frances and I bathed our tired feet in hot water. Sitting on the side of the bathtub, we discussed our spirits-loving friend and our first Christmas ball at the Pitchfork.

The main gate to the Pitchfork Ranch appears above. The road is lined with the trees Mamie planted. Inside the Big House, below, D holds Anne Hamilton, while Mamie relaxes at the right.

Above: The Big House, Pitchfork headquarters. *Below:* The backyard at the Big House.

Clockwise, from upper left: D visits with Pitchfork owner Eugene Williams, who leans on the mantel of the living room fireplace. The Grands, Anne and Burns, look over their grandfather's shoulder as he reads a book he got for Christmas. Mamie's Aunt Fannie poses for her portrait. Mamie's mother is shown with her sister Lizzie.

Above: Ranch duties included representing the Pitchfork at area celebrations. Here the chuck wagon is ready to pull out for the Fourth of July Stamford Rodeo. Mamie's niece Anne McGuire, standing by the wagon in an all-white suit, is to be the ranch's sponsor at the rodeo. Burns (age four) and Anne (age seven) Hamilton are on horseback in front of her. *Below*: Mamie and D watch Anne on Cinnamon and Burns on Pepper, as they prepare for a ride.

Above: The Grands enjoyed ranch life, and their grandfather insisted they learn good riding habits, which they demonstrate here. *Below:* Burns on Keno.

Above: Mamie with Terence Cuneo, a British artist who painted many Pitchfork scenes. *Below:* Christmas at the Big House. *From left:* Willie McGuire (Mamie's sister), Gordon McGuire, Anne Hamilton, Burns Hamilton, D and Mamie (standing), Anne Simmons, Annie Sypert, Charlie Simmons, and James Sypert.

Above left: Anne Hamilton and Keno. *Above right*: Anne in her wedding gown.
Below: Mamie, "a true romantic, a lovely, gracious lady."

Above left: D Burns. *Above right:* Mamie, preparing one of her famous salads. *Below:* The Pitchfork. This is the road down the croton breaks to John Ballard's house in Croton Camp.

Clockwise, from upper left: D and Mamie in the Pitchfork buggy at the 75th Reunion, Abilene, Texas. Burns and an unidentified ranch hand stand at the water bucket near the fence; behind them are (*from left*) Grubbs, John Ballard, Paul Vinson, and Garner Vinson. Longtime foreman Coy Drennan with dog Troubles. Veto Austin and his wife.

Above: A chuck-house Christmas party, a time for all the hands and their families to gather. *Below:* Cowhand Jack Meyers poses with Jimmie Smith and Jimmie's little sisters.

Above: Veto Austin watches son Dickie on a bull. *Below:* Ed Nolan, Pitchfork born and reared, rides out.

Hugh Vinson, one of the Forks' wagon cooks, prepares chuck, above. Wagon cook Chalma Reid (*left*) with Bill Allen and cook's helper Slug Mayo (*right*) are shown below. Allen, an old-time cowboy, lived at the batch camp where Roy Rogers' movie *McIntosh and T. J.* was filmed.

78

Above left: Chalma Reid preparing chuck. *Above right:* Lunch at the chuck wagon. This is Burns Hamilton. *Below:* Eating chuck from the wagon. From the left they are Buddy Moore, "Prairie Dog" Martin, and J. R. Edwards.

Above: Getting a little rest after lunch at the wagon are, from the left, Pete Drennan, J. R. Edwards, Buck Craft, Paul Vinson, and Jimmie Smith. *Below:* Heifer yearlings at the Forks.

Above: Bringing in the morning remuda at batch camp. *Below:* Saddling horses without a corral.

Above: Boyce Hart. *Below:* Culling cows for shipment are from the left, cowboys Paul "Killdee" Hudman, unidentified, "Prairie Dog" Martin, Delbert Byrd, "Suckerod" Osborne, Billy George Drennan, and Coy Drennan.

Above: Flanking calves for branding. Shown, from the left, are Grubbs, unidentified, Ed Nolan, Newt Bigham (with calf), and Keith Slover. *Below:* Branding calves. These cowboys are Jack Meyers, D. Cockran, unidentified, D Burns (with brand), Dean Nolan (behind D), and unidentified.

Clockwise, from upper left: Ed Nolan (standing) watches as D Burns brands a calf. Burns Hamilton sits with a newborn calf after roundup. Tommy Smith waits with D Burns's horse Douglas. Dragging calves for branding are Dickie Austin and Bainey Smith.

Above: A herd of purebred cattle grazes on the north side of the ranch. *Below:* Mamie is introduced at the dedication of the Ranching Heritage Center, Lubbock.

10

Lennie

The old Buick was fairly groaning under the weight of the balled shrubs. Crepe myrtle, lilac, jasmine, pussy willow, forsythia, and redbuds were stacked to the top in the back seat. The turtleback was tied up with rope, and crab apple, peach, pear, and apple trees protruded a full six feet beyond the car. On its top the smaller plants were tied in two sacks.

The two largest trees, gifts from the nurseryman who had found they crowded his stock and had feared they were too big to move while still in leaf, were tied one on each fender. They practically obscured the highway from view and no doubt gave a feeling of wonder and awe to those coming toward me. Never have people been nicer; they gave me the entire road!

Being a scant five feet, I had to stretch my neck considerably to see where I was driving. Just as I was maneuvering the last dangerous curve out of Lubbock, a car pulled close to mine. I recognized two friends, at least I had always considered them so. They were screaming with laughter, but I distinctly heard ". . . I'd have bet five dollars it was you!"

I should be going to the psychopathic ward, I thought. What possessed me to order all these shrubs? What comes over me the minute I get a plant catalogue in my hand? I remembered the Sunday afternoon that I'd made up that order. We were sitting on the screened porch, the most pleasant spot of that large comfortable house, looking out over the valley. We decided to make our garden here, since the large trees in the front of the house gave us too little sunshine for grass and flowers.

"I'm going to plant redbuds and forsythia down by the creek," I said. "I think they are so much prettier in the distance. Drifts of daffodils and iris along those rises. A few tamarisks would be lovely scattered among the cottonwood, mesquite, and wild chinaberries. That clothesline has to be moved. What do you say to grapevines along the entire length of that fence? I want oceans of greenery everywhere—"

"Uh huh," said D, not bothering to look up from his paper, "I think that would be fine." "Sweetheart," I begged, "please take some interest in this. You haven't heard a word I've said." "I have, too. You said that you were going to plant grapevines on that clothesline." I was outraged.

"Get the shotgun Mayme, quick! Here's a rattlesnake!" I looked. Sure enough, not two feet from his lazy chair lay an eight-button diamondback, but a screen wire between them made the difference. If D moved, the snake would crawl away. I didn't keep that .410 on the porch shelf for nothing. Anne later told it briefly in a poem:

> The gun was got,
> the snake was shot,
> and Mamie went back
> to her garden plot.

"Do you think two dozen polyanthus roses will be enough to go along that wall?" "How much is all this going to cost?" "Haven't added it all up yet."

I never did, and it's a pity I didn't, I thought, eyeing a dark cloud in the north and trying to keep the old buggy down to the wartime 35 miles per hour requested by our government. I'd not have all this stuff to put out now. I thought longingly of Old Smokey, my erstwhile yardman; it would take more, a whole lot more, than his making beer for the cowboys to cause me to fire him now, if only he were with us.

My car swerved to the right as a cold wind hit my face, the first norther of the season, and a lulu! We seldom have one in October, and here I was in a cotton suit with eighty miles to go. Thank heaven for a good heater, but wouldn't it ruin those flowering quince wedged down between the heater and the seat? I could see the tag on one of them, $2.75. What if they were in bud and would never know they'd been moved, as the nurseryman said. That was too high. What if my extravagance got D fired? What was D going to say when he saw that nursery on wheels? Yes, definitely my head should be bored for the simples. The speedometer was on sixty. I couldn't help it, I had to get home and start on these plants. Maybe I could get some of them out and store the others in the basement before D came in.

The tumbleweeds and sand were flying in front of my car. I almost passed, without seeing him, a black man panting his way through the thick dust on the side of the road. D's warning, "Mayme, you're going to get killed! You must stop picking up hitchhikers," passed through my mind, but it was getting colder every minute. He was a long way from any little town, and besides he might need a job. Of course, the seat beside me was packed and jammed, but he could stand on the running-board (a '39 Buick had one) and put his head in out of the wind. He came running when I stopped and poked his pleasant but surprised face through the small opening above a nandina. "You ain't got no room, is yuh?" he asked in the highest, most unusual voice I had ever heard come from such a huge body.

"I was afraid that no one would pick you up, and I thought that you'd rather ride outside than walk. Who are you and where are you going?" It soon became evident that he was almost entirely deaf and that I'd have to scream at the top of my lungs to make him understand me. After learning that he was leaving me in sixteen miles, I lost no time asking him if he'd like a job.

"What does yuh pay?" he inquired.

"Whatever you are worth," I yelled.

"You is gettin' ready to break yo'self, lady, 'cause you is lookin' at the best wukker in the country."

I'd heard this kind of talk often enough, and generally exactly nothing came of it. "Do you know anything about putting out shrubs?"

"Ah reckon I does. Ah knows all they is to know about scrubs."

"Who have you worked for? Where did you learn so much?"

"In the penitenchery," he proudly answered.

"What were you put in the penitentiary for?" was my shocked question.

"De judge say, ah don't know mah things from de udder fella's." The most provoking thing about D Burns is his always being right, I thought. Oh well, no harm done. I can let him off at Ralls.

"Mah name's Lennie, what's yo's?" came from the car window. "How you fix yo' holes fo' to put yo' things in? Ah digs a real big hole, lots bigger'n de scrub, and puts in fertilize and den puts in leaves and po's de water in de hole and puts in de scrub an' mashes de groun' and waters it some mo'."

This sounded too good to pass up. By nine o'clock that night, most of the plants were in their planned places, the others neatly heeled out. My voice was completely gone from screaming directions in that cold wind, but Lennie's work was all he had advertised it to be.

When D finally came in, I told him of my treasure, but said, "My throat is killing me. In the morning I want you to take Lennie to the basement and show him how to start a fire in the furnace. Then have him come to my bedroom to make a fire in the fireplace after first knocking on the door."

About five the next morning, I was awakened by a fierce pounding, and before I had my eyes open, Lennie was saying, "I'se done made a fire in the furniture. What yuh wants me to do now?"

It was three days later that Lennie got round to telling me about a wife and asking if he could use the Ford to drive the seventy miles after her. Even then he forgot to mention the baby that he later said was the cause of his being six hours later than he had promised in getting back to the ranch. "We had to take the baby to the doctuh," Lennie explained.

All the cowboys were standing round watching them unload the car, for already Lennie had established himself as a character. "What's the matter with the baby?" I screamed into his ear. "De doctuh say we got to have him circumstanced" was his equally loud reply.

11

Misunderstandings and Then Coy

D was told when we first came to the ranch, "There's been trouble here for a long time, D. I hope you can get it straightened out." He was told also that the men on the Forks had been given the right (which they fully exercised) to bypass the manager and go directly to the owners with their complaints. "I'd clean house, D." By cleaning house, they meant firing every man on the Pitchfork payroll and asking each to hire to D if he wanted the job and if D felt he would fit into his operation. To D it seemed like a hollow gesture under the circumstances. He had not run his own ranch for years. He had no organization to bring with him, and it would have been impossible under existing conditions, the war and all, to have put a good cow crew together. D was a cowman and a good one. He had always gotten along well with people. He knew there were some good families on the ranch who were familiar with the country. Some of them had been working together there for years. Besides, D liked and trusted the Williamses. So despite the warning of cautious friends, he tackled the job as was.

One Sunday afternoon two men from neighboring ranches, who had tuned into the rumblings of their cowhands about things they had heard from Pitchfork hands regarding their new boss, came to apprise D of the situation. The ranchers knew what a splendid job D was doing with the help of George Brock and Roy cross repairing fences and building gates and cattle guards. Out of respect for his ability and dedication, they decided to reveal that Murd, who had aspirations for the manager's job himself, was at the root of the trouble. The man D trusted most was stabbing him in the back. "Remove the cancer, D," they advised, "and things will straighten out." These men had no ax to grind. They came out of friendship.

Up to the time of this disclosure, we were baffled. Once aware of the cause of our troubles, D was rejuvenated in spirit. He determined to go to Saint Louis and present the facts to the Williamses and the Pitchfork directors. As D was packing his bags, Mr. Joe Bridwell came by. "I'm glad you're here, Mr. Bridwell. I need your advice." D related the information he had just received.

Mr. Bridwell replied, "I regret the necessity of your trip, but I feel you're doing exactly the right thing. I believe that the Williamses will understand and be in your corner."

"Joe, I'm not at all sure that their decision will be in my favor. Murd has been on the ranch longer than I have. I have no hole card. I've sold my ranch and given up my job."

"Don't be too concerned about your job, D. I know lots of ranchers not living on their places who would be glad to have you as a manager. I'd like a fellow like you in my organization."

D broke in, "Mr. Bridwell, I came here to stay, and no one man or a dozen men are going to run me off unless the Williamses don't want me."

Mr. Bridwell put his hand on D's arm. "I'm proud of you, D, and I'm pulling for you."

For just a moment there I felt that I'd like to get away to any place where we'd be free of dissension. After hearing D's words, I knew I'd never willingly leave the Forks.

Next morning the information came through in D's voice from Saint Louis. "Darling, everything is all right. We're staying, but somehow or someway, I'll alter the things that are making life so hard for you." I settled down to await a better water supply, better lights, better phone service, and, I hoped, better understanding with our neighbors. But D could not do that for me. That I'd have to do for myself. I'd tighten my belt.

The ever-thoughtful Williamses urged D to show Murd every consideration. To save him as much expense as possible, the ranch would move him when he found a job, besides giving him a month's salary. It was several weeks before Murd completed his arrangements. Many of the ranch people seemed to want to stay on the good side of Murd in case he was successful in ousting D. At the same time, they wanted to keep their jobs if D remained in the saddle. Above all, I think they were really wanting to stick by the man who could best serve the interests of the ranch. As Veto later put it, "Mr. Burns, I don't pay too much attention to what I hear about a feller. I just watch him a while. And if you're not a good man, I'm no judge of character." I think they all just watched D for a while. That Robert Koonce and Roy Bradford were the first to decide D was capable and sincere there is no doubt. They showed it by their attention to their jobs and by their courteous and kind treatment of D, their acceptance of him as their boss, and they showed it by their words at the first Christmas gathering.

Although there was joy in knowing that Murd was leaving, the next crisis was to find a permanent replacement, not only for Murd but also Harve Adams, who had taken a job managing a ranch near Big Spring. Both were top hands and it would be difficult to find their equals. And how I would miss little flaxen-haired Dugan!

One day was so much like another, but July 1, because it brought Coy, stands out in our list of days. When D crawled out at four that morning, he said, "She's rainin' cats and dogs out there. We can use it; it'll give me a chance to catch up in the office. Have to go to Spur, too." It was heavy weather, both in the skies and in our hearts. Today, I thought, will be just like yesterday and the day before. I had come to dread going to the chuck house without D. The ranch people were so chilly and impersonal that I decided to have crackers and cheese and a cup of tea at home. I had done that pretty often lately.

I wished that D could find two men to take Murd's and Harve's places. As much he needed good hands, even more he needed a friend, someone he could confide in, someone he could count on and who would give him some cooperation. It was lack of cooperation that was bogging him down. How much longer could he possibly hold up? "Somewhere," D had said, "there's bound to be the right man, if I could just find him."

Then out of our blackest day, with no warning or fanfare, came such a man—Coy Drennan. By accident, D ran into Coy at Spur. Coy asked D if he needed another hand. D, buoyant when he came home that evening, said, "I can't tell you what this means to me, Mayme. Coy's the best hand in the country. He's likeable, and he knows our range. I don't know what's the trouble at Swenson's, but I sure feel lucky to get him."

Coy's coming was a great turning point in restoring D's spirits. D took heart and hope. So did the anxious ranch. We take a deep, old-fashioned breath just thinking about it, because from that hour nothing was ever quite so bad again. For D had a friend. Coy shared with D the extra burdens that the war had brought us, tasks too prosaic, too onerous for the boys to perform. Milking cows? Cleaning chicken houses? They'd never stoop to such degrading chores. They couldn't be done on a horse, and going about a ranch on foot was close to disgrace. We happily admitted our debt to Coy. Not only was D assured of a capable, willing ally, but Coy's being here had great practical effect on the younger boys at the ranch. His compelling personality inspired and generated a new enthusiasm among them. If the popular Coy Drennan, wagon boss of the SMS for years, could juice a heifer, well, maybe a budding cow hand wouldn't lose his wooliness if he tackled one. Coy had grabbed a milk bucket and gone to the cowpen with D from the first day. Yes, things had been that serious. D, who had risen at four o'clock, had also been doing the milking. It wasn't long before Coy told him, "Mr. Burns, you go on to your office. I think these boys and I can get this milking done."

We were delighted with the turn events had taken. After two years of strain and despair, the sun was shining again for D. Coy was the support he had needed. The work was no less hard, but now D had a friend beside him, someone who could carry out his orders, someone he liked and who liked him. Even I was not a complete disaster.

Coy was of much value to D in many ways. He did not have the tendency of the old hands to say "It can't be done" or "It never has been done that-a-way on the Forks." He did not resent the reorganizing and changes D thought it necessary to make. He helped to bring them about by getting the younger men to understand, work harder, and do a better job. He felt a part of those changes. D talked everything over with Coy. It gave him a chance to pool his thinking with that of someone familiar with the country and the former workings of the ranch.

Coy must take much of the credit for our present pleasant state of affairs, for it was he who started the pot boiling. In a dozen small ways he set examples for the other men. For in truth, the Pitchfork suffered more from a lack of interest than from lack of hands. Coy was the first man D had hired, the first man, that is, to take up his abode at the ranch, to make it his home and to make the Pitchfork a hand.

Coy offered what a ranch demands of its foreman, a fearless likeableness. He could take a drink or leave it. Never ostentatious, he was not lacking in level-headed courage and self-confidence. "Never heard of Coy having a fight," someone remarked. "No," D said thoughtfully, "but I don't want him to hit me."

Coy was known as the handsomest cowman in the country. Though he made no effort to court the crowd's attention, his black hat, black neckerchief, and white jacket easily set him apart. That black hat, which no one ever knew him to take off, was not hard to find among the white Stetsons the other men wore. But he had a lot more than good looks going for him. He drew his own conclusions from everything he saw, and he remarked upon them. He never hesitated to speak out on any issue. And he nailed home some truths at the same time. After a particularly discouraging day on a roundup, D was offering him consolation. "Coy, you can't win 'em all. You're gonna have some bad days. Cattle are hard to work." Coy, philosophically reflecting upon some minor discord existing among his men, replied, "Cattle are not as hard to work as men."

I knew that Coy had come to stay as soon as I saw him buckling down to the job of building morale. "Never had victuals like this at a chuck house." Mrs. Clary, the cook, beamed; Coy had already started making friends. Concerning D, he said, "He's a good un. Never asks a man to do nuthin' he wouldn't do hisself." It gave me a warm and happy feeling all over. I wanted to shout, but I was afraid I was going to cry or start giggling.

Coy showed me at all times great respect. He had patience with my hobbies, interests, decorations, flower arrangements, and especially my dried bouquets, and he did not consider me eccentric because I roamed the creek hunting grasses and flowers to press and use on our Christmas cards. Instead, he hunted them too, and sometimes brought me interesting specimens.

But it was his great interest in living that I enjoyed most about Coy. Everything that he saw, every piece of furniture, every growing plant, every bite of food, was an adventure. He wanted to know and he found out all that you knew on any subject. He wanted to know, for instance, "How do you make those things stay awake in the house?" He pointed to some profusely blooming morning-glory runners crammed down in a pitcher on the shelf above the bookcase.

Never once do I remember going to Lubbock to pick up baby chicks that the weather didn't take a turn for the worse. During the most vicious norther of the year, under the delusion that the chicken house would be warm and ready when I returned, I made such a trip to get some day-old chicks. But when I got back, nothing had been done to heat the brooder house, nor could I get anyone to take any interest in my predicament. Here I was with five hundred cheeping babies on my hands and no heat. Even the nails on the wall were white with ice and frost.

Then I heard a welcome voice from the outside. "Looks like you need some help." It was Coy. I was trying to keep the chicks warm by putting hay on the floor. I asked Coy if there was any way to use the coals I had seen under the washpots to help us heat this house. While I was adjusting the kerosene stoves, he brought a washtub of coals and ashes around which the chicks could crowd for warmth. The moment of kindness and interest paid for the two years' struggle I had had in raising some chickens. He and I in the middle of the night tried to save those little chicks. He gave me some sound advice. "Mrs. Burns, it will pay you to get older chickens, two weeks old at least, and you should get the county agent to help you." I felt the trickle of tears when I said, "Thank you, Coy." He turned away quickly to save me embarrassment.

12

The Big Bedroom

D, stepping knee deep through magazines and scrap books, asked suspiciously, "What are you planning to do in here?"

"Oh, I haven't got it all figured out yet. I want to get a bay in that corner and some bookshelves on this wall. I hope I can do something interesting over that—"

"Let's not get too tricky, Mayme."

"Tricky?" Of all the belittling and unflattering words, tricky! "It was not my intention to be tricky, whatever the word means," I said with what dignity I could muster. "It smacks of trapdoors, secret panels, and disappearing acts. But I do hope to do something interesting."

"Interesting, perhaps, but not startling. It was those startling features of yours that caused us to be so long selling the San Angelo house. You said so yourself."

"A whole week," I put in, "and I said it was my most attractive features that those people didn't appreciate."

"Attractive to you." Here we go again, I thought. "Look, Mayme, why can't we ever have a house like anyone else's? Just a plain house? They've told you we can't get a bay on here because of the pitch of the roof. Now—" He jerked a pencil out of his pocket and drew a rectangle on the back of an envelope, representing a room 16' by 22'. He slashed off one end for closets, drew an X in the middle of the other end for a door, and said, "Now, put the fireplace anywhere you want it. Right here would be a good place." Another X in the middle of the east wall. "We can have a fireplace like the one we had in San Angelo with the woodbox beside it, opening from the outside. And that perforated pipe for a lighter was convenient."

"So glad you liked it, Mr. B. I was beginning to think— I feared— that you didn't approve of my style of architecture."

"There it is," D said belligerently, thrusting the seven-minute blueprint at me. He didn't intend being sidetracked from his argument or peeve. "It's perfectly simple."

"Isn't it?" I asked sweetly. "Sixteen by twenty-two, when anything less than a thirty-foot room gives both of us claustrophobia. Why go to the trouble of doing anything if those few feet are all you're going to add?"

D smiled with maddening superiority. "My dear," he said, "you are a chicken raiser second to none, a splendid cook, and a decorator of some ability, but one can't add twenty feet to a room where there is only ten feet of ground." He drew me to the window overlooking a fifteen-foot bluff. "We'll be teetering on the bank as it is." He was delighted at having won an argument so easily. We generally wore one to shreds.

"I'm planning to build the bank out." I said it softly, cautiously. I'd been waiting for just the right moment to broach the subject. Somehow this didn't quite seem the time. D is allergic to new ideas. I'd thought perhaps after a highball, or over a good thick steak, a sprinkling of guests wouldn't hurt. You know, it's amazing how just plumb sweet D can be sometimes, when there are guests, about something I'd sorta dreaded to mention. I could use a few now, kinda influential ones, but there wasn't a guest in sight.

"Build the bank out?" D raged. "Only twenty feet of bank, fifteen feet deep! You must be crazy Mayme. What do you expect to hold your bank up? The first hard rain would—"

"A rock wall ought to hold it," I reasoned.

"A rock wall?" D was wild.

"And I've found the most beautiful rock right under the hill, and a cedar pile fence with the poles wired together—you know, like that lovely one you built for me in San Angelo, to go down there."

"Down where?" he stormed.

I waved in the general direction of the creek. I find I have to be a little vague and indefinite with D, for the more definite I am about my plans, the wilder he becomes.

"Do you realize," he asked, "just how much a rock wall would cost? That we don't own the Pitchfork, and it would take hundreds of loads of dirt to build a bank, and that you are going to lose this job for me?"

"It could be landscaped the sweetest— Just let those banks drip off down there. They'd love it," I promised.

"Like hell they would! Mayme, we hardly know those people! What makes you think they'd like your ideas?"

"Those imported tweeds, sulka ties, and that cocktail kit from Abercrombie's."

"I don't even know what you are talking about, and I don't think you do, either. I think you're trying to change the subject."

"Isn't that your ring, darling?"

"Saved by the telephone!" I said to Mandy, who had come out to talk about lunch, but hadn't been able to get a word in edgewise. "Puts me in mind o' Jeet," she said, "he's ag'in anything a woman favors." Whew! The first bout was over.

I wish you could see the room now. It's almost exactly like D wanted it: a large bay with a dropped ceiling, recessed windows with bookcases underneath, weathered beams—but the loveliest part of all is the view from the south and east windows. The gentle slope of ground some forty feet below.

13

Hefflebower Dance and "Tawm" Dowdy

A long-distance call let me know that the Hefflebowers were having a dinner-dance at Abilene on Friday evening. "Could you make it?" Marie had asked. "You'll just have to, as you are the honor guests." Marie was the wife of General Ray Hefflebower, who was commanding officer of Camp Berkeley at Abilene during World War II. I was about ripe for another dance, I told her. It had been at least a year since our last one, that bruising affair at the bunkhouse on Christmas.

She said, "Anne Smart wants you to stay with her. She is having about twenty in for cocktails before the dance, just your closest friends. Come early and dress here. It's formal, of course."

I suffered some misgivings. D has little liking for formal parties. Getting him into evening clothes might involve the use of chloroform, but I'd dig them out of moth balls right away, I thought, and start airing them and take them to the cleaners later. I'd wear the "spo'tin'" dress.

All that day as I worked with the county agent dusting hens, spraying the hen house, roosts, and nests for mites, blue bugs, and lice, and putting fresh straw in the nests, I kept wondering how and what I could say to get D to that dance. But I knew what he'd say. "Hell, no!" (I'm sorry about that, but that's the way they talk on a ranch.)

All day I kept thinking up approaches, how I'd broach the subject. "Darling, do you want to do something to make me happy?" There was a time he would have answered, "Don't I always try to make you happy?" But he wouldn't answer that way now. No, I'd not risk that one. I'd say, "Honey, guess what? The Hefflebowers are having a dinner-dance Friday evening. They are honoring us. Do you suppose we could—" "It's out of the question," he would snap before I could finish the sentence. So I dropped that one, too.

After craftily planning all day what I'd say, I decided on the direct approach. Surely I wasn't afraid of D. I simply told him about the dance and said I'd like to go. *"Dance?"* D looked as if he didn't know the meaning of the word. "Dance," I repeated. "Who could think of a dance in times like these?" "They did." I was in a mood to defend my position. "They know one can't go on day after day, twenty-four hours a day, just working. That you must have some rest and diversion and pleasure."

"Pleasure! Mayme, I've got a job to do. I get my pleasure out of doing it. I thought you did too." He was amazed at the whole idea. "It is incredible, ridiculous. It's not like you. I don't believe it. We have to put this ranch first. We cannot go," he said with finality.

I'd had ranch up to my eyes. Disappointment, hurt, anger, and self-pity poured out. "D," I said, "if you really wanted to go to that dance, you'd manage it some way. If you had not been out of that entrance gate for ten months except to run an errand to Guthrie or Spur for the ranch, you'd like to see someone else, somewhere else, too! I know your trips are business, but you do make them. You meet new people, see old acquaintances, get a change of scenery, a change of pace. I'd like something like that myself once in a while to regain my identity."

D did not seem to have heard a word I'd said. He dredged up all the reasons we couldn't go. "And on that particular Friday I have to deliver nine hundred cattle to Narciss shipping pens," he said, then went behind his newspaper.

Several minutes passed. I became aware that D had put down his paper and was about to say something. "I'm sorry you feel like that, Mayme, and I'm sorry I can't make it. It was a nice thing for the Hefflebowers to do. Why don't you go?"

D was holding the high card. He knew I couldn't and wouldn't go to a dinner-dance without him. "D Burns," I returned to the attack, "you could manage it if you wanted to go as much as I do."

All right, Mayme," he shot back. "If a dance means that much to you, we'll go." As a final touch, he said, "I may lose my job over it, but if it's that important to you—" He stalked out.

Tenderly I packed our bags with every immediate need, stuffed our evening clothes with tissue paper, laid sheets between every fold. There wouldn't be a wrinkle. I lugged the bags to the car, anxious to save every minute. I, myself, was manicured and marcelled like a Hereford ready for the show ring. He'd be home at five, we'd leave for Abilene by six, just a bit over a hundred miles, we'd be at Anne's by eight.

Five o'clock, no D. He'd be along in a few minutes; D was punctual. I'd draw his bath. When he hadn't got in by six, I knew we couldn't make the cocktail party. Oh, well, something had detained him. Anne would understand. I'd call her. Six-thirty, seven—why hadn't he come? I was furious. We'd have to dress here. I brought all of our clothes from the car, laid D's on the bed, and started dressing.

I'd have to pull my dress up around my shoulders and sit on the edge of the seat all the way. D could have made it if he'd really tried. He was getting like all the other men. Women's affairs, social things were not important. D had never been like that. I couldn't stand it if my sweet, considerate D got—got? But he already was! He didn't care about anything but this ranch anymore. I'd just as well face it. What twenty years of marriage had failed to do, this ranch had done in one.

There was his car! I'd not be very nice about this, just as well let D know that I didn't intend to be treated— A knock on the back door, so it wasn't D then, after all.

"Lady," came a voice from the darkness, "will you call an ambulance? A fellow's had a wreck back there on the highway. He's unconscious. I was afraid to move him."

"What kind of car was he driving?" I broke in frantically.

"A Ford. He passed me goin' like blazes."

"How was he dressed?"

"Well, I don't know hardly, lady, but he's a ranchman. He had on boots and spurs."

Panic seized me. It was D, of course. Oh, my darling, you were trying to get here! Oh, darling, darling! Somehow I got to the phone, somehow managed to call an ambulance, somehow got blankets. "Could I go back with you?"

Oh, D! D, why did you hurry so? The dance didn't matter, it wasn't important. Oh, God, dear God, let him be alive. Let him be all right. We could see the car, all four wheels in the air, several minutes before we stopped. It looked as if someone was sitting on top of it. Something was wrong with my mind. Oh, God, don't let this happen to me now. Let me think clearly. I shook my head, but he was still there. He waved, waved a bottle. He didn't look like D. I stumbled out of the car, my knees, what had happened to my knees? I couldn't stand up, my knees, my mind, my— Their voices sounded very far away.

"Are you all right?"

"Shure, shure, I'm all right. I'm all right. I'm all right—hic— but I'm drunk. Drunk ash hell."

It wasn't D, but where was D? Maybe lying on the highway, maybe he was dead. Oh, darling. But I'd have to take this man to the house, keep him for the night.

His car was a shambles, but he didn't seem to mind. He waved his hand toward it in an uncaring way as we left it there in the barrow pit. He spoke of it in the past tense. "She was a good'un while she lasted, but the best of friends got to—hic—part." (Later Tom was wont to recall in reverent detail all her good qualities. "She was a runnin' Jessie, nine years old and run like a three-year-old. I never spent a dollar on that car for repairs, she'd run on gasoline or coal oil, never made no difference.")

But now the disheveled stranger was talking to us. "I was lookin' fer a job. Where you all live?" Then, in amazement, "Pitchfork Ranch? Hic—now ain't that somethin'? Uster work there. My name's Dowdy. Tom (he pronounced it "Tawm") Dowdy. What's yourn?"

"I'm Mrs. Burns."

"And my name's Jameson," came from my fellow rescuer.

Tom thrust out a horny hand. "Pleased to meetcha, Mr.— hic—Jameson and Miz Jame—" he stopped short. "What did you say your name was?"

"Burns. I'm Mrs. Burns."

"Now ain't that somethin'?" Tom grinned knowingly.

"I live at the Pitchfork. This gentleman—"

"Widder?"

"No, my husband's—"

"Tha's all right, don' make no difference to old Tawm. Anything goes with me. Well, ain't this somethin'? How come you two—?"

I tried again. "My husband's the manager of the Pitchfork. He might give you a job." Might? D had run the wheels off his car hunting help, any kind of help, for any kind of work. "What kind of work can you do?"

"Now ain't that somethin'?" Tom appealed to Mr. Jameson. "She asks me what I can do. Lady, I can do anythin'." He gave me the steadiest look he could. "Anythin' you got to do. If hit's work, I'm yore boy."

"Do you run a tractor? Mr. Burns particularly needs—"

"Do I run a tractor? She asks me if I run a tractor," he confided to Mr. Jameson. "Now ain't that somethin'? Lady, you're lookin' at the best tractor man in the state o' Texas. What kinda tractor you got?"

"Oh, Internationals, Fords, and a Twin City, I think."

"Did she say Twin City?" Tom asked incredulously. "I'm yore boy, Lady! This here's the luckiest night of yore life. You ain't never gonna regret pickin' old Tawm up. Now I don't know what yo're doin' out here on the highway, or how come you two are out here. Hit don' make no difference to old Tawm, but you got the best tractor man in the world." Tom's head dropped forward; he dozed.

"Looks like you have got a tractor driver," Mr. Jameson ventured.

"She aint' got nuthin' else," Tom put in. "I'm the Twin City-in'est thing in the world. I'm yore boy." He clapped a hand on my gold lamé-covered knee.

The car stopped at the house. Tom stumbled out. "Where's that Twin City?" he wanted to know.

"It's at the Farm Camp, Tom. Mr. Burns will take you up there in the morning."

"Run 'em night or day," he hiccoughed. "I'm yore boy." Tom staggered around unsteadily trying to help with the blankets and medicine. He noticed my long dress. "Been on a pic—nic?" he asked. Then, seeing the Buick, parked beside the gate with the back door invitingly open, he crawled in and lay down.

"Let him sleep right there," Mr. Jameson suggested. "He won't even move until morning. There goes the ambulance!" We could see its lights on the highway. I had forgotten all about the ambulance. "I'll go explain. I'm a highway patrolman, Mrs. Burns. I've been on a vacation."

The phone was ringing insistently when I went in the door. "Where in the world have you been? Asleep? Mr. Burns is trying to get you from Paducah," said Mrs. Street, the operator.

"Mayme." I could barely hear D's worried voice. "It's going to be late when I get in. Didn't want you to be worrying about me. We've had the devil with these steers. They've tried to run all day. Everything's gone wrong."

"I love you, darling," I shouted.

"What?" asked D.

"I love you."

". . . can't hear you."

Mrs. Street chuckled. "Want me to tell him, Mrs. Burns?" (That's the beauty of having your own private operator.)

There was a streak of grease on the gold lamé dress; there were rocks in my gold slippers, but there was a song in my heart. D was safe. Three days later, D asked, "Mayme, when is that Hefflebower dance?"

D sent Tom to the Farm Camp where he proved to be just as good as he thought he was. Roy Bradford, our Farm Camp manager, said he'd never had a man who could come as near making a tractor sing. But the minute Tom got his paycheck he'd go into town and get drunk. Sometimes it would be three or four days before he'd show up on the job, then D would threaten to fire him if it happened again. Every month he swore off liquor for life; every month for eight months. Tom was a deal, don't think he wasn't, but he favored me with his friendship and often stopped by our house to visit, or, as he said, to pass the time of day. "I'm a reformed character, Miz Burns," he'd tell me at these times, "And I owe it all to you."

D and Coy got a great kick out of this. I'd made the mistake of telling them the things Tom said the first night he came to the Forks, so the forty-three-year-old tractor man was soon known as "my boy." "Seen yore boy over in town last night staggering around like a locoed cow," Coy would say. Or D: "That boy of yours lost out in his bout with the bottle again." Even Mandy, who seldom joked me, commented, "'Pears like yore boy's powerful apt to get drunk." It was not until six months later that I knew Tom also considered himself my boy and intended to make full use of that fact.

"That you, Miz Burns?" a loud voice said on the phone. The call was from Spur, collect. "Yes?" I was pretty sure who was on the other end of the line. "You know who this is?" The voice was brimming with eagerness. "It sounds like Tom," I said. "It ain't nobody else," he answered, and he couldn't have been more pleased that I had recognized him.

"Miz Burns," he continued in his hopeful mood, "did you say I was yore boy?" I admit a moment's silence. Then, "I certainly did, Tom," I told him frankly, but somewhat ruefully. "Well," he said in a that-being-the case manner, "you'd better come over to Spur and git yore boy, and Miz Burns, you'd better bring about twenty-five dollars, 'cause he's in trouble. I'll be at the Saxon Hotel, if they let me out of here. The sheriff wants to talk to you."

This was the sort of thing that happened the minute D drove out of the gate. This time he'd betook himself to Denver and wouldn't be home for a week. Coy was out with the wagon. There wasn't a man within miles. If there had been a man, or six men, at headquarters, they'd have been too busy to go to Spur.

Tom reeled out of the hotel when he saw me. He waved a beefy hand to some men who were standing on the porch of the small inn. He was having a hard time managing a burlap valise and some laundry. Tom was in a state of bleary disrepair, his eyes bloodshot and his breath reeking of liquor.

I helped him put his bundles into the car, all except one brown paper bag, which he held tightly under his arm. Then I slipped under the wheel, reached across and opened the door on the other side for him. Tom stood beside the open door holding onto the handle. "Get in, Miz Burns, get in," he said thickly. Humor a drunk, I'd heard; it might take a deal of humoring before I'd get him home. I made an exaggerated motion as if settling myself in that seat. "O.K., Tom, now you get in." It worked. He fell in beside me. Tom had had more to drink since he had called me. He could scarcely talk; his words were punctuated by hiccoughs. He sat up with difficulty.

"To whom do we give this money?" I asked, wondering if he would understand. Tom spoke right up, "We give it to the Law." But he was nodding before we'd gone a block. He roused when I stopped the car at the sheriff's office. "Never slept much last night;

never got to bed," he apologized. Tom went toward the jail with his check as fast as his uncertain feet could take him.

Once more in the car, Tom said, "They think a heap of you at the jail. They let me out soon as I talked to you. They say yo're a—hic—lady." Tom closed his eyes again but opened them as I rounded a corner. He tapped me companionably on the shoulder. "They shore did, Miz Burns, they said you was a lady—drunk or sober!" Tom hiccoughed loudly and went sound asleep. We were almost home when he awakened. He said remorsefully, "Ain't mad at me, are you?" He seemed quite sober now.

"No, Tom, I'm not angry with you, but I don't know what Mr. Burns is going to say about this. It looks like—"

"I wish you hadn't a-mentioned his name." Tom held his head in his hands. Suddenly he dived for the brown package between his feet and came up with a bottle. "Take a drink of this, Miz Burns, an' things'll look different." He was fumbling with the stopper. I was glad to see Floyd and Tex standing by the shop door. At my signal, they came to help, saw the situation, and in a minute had whisked Tom's liquor out of sight and into D's office.

The string had broken on the package of laundry. Tom was busy trying to gather it up while shielding me from the immodest sight of men's long drawers. This accomplished, he suddenly remembered. "Where's my—What'ud you all do with that sack o' stuff?" No one seemed to know what he was talking about. No one had seen a sack of stuff—they said. Tom glared angrily from Floyd to Tex, "They're thieves, Miz Burns. Watch yore purse. Yo're dealing with a pair of thieves." He lurched forward. Tom was pretty sick. We have understood since there was a bit of nipping at the bunkhouse that night, courtesy of Tom.

Next morning he felt some better, not much, but some. He walked down from the bunkhouse to where I was working in the yard. His face was greenish-gray; his voice worried. "Miz Burns," he told me sadly, "I been stabbed."

"Stabbed?" I asked, incredulously.

"Stabbed!" he repeated.

"Not stabbed with a knife?" I couldn't believe it.

"I was stabbed yestiddy and I cain't figger out who done it." He looked as if he just might believe I had done it.

"Tom," I asked, "are you sure?"

"Am I shore? God a'mighty, Miz Burns, a man knows when he's stabbed, I reckon." He jerked his shirt tail out and twisted around to show me his injury. There was dried blood on the shirt and on his back, but I saw no wound.

"I can't see the place, Tom," I told him. "Let's go into the hospital room so you can take down your trousers, and I can get a close-up of this cut."

This suggestion met with immediate opposition. "Miz Burns," Tom said sternly, "if you want to see this place, I think we orta look at it right out here." Tom unfastened his belt and one button of his Levi's. The cut was barely discernible, about the width of a dinner knife, but when I pulled it open, I could see an inch down into it, and I didn't know how much deeper it went. All I would see was fat; the wound itself was perfectly clean. Tom refused to let me take him to a doctor, so I filled the place with sulfa ointment. The next day Tom was riding a Twin City.

When one thing or another brought Tom down to the ranch headquarters, he always made it convenient to stay for a meal. He said it was a break in the "monotomy." It was a break in the "monotomy" for us, too. Tom's periodic visits enlivened our days. Tom was a departure from the norm. His conversation, punctuated with heavy belches, was always the unexpected.

"Gravy, Tom?" I'd ask. "Well, Miz Burns, wouldn't care if I takened some I guess. Hit don't come in bottles," he'd answer. Tom was a card and knew it.

The actions of Tom's digestive organs were unpredictable, and uncontrollable, I suppose. He burped with noisy regularity, but sometimes I believed he gave especially impressive demonstrations for guests. "Where's the bakin' sody?" he'd ask loudly. Tom did everything loudly. Standing in plain view of us all, he'd gulp down an Arm & Hammer cocktail. Almost immediately, relief of room-rocking proportions would rumble forth. "Feel better'n I have in a long time," he'd say, fishing for the turkey quill from his pocket. He scorned the use of toothpicks that the cowboys reached for.

Once when the dining room was filled with visitors, Tom made such a request, and in her haste, Mrs. Clary handed him the Twenty Mule Team Borax. Tom put a heaping teaspoonful in a glass of water, stirred vigorously, and polished it off at a single draught. We waited fascinated, unbearably fascinated, for the reverberation, fork and knife suspended. It was impossible to ignore. One could not go on talking, acting as if nothing were about to happen, when you knew that even the window panes might be shattered. They almost were. Tom gave his prize performance. "Wups," he said, almost gently. "Wups! What the hell?" Tom's burp rose to the occasion. "W-U-Ps!" And to our amazement and his, before he reached the door, Tom was blowing bubbles all over the place.

After a year of stormy passages, D fired Tom Dowdy. Tom, with his few belongings, was going toward the highway. "There goes the best tractor man in the whole country," Roy Bradford said, with more than a little regret. The words were strangely reminiscent of Tom's own brag. In another moment he passed out of our view and out of our lives. One of the Pitchfork's real personalities had gone.

14

Tom and Walker

About 1948 two old Matador hands, Tom Thornton and Walker Williams, drifted over to us from the big spread to our west. Tom hobbled around as if there were nails in his boots, but D said (there are only a few years between them), "Tom's not an old man, he's just been badly broken up."

None of the Pitchfork regulars had to be told that we had acquired a pair of top hands. Their reputations were well known in Texas, Arizona, Wyoming, and Canada, and it didn't take the younger cowboys long to find out that Tom was hard to beat to a maverick yearling in the brush. He and Old Feathers, a good sorrel horse, were usually first at the catching.

Veto had said when we first went to the chuck house, "Why don't you sit here, Mr. Burns?" He indicated the first space on the bench nearest the kitchen. "That's where Rudolph always sat." D patted the number two spot for me to be seated beside him. Thereafter, the Austins thoughtfully kept those places for us if they knew we would be over for a meal. Most of the men sat in any spot that was available, but a few like Mr. Deaton and Roy Callicoatte who had been there a long time were a little put out when they found someone else in their places.

When Tom came to work with us, he chose the place on the bench next to me. I liked the arrangement. Tom was clean, courteous, and always good for some chuckles. He had a wicked sense of humor. "Ain't it a shame when a feller wants to be a gentleman so bad and don't know how?" he leaned over and asked me quietly once when Murd was doing some rather loud bragging.

If you hear more of Tom than Walker Williams, it is because the latter was less articulate and less often at the chuck house table. Walker was the first man D sent to Croton "batch camp," at least twenty miles from headquarters. Much work was to be done there. It required a man of good judgment, not afraid of work, who wouldn't mind living alone and cooking for himself. Walker had the qualifications. He had assumed a similar responsibility at the Matador and had done a good job of it. He did a good job for us too.

You knew exactly where Tom stood on any subject, whether he was disgusted, amused, or just not interested. His observations on the chuck-house chatter and the rest of us made good listening. His sidekick, Walker Williams, came to lunch with us from his lonely job at the Croton line camp one Sunday. "Pass the butter," Walker requested, opening a big slice of hot cornbread to receive it. "That's the first time I have ever heard Walker speak," I observed to Tom. "Ain't seen nobody fer a long time, and he's full o' talk," Tom explained.

When a man who had been on the Pitchfork for about three months told Tom he was thinking of quitting, Tom replied, "We thought you already did."

"I'd like a go at the old gentleman you call Tom for one," Mr. Terence Cuneo, the eminent English artist who was spending two weeks with us preparing for his British exhibit in New York, told me after he had carefully surveyed our crop of picturesque subjects for study. Although Suckerod, Billy George, and Prairie Dog enjoyed sitting and were flattered that Mr. Cuneo would think them interesting and typical subjects, Tom refused. When he was asked for his consent, Tom wanted to find out where that portrait would go. "Will the picture stay here at the ranch or in Texas? I ain't lost nuthin' in England."

Once in the chuck house several of the boys were discussing the rigors of ranch life in the old days. Some commented on the low wages they had received. One cowboy said, "I was workin' for thirty dollars a month." "Heah," Tom broke in, "but in them days dollars was a-bringin' a buck apiece."

Coy had a philosophical way with words, Ed had more flair, Tom was caustic. If the flavor of their *bons mots* was different, the effects were equally pertinent or devastating. Witness Tom's handling of a visitor who, observing Tom's age and the fact that he was in charge of the riding horses, expected him to be omniscient concerning them. If Tom had thought the question a sensible one worthy of consideration, he would have explained in detail. But having been asked how to keep a horse from slobbering, Tom gave the lengthy reply, "Larn 'im to spit."

Equipped with a wry sense of humor, Tom was a man of legendary likes and dislikes. A story in which a cowboy is bested was one of the things he disliked, but he couldn't resist one in which a cowboy outwits a city slicker. Tom was a little short with dudes himself. "Why do you people always have this kind of bread (meaning cornbread) with your beans?" he was asked by a chuck-house visitor. "Helps us to clean up our plates," Tom answered. Another newcomer wanted to know if Tom had been on a ranch all his life. "Not yet," was Tom's laconic reply.

Tom had no explanations or apologies in him. "Yer friends don't need 'em, an' the rest ain't gonna believe 'em." He was full of homespun philosophy, coupled with quick and pointed repartee.

"Where are the other boys?" D asked, noticing Tom coming in alone for lunch. "Up at the gate signin' autographs. A group of Tech coeds waylaid 'em up there, but they was defendin' themselfs purty good."

Tom was a great competitor, whether he was pitching horseshoes, roping, or riding. Tom was usually the first man on the job in the morning and generally the last to quit in the evening. "What are you in such a hurry about this morning, Tom?" I asked. "I have to hurry or I'll fergit where I'm going," Tom answered.

Tom had been pretty wild as a young man, was known as a fighter, drinker, and hell-raiser, but somewhere along the line he had made the decision to be a gentleman and had established a set of values, the code of morals by which he lived. A gentleman in Tom's book was a man who kept his word, paid his bills, was "respectful of wimmen," and was loyal to his outfit and his employer. He saved a certain amount of his salary each month. He thought of money not as a means of authority but as security against old age. "Don't want to be beholden to nobody, an' don't want to be in nobody's way."

Tom could not bear to see horses standing for hours saddled and bridled. Many visitors would ask for a horse to ride at eight o'clock in the morning, then decide to sleep late or change plans and leave them tied to the fence all day, fighting flies, gnats, and mosquitoes, without water or food, but this wouldn't happen if Tom came by and saw them. "Have them people been ridin' yet, Miz Burns?" he'd come to the house and ask. If my answer was no, he'd take the horses back to the corral, hang up the saddles, and turn them out. Never again would he ready a horse for riding for that person. This went for owner, family, or visitors alike. Tom was not notably humble. "I'd rather be fired first, an' I'd be glad to tell 'em so."

Tom had a gentle gruffness with children, and under his guidance, ours became experts at horsemanship and fairly proficient at a few ranch jobs. He let them know that he was the boss when they were under his instructions. He'd explain these things in words they weren't likely to forget: "The first lesson to learn if you are goin' along with a cow outfit aimin' to work, you take orders." I believe it was Tom who told young Burns that a bull wasn't very smart because he couldn't keep his mouth shut. "If he ain't eatin', he'll be a bellerin'. You can locate him that way."

Tom said that they were the best-mannered children he had ever known. "No matter how big a hurry Miz Burns is in to get off anywheres, Anne and Burns'll hunt me up wherever I am to say 'Thank you for getting our horses for us and taking care of them through the week.'" It was always a chore to get them into the car to go back to Lubbock. They loved Tom, appreciated the many things he did for them and taught them, and were always anxious to please him, but they were stalling for an extra few minutes on the ranch.

Tom believed that young new hands, or punks, were far more trouble than help. We got a fine example of what he was talking about when Bill Severn and his friend came from Iowa to work at the Pitchfork. But if a new boy had guts and wanted to learn, Tom would take infinite pains to show and help him. On one occasion when Tom was breaking in a new hand, he got down off his horse to examine a windmill. The boy rode off. His excuse was that he'd just wanted to see what was over that hill. Tom told him he wasn't going along just to see the country and "You can't sleep very sound while yer ridin' thet horse."

15

Mandy and Jeet

D told me of a couple who were up at the Farm Camp, according to reports a queerly turned pair, but the Bradfords believed they were of exceptional character. Bates was their name, Jeet and Mandy Bates. It was Jeet who was employed by the Pitchfork to feed the pen full of hogs and do odd jobs at the Farm Camp. The woman did not work regularly, but she had helped Mrs. Bradford through the heavy harvest season just past when there were so many extra hands. She had done an excellent job. The Bradfords thought she would suit my needs perfectly and would be a prime comfort when my guests arrived, that she would be kind and uncomplaining and would be willing to take the long hours in the kitchen.

D said the Bradfords could manage without Jeet for a time, that they themselves had offered to let us have the Bateses just to help out through the emergency. But Mandy and Jeet were proud and touchy folks, Roy Bradford explained, and might not consider coming at all. The situation was a ticklish one and would take careful handling. "They think it's one thing to work beside a feller and another to work for him," Roy said. "They ain't never been bossed and ain't aimin' to be." I came to appreciate this observation about the Bateses after they had been with me some time. They were not ingratiating to their superiors; they knew no superiors. Mandy bowed to knowledge and righteousness. Jeet didn't bow.

There are many reasons why I remember that first day of Mandy and Jeet's. "He's brought his dog and his cat—Jeet sleeps cold," Mandy told me. They were mountain folk. You knew it at once. They had mountain looks and mountain ways.

I watched them come from the car together. Mandy was a tall beanstalk of a woman of about my own age, with a knot of hair on top of her head. Her skirt was long and she wore a man's jumper. She had a quick, determined step, a birdlike alertness. Jeet walked in slow, aimless fashion behind her. He was more than half a head shorter. A dyspeptic-looking character, but straight and slim. He presented a ludicrous appearance. Red suspenders had his pants hitched almost under his arms. Above a stiff-starched shirt bosom an enormous Adam's apple worked continuously up and down. From the first minute that I sw him through the window I had trouble keeping my eyes off that Adam's apple, particularly when he talked, for his voice seemed to go up and down with it. So did his tobacco-stained mustache. I walked to the kitchen door to greet them.

"Yard's big as a cow pasture," I heard Jeet say. "A body could set a gyarden in here," Mandy remarked. A jerk of her head indicated the newly built-up ground. None of this how-de-do nonsense about her. "Come spring hit orta be galore." I wasn't sure what the word meant, but felt somehow that it carried approval. I knew an immediate friendliness for this strange woman. Words or no words, we would understand each other.

"I'm Mrs. Burns," I ventured, though it seemed a shame to inject so banal a fact, spoil the dreamlike quality of the moment.

"Calculated you was," Mandy replied. Her face was not a happy one; worry wrinkles stamped her forehead. But kindness was there and a heart-touching warmth. She was at ease in the world. "Ye mind me o' someun." She looked me slowly up and down. "Ye put me in mind of Miz Majers. She wasn't pretty neither." Vanity is not among my vices—I go in for good works. "Well, a body cain't help their looks," she comforted me.

Jeet looked at the sky. "Rain's gone," he said. No formalities here either. He knelt at the corner of the flower bed and sifted some moist soil between his fingers. He, too, bore himself imperturbably.

They came inside reluctantly. It was plain their interest was for the out-of-doors. So was mine, for that matter. I could grub around in a garden forever and find it comforting just to sit under a tree, but guests were due by nightfall and napkins were to be washed, bread made, the house dusted, a thousand things.

This was in the early stages of my life as a ranch woman. I was still trying to manage this place as I had my small house. Oh, how I longed for my two-bedroomed, two-bathroomed home, with a hot water heater that worked! Now Mandy stood, her feet wide apart, surveying the scene in my kitchen. "Things piled up on ye," she observed.

I had started to mop the kitchen floor—the pail and mop were in evidence—but had stopped to answer the phone and to work back the bread before it overran its crock. The napkins were soaking in a dishpan on the drainboard. At ten o'clock a plumber arrived from Paducah to see if he could do anything about the lines to the water tank. We hadn't been able to get a drop of cold water for over a week. I showed him to the basement. When we came back, Mandy, her skirts tied up, was mopping the kitchen floor. You knew that she loved cleanliness the way she scoured and rinsed that linoleum and dug into the corners. She put a broom in Jeet's hand and told him to hump it. "Ain't humpin' it so's you can tell it," she said, going out the door to hang the napkins on the line. "Aggervates me beyond reason." Mandy spoke as if she were thinking aloud, and that's what she was doing. In time I became accustomed to these mumblings, listened for every word, for what Mandy thought of a thing or a person she was apt to say in these asides, even if the person was standing in the same room. Her estimates were invariably correct. She seemed to see right through one.

How easily Mandy gathered up the strings of my confused household. She put Jeet to laying fires and carrying wood while she changed the beds, dusted, and washed up after me in the kitchen. Once we heard a noise from outside. It sounded like wood falling. Mandy said, "Tripped over his big feet, I'll bound ye." She did not look up or stop scrubbing the pan she held in her hand. "Scamped her work," she absently remarked, and it took a while to figure out that she was speaking of the girl who had gone only last week. Jeet complained to Mandy, "It's a mort of work to be done around here." There was a lack of enthusiasm in his voice for the chores, but when lunchtime came he was happier. Mandy had boiled a big pot of roasting ears. "This here's the eatin'est corn ever I tasted," Jeet said. Butter was dripping off his elbows. But he had no appetite for the party leftovers we'd set out of the refrigerator—olives and celery. "I leave all sich for the fools as likes 'em," he stated bluntly.

From this simple and firm beginning came the most rewarding friendship. When Mandy left that afternoon, she said, "Leave me know when ye want me. I'll lift ye come trouble or sickness." Come company, too, I hoped. My hopes more than came true. Mandy lifted my burdens of work and my burdens of spirit. She found cobwebs, too enchanting to destroy, at least before she had shown them to me. "Happen you ever noted the sun a-shining through a spider's web?" She had come from the far end of the house to ask, and I would behold a gossamer web of jewels, diamonds, and sapphire. She discovered and later pointed out beauties and wonders that had long been there for us to look at but that we had somehow failed to see. Her finds were always worth the seeing. It was after a trip to the garden corner where she showed me three baby rabbits rolled in a furry ball, their soft nest hidden by tall grasses, that she announced, "I like you, Miz Burns," then voicing her thoughts, murmured, "but it's plumb amazin' them as don't."

Mandy took long walks when time permitted. It took the sameness out of her days. "Ain't fog a wonderment to you?" She reveled in its misty loveliness. The smallest things gave her much pleasure. It was her awareness, her delight in the small things around her, that I admired most.

Mandy could make a little go a long way in the kitchen. When I got off without planning a meal, I didn't come back to find she'd raided the emergency shelf. If there were bits of steak or roast in the refrigerator, she'd make a delectable hash. And since we always had homemade sour cream, she often concocted a stroganoff. She had watched me use spices and wines and soon developed just the right touch with them. "Gives it oomph." She was mightily pleased with herself when she could squeeze in a word like *oomph* that she had filched from us. We adopted many of hers, too. The children said "laughed master" as often as Mandy did and knew exactly what it meant. I was indebted to her for *swivet*. Couldn't get along without it. Mandy was stricken that her biscuits were not her best. "Ain't fitten for pigs." But light bread was her specialty. Mandy's long, brown loaves were fit for kings. She had a way with cornbread and a strong right arm for whipping up Irish potatoes. She did not believe in mixes or synthetic anything. Trying to convince her that imitation vanilla, cream, or pepper were fit to use was a waste of breath.

She seemed eternally grateful for the Pitchfork. "Where better'd a man betake himself fer shelter and vittles 'un the Pitchfork? I give grace we found it. Afore we hit here after leavin' the Majers there was days we never had side meat and not a lick of sweetenin'. We was plumb froze fer marrow bone and spare ribs, had nothing' but leather bread." "Why did you leave the Majers, Mandy?" "Accoun'o

Jeet," she said, "always aimin' to see the higher side of the hill and when he gits there he'll find jest another hill, but he'll think the grass'll be greener on the next'n over there." "Has he learned nothing, Mandy, from those past experiences?" I asked. "Never lingers none in the past. Allus expecting someting just ahead of him."

Mandy and I worked side by side in the kitchen. She never suggested that I go ahead on, that she preferred the kitchen to herself. Mandy was wonderful company. We talked as we worked. One day I remarked that there seemed to be less ill feeling than usual. "Do you think," I asked, "that they are getting to like us better?" Mandy summed it up in one of those sentences of hers. "You've set foot in the doorway to friendship," she told me. "Take keer you don't stumble."

I listened, as we worked together in the house, to Mandy's thinking aloud. She berated them as would leave a ring in the bathtub. She lauded those who had the good sense to clean their boots outside and not "come traipsin' mud all over the place. They was scrapers and brushes by every door, wasn't they?" Her growling about folks with money (these might be our friends, our families, or the Williamses). "How come they turning their children loose to wreck other people's things? They's a damage to property, that's what, racin' over that chicken-house roof like all tarnation and we got to mend the leaks." She'd complain about food left on their plates. "Vittles cost money and they come outta our pocket." Like D, from the day Mandy joined the Pitchfork payroll, the ranch was hers and waste of any kind was like poking fingers in her purse.

Our needs were suited perfectly. Mandy was kind and was willing to take long hours when they came. She ran my house a bit high-handedly, but I was glad enough to turn it over to her. It gave me time for the chickens, the yard, the vegetable garden, building walks and terraces, or whatever project I had going. Her word was law. "I don't work on a Sunday," but on Saturdays she carefully prepared something that would be good cold for Sunday. Ham, roast chicken, tongue, some of the congealed salads she had learned to make from my cook book, and always there would be ice cream, custards, and pound cake for dessert. We ate when Mandy called, "It's ready." "Mandy," I ventured once, "Don't you think it would be nicer to step to the door and say 'Dinner is served'?" "No call to say dinner is served when it ain't," she answered. Serving was against her ingrained principals. Being at the mercy of another's moods was not to her liking. "Makes me balky," she stated. "I'll just set the vittles on the table." She did, and what good vittles they were. The bell? The rebel in Mandy emerged. As she had explained before, "I don't like that bell. There warn't no such foolishness at the Majers. I set the vittles on the table and they jest et. A man orta have as much sense as a mule," she argued. "Leave a mule see his feed in front of him, he'll eat it."

All of her days she walked as nearly as she could down God's pathway. She was good for goodness' sake, not from fear of punishment or hope or reward. And she had a wisdom not taught in school. "Mandy, sometimes I feel as if I don't have a husband anymore." She added up our domestic picture with two short sentences, and to herself. "Been used to getting more attention." Then, "Reckon Mrs. McArthur was too."

I worried about D. Mandy worried about me. She turned her diagnostic eye on me. "Ain't so peart yerself." She thought I could end the day less tired if I'd take out every so often to rest. "Set down and put yer feet up now and agin. You orta slick up today with them folks a-comin' an' all. Rest up too. I wish you hadn't a got that scrub brush haircut." It was a deplorable haircut, but the best I could do at Spur. "Don't aim to rile you, work if yer bound to, but it ain't helpin' yer looks none." Mandy had many gifts: truth, simplicity, kindliness. But diplomacy was not among them. With her keen analytical mind, she read me like a book but judged me kindly. "Well meant" was her estimate. Mandy did an uncomfortably accurate job on me, and the things she said struck home. They made a certain amount of sense, but I could not always follow through. Put my feet up, indeed. I'd have loved to put my feet up. I'd have loved stretching out on the bed under a mound of cold cream. Why, if I even sat down beside my overflowing sewing basket to catch my breath while I turned a shirt collar or sewed on a button, there'd be something more urgent pop in mind—letting the chickens out, changing the garden hose, keeping Jeet at work. One day Mandy looked at me solemnly, judging whether I would understand what she was about to say. "Overhasty. Got no patience to wait for what God send you."

Mandy was blunt about my shortcomings, even more blunt about my appearance. Was Mandy trying to tell me, was she saying that at root my plight was of my own making, at least partly? Five years and ten pounds ago I'd worn that square dance dress to the first Christmas dance. Eating like a dray horse, I had gained twelve pounds in my first year. How could I, and run like I did? I have never seen 111 again.

I'd come in from the yard and collapse on the nearest chair. Mandy would say, "You look whacked." If that meant bushed or completely exhausted, I was whacked. But Mandy was altogether reviving. She'd put a glass of iced tea in my hand, rub my shoulders and my feet. "I know the next Mrs. Burns gonna pleasure that yard."

"'Pears to me you and Jeet got the same thought regarding work, but a different manner of treatin' with it." I'm afraid I showed my surprise and consternation at being laid along side Jeet, so to speak. He couldn't be termed a wheel horse in anybody's book. "Jeet ain't afeerd o'work," she went on reassuringly. "He can lay right down beside it and go to sleep, whilst you sails by it lookin' tuther way in hopes o' ignoring it whilst gettin' to the yard."

Bit by bit she told me the story of her life. How had it happened that she hadn't married earlier? Why Jeet? She had reached the fatal age of thirty and her family thought it might be her last chance, and "none other had come a-courtin'." Mandy's lover had been killed in the First World War, but she had his memory for all of her days. Mandy measured her life by it. "That was five years after Amos died." And, "Shoulda married him afore he went away. I wanted learnin'," Mandy said, "but it never fell out that way." Some times she talked about the children she had wanted and never had. Those children were very real to Mandy. She spoke as if they had actually been born and she had lost them. Junior would be goin' on twenty-eight. Slim's the spitten image of him—same build and jaw. They would have been well mannered. They wouldn't have answered back, and they'd have had a feeling for nice things. Children with gumption and horse sense, too.

But she was never bitter about her lot. She had married Jeet; she understood him and accepted him with his superstitions and avoidance of work. Mandy saw the positive side of Jeet most of the time, such as his knowledge of growing things. "Fer all he's so slow,

Jeet gardens master." Yes, Jeet was a good gardener. He knew that the yellow pumpkin ripening among the corn should be gathered at first frost. He knew when to dig the potatoes, and potatoes turned by his fork were smooth and whole and not mutilated by careless thrusts and prods. He knew when to take up the carrots, onions, and turnips, how they should be stored in the root cellar, how to wrap pears in newspaper so they would keep until after Christmas, to put green tomatoes away in corn meal for ripening, and to transform our homegrown corn into plump and snowy hominy. He could make flavorful sauerkraut from the bursting heads of cabbage. He knew all this and more, but he was too lazy to do any of it unless one worked beside him. He was apt to be tired.

There would be popcorn for winter evenings because one day in May Jeet had said, "Time for putting popcorn in the ground," and I had jumped at the idea. He never seemed to realize that these observations might make work for him. It is possible that he enjoyed the importance of having his suggestions acted upon so much that he made them at the risk of having to carry them out. At any rate, he kept right on making them. "Leaves air gone," he'd say. "Gutters orta be cleaned."

All he knew was weather, gardening, chickens, pigs, and cows, things belonging to the soil, but he knew those well, if not scientifically. "A rusty file in that drinkin' water's a whet more useful than disinfect," he'd argue. Even Mandy did not know where he'd picked these useful bits of information or his odd superstitions. But she said, "He come of plantin' folks."

It came the time of year for grafting, and the man from the nursery talked and explained to Jeet and me the art he knew and loved so well. He spoke of scions and grafting wax. He gave us a pair of pruning shears and a special kind that would save our hands and our hours. They saved us work, but they did not save the lower limbs of my shrubs. Jeet pruned *Cedrus deodara* as far as he could reach with the stepladder and the euonymus and the wax-leafed ligustrum to one skinny stalk. He'd never had so much fun in his life.

After that visit Jeet lost all interest in anything but pruning and grafting. Those pruning shears, a jack knife, and a blab of grafting wax were always somewhere on his person. He whittled on every pear, apple, peach, and pecan tree on the place. His concern was all for the inner bark, and with that jack knife he was bound to find it. He'd stick a scion on anything he came to, and it lived and bloomed and bore fruit.

This was the only work Jeet did without strong urging. Jeet was a believer in work as it applied to the other fellow, however. He discouraged idleness in the boys. "Swing that hoe—." But to him, a hoe handle was only something to lean on. Even the mildest form of labor tired Jeet. "I can't make him understand, Mandy. He just looks at me." Mandy thought he was being intentionally wooden.

He gave you some good ideas, but he felt no obligation to carry them through, to put his hand to any work. Mandy supplied in character what he lacked. They were a pair, weren't they? Without her, Jeet would fall apart.

Jeet's lassitude was of the body, not of the mind. He had a real contempt for laziness and spoke out against it. He had small patience with them as versifies—hiding laziness behind talent. "Jest something to hide their laziness behind." He emphasized the wording scornfully. Jeet's position would have been far more persuasive if he had not had such opposition to work for himself. And Jeet, whatever his inclination, could not avoid a bit of work. Mandy saw to that.

Often she wondered aloud what he was dreaming about when he stood, rake, hoe, or pruning shears in hand, gazing into the distance for a good half-hour. What was he experiencing when he sat chin in hand, leaning on the chuck-house table, oblivious to all around him, lost in contemplation? Mandy complained mildly of these characteristics and grumbled to herself and urged him to greater industry, but she never berated him.

One fall evening Jeet informed me, "We're scant a kiver." This hinted the first cold spell of the season, and I dug up some extra blankets for them. "Jeet sleeps cold," Mandy explained. "He puts his sweater and his coat on over his unions when he goes to bed. He makes the dog sleep on his feet, puts a hot iron on his back, crams pillows around his shoulders, and gathers me up like a feather bolster to keep his stummick warm."

Weather was one of Jeet's specialities. He got out of bed only at Mandy's insistence, but once outside he studied the weather, and he studied it from every direction. First he sized up the situation in the south, then he'd walk to the east bank. He'd sneeze a few times and, gazing into the sun, he'd satisfy himself on that score. Jeet had to back away from his house a distance of a hundred yards or more before he could see over the housetops and trees. Jeet always looked from the same spot. He stood on the first rock that led down the bank and gazed intently into the northern sky. If the skies were clear and we needed rain, he'd shake his head sadly. "She's clear nor any bell." Or if there was work to be done that called for fair weather, and the sky was cloudy, it was, "Don't look anyways good." "Looks like she's gonna come one," could mean a norther or a sandy. With an air of saving the worst for the last, Jeet would scan the western skies. "Ummmm—"

"Jeet knows when it's going to rain and when it isn't," Burns said. "I'll go ask him." Jeet solemnly reported it would not rain that day. Formerly, wild geese had been our most trusted weather prophets. The weather man via radio was not as reliable as our own Jeet. Burns said, "That's because, Mamie, the weather man's reportin' on a lots of towns, like Germany and Texas and New York. But Jeet's reportin' on right here."

Jeet talked little except to Mandy. To her he'd keep up a monotonous drone of conversation. We could hear it from our bedroom, when they were eating in the kitchen, without hearing the words. I don't know if Mandy really heard them either. We never knew what he said exactly. She seemed to have the ability to listen, even to answer, with "uh-huh" or "huh-unh" or "well," to go on with her work and plans and thoughts of her own.

Jeet hummed a doleful tune when he saw a ring around the moon. It sounded like the moan of a dog when he sees a buzzard sailing overhead. Mandy said there were two tunes that he sang, one when we needed rain and one when we didn't. We never heard but one of them on the ranch, of course.

Born on a lonely farm in the hills of Arkansas, Jeet was a mass of superstitions and old wives' tales. He'd raise his eyes unseeing and otherworldly. He strung his walls with horseshoes. He cut a willow tree that touched the eaves of his house. "Had air a body died in here or been very sick? Death lyin' in wait for somebody," he explained. Jeet thought anybody'd know better than to let a willow tree touch the roof. Peacocks have long been considered unlucky. Jeet wouldn't stay on the place with one. He said only a stolen cat was fit for a mouser. "Airy thing I ever stole was a cat." The Bateses were scrupulously honest.

Mandy's superstitions were not on a lively scale. She was not afraid of man or devil. Jeet was full of fears and superstitions. He often had the feeling that some misfortune awaited: "Seen a streak of blood in the sky." He suggested we hang rattlers about Burns's neck to make teething easier. Jeet said it was an evil time. He'd had a week-long premonition that something was going to happen. Mandy thought his trouble lay in his liver.

Jeet wouldn't work with a certain Negro on the ranch on the insufficient grounds that a blue-eyed Negro could cast a spell on one, and he'd come to us on Friday the thirteenth, too.

He had endless folk tales and superstitions regarding the coyotes. Jeet said a coyote had the evil eye, but the roadrunner was a luck bringer "unless we was foolish enough to kill one." Then, Jeet said, one was indeed in trouble. He said if I'd cook a coyote and feed it to my chickens, "nary 'nother coyote'd come nigh 'em."

Jeet had dreams powerful in meaning. He felt a first omen of dread at the sign of the Pitchfork Ranch; he thought it looked like a swastika. I wasn't the only one who had considered the changing of that brand! Jeet suspected that Pitchfork was a hex sign. Hadn't it rained on the 6666 and the Matador? A new crop of fears had assailed him. No use telling Jeet those old notions had been disproved.

Legend and superstition were deep-rooted in all country people. Jeet had a snake-bite cure in which his faith rested confidently. He'd mumble words to the moon; what he mumbled we never knew. And he knew how to conjure. Mandy did not object to the medicine or Jeet's marks and signs. Jeet knew when disaster was going to strike by the way his dog behaved and the way the west door kept opening of its own accord. He believed in ghosts and was sure of their visitations. Leave any place, he advised the boys, when haints set in.

The children took some stock in Jeet, especially his weather forecasting, but they adored Mandy, and she returned with deep affection of her own. She told them tales, "dreamy stories," Cups said. "Sharp now," she'd admonish the children, Cups and Burns, "they's rattle bugs about." The first time I had occasion to call the children from their play, Mandy said, "Leave 'em be. They ain't doin' hurt, I reckon. Eatin' their white bread now, an don't know it." Mandy called Burns venturesome. Mandy's quick dark eyes watched the children sharply. She seemed impervious to their roughhouse and thought they should be allowed, when they were reproved, a comeback. "Sass ain't bad," she said. "If they can speak their piece, they won't be carryin' hurt around to fester."

Mandy believed in homemade fun. "Airy body to holp?" she'd ask, starting toward the kitchen. "Popcorn balls are mighty tasty in rainy weather." Or "Iffin the peanuts was shelled, we could make brittle." Or "Takes mor'n one to pull candy." Mandy spoke roughly but she was kind. "Where at's them young'uns?" She was carrying a tray with huge bowls of ice cream.

Mandy wasn't used to having her way. She raised no objections to Jeet's plans. She uttered not a word against leaving, but she had fallen into a silent mood and one felt she would rather die than go. I like to believe that the time here with us was the easiest Mandy had ever known, that she knew how much I needed and appreciated her. Mandy and I were alike, not in the facts of our lives, but deep down we were the same kind. Because Mandy was the kind of person I wanted to be. She had been happy here as never before in her life, "'scusin' Mis Majers," she said. The things I had grieved for yesterday or the day before were small and unimportant. They were just things. I could buy another luster pitcher, not Cousin America's, of course, but somewhere, sometime I'd find a blue and brown pitcher just that sweet size. Sheets the laundry had lost could be replaced someday. But no more in this world would I find another Mandy. For no price would I find such loyalty, such honesty and kindness, such quiet wisdom. Mandy couldn't be replaced. No one I had known, except my mother, had so well practiced what she preached.

I have not heard from her. "No need writing between friends." My eyes were moist but they were shining. Mandy didn't want to go. She had endured grinding poverty, she had been desperately close to starvation. She felt security here. She was determined to outlive any hardship and to follow her man. Hers was not a sad face, yet a harsh, barren life had left its mark. Even I had not realized how heavily I leaned on Mandy—not just help in the household chores, but her loyalty, her sage advice. Mandy could whip out clear as a whistle a reasonable explanation for my behavior. I was sometimes amazed. I had attributes I did not know I possessed.

I even missed Jeet.

Mandy was more than good help to be missed. She had been my friend. How the place missed her. She didn't want to leave us. She knew how terribly we needed her. "Hate to leave with you standin' in need o' us like you do." And she knew how deeply I cared for yer. I wanted to tell her how I leaned on her, how I appreciated her, but it would only have caused embarrassment.

16

Ed Nolan

We did not feel the loss of those who marched off with Murd so much, because others came with Coy. "There is an old hand that would like to come back and work through the season with us," Coy told D. "He was raised on this ranch. He knows all the canyons and every cow trail in this country, and he is a real hand in the brush." With this recommendation, Ed Nolan came back to work at the Forks after an absence of nineteen years. He had a wife and six children now, but they would stay and manage his small farm at Calgary, he told D. "It's a right sharp snort from here," he said. "But I can go back now and again on Sundays if you can furnish me some gas." D could do that, as we and other ranchers were allowed ample gas for our transportation needs.

It was down the long table of the chuck house that I first saw Ed. Cowmen are imposingly robust as a rule, big and brawny. Ed broke all the rules. He was intense, small, and frail looking, but I knew at a glance that he was tough as a pine knot. His life's story could be read on his weather-creased face. His eyes wandered contentedly over the place. He sat beside Coy, and all of us were fascinated by his animated mannerisms and conversation. His words were more light-hearted than Coy's droll remarks and responses, but just as entertaining.

"I'm purty prideful about this ranch." His rare high spirits pleased us, and we strained to catch every word. "You see, I come here three months before I was born." All the years of his young life he had spent on this ranch. All those years when he was learning to handle a horse, a rope, and to read the mind of a cow. His pa had worked on the ranch and his ma had cooked for the men. He spoke of his boyhood. "I done my courtin' here," he said. 'I was single and plenty interested when Wife's folks moved in to take over the chuck-house job. She was sixteen and purty as a speckled pup."

It was a rainy day, and there was no reason that we couldn't sit

as long as we wished at the chuck-house table, listening to Ed re-
count the variety of jobs and experiences he had enjoyed on the
Pitchfork, riding line, bogging, plowing fire guards, haying, fighting
fires, fencing, freighting supplies, doctoring sick cows, and driving
Mr. Gardner. He explained the difficulties of ranch life in the early
days. Before the advent of tractors, it had been necessary to make
fire guards by using turning plows, or sulkeys, or gang plows hitched
to mules. Ed had been a scrawny thirteen-year-old when he first
drove for Mr. Gardner. (He wasn't much bigger now.) One could
not miss the veneration he felt for Mr. Gardener.

"We trapped wolves, skunks, and turtles. Mr. Gardner paid a
bounty on the wolves. We done anything ast of us to stay on the
payroll."

Ed was an ideal storyteller. He put himself so thoroughly into
the subjects he described that the events, though they may have
belonged to Mr. Gardner's Pitchfork, seemed to have happened
only last week. He was a storehouse of Pitchfork history and knowledge. He probably knew more about the Pitchfork's physical past
than any man alive: how many acres in the first purchase, how
many men they worked, what they were paid, what Mr. Gardner
thought important, and what he did not allow (drinking, gambling,
marrying). Ed had lived here most of his life and had seen all the
changes. His mind was stocked with tales of cowmen, cowboys, and
ranches and with stories of bottomless pits, the horses he had
known and loved, and things he had seen and done on this ranch.
He seemed as much a part of the locality as the mesquite.

He loved to tell the stories of his youth. He remembered the
Pitchfork at the turn of the century and the stories his father told
him of earlier days. His speech was vivid and inimitable as he recre-
ated the color of events he recalled from the past. He told me the
stories of Buttermilk Gaines and Peely Ripple, two old fellows who
had worked on the Forks in the early '80's. Once they had ranches
of their own; their land lay side by side. Hard times had fallen upon
them, and their friend, Dan Gardner, had given them jobs. The
greatest of friendships existed between them. A liking for cattle was
their strongest bond and a liking for the bottle, their common
weakness.

Buttermilk had been a bad man in his prime, had killed a fellow or two. His trigger finger still held the power to keep tongues respectful among the Forks hands. Peely, quiet and unassuming, was exactly the opposite of his friend. Legend had it that years ago these two were drinking in a saloon and started a discussion that ended in argument. Emboldened by drink, Peely had said, "jest fer a little, I'd slap hell outta you." Brash words for a fellow to use to Buttermilk Gaines. The crowd parted for the action. Buttermilk fixed a keen gray eye on Peely. "I got a durn good horse out there at the hitchin' rack. I'll jest give you that horse if you'll hit me." He advanced a few steps. Peely thought a long second. "Let's go look at your horse," he said.

"I come upon 'em once talkin' about dyin'," Ed related. "Hope I ain't sick no time an' I hope they ain't no long faces at my funeral," Buttermilk had opined. "I hope everbody's plumb merry. I hope they have a band, an' I don't keer if they dance." Peely was scandalized at this lack of reverence. "Well," he announced, "I'd want a few tears shed over me. I got no mind for hilarity at my grave, an' I hope when my time comes to go that I'll be sick a long time, thet all my fam'ly an' friends'll come. I want to linger and linger and linger, an' then get up."

According to Buttermilk, Peely was a pessimist. They used to pass bets on the weights of their cattle. Buttermilk always overshot them; Peely always under-guessed. Especially once. He was coming in from delivering his cattle, long-faced, morose. "What'd they weigh?" Buttermilk had asked, and Peely had answered, "Not as much as I thought they would. Didn't think they would."

Ed missed his family and would drop by the house on evenings, especially when the grandchildren were there, to visit. The children loved his stories. He told them about his own youngsters and how they wanted to move to the ranch. "They'd be here right now if we had a house for you or if one could be found anywhere close," D told him.

Burns and Cuppie liked nothing better than popping corn at our fireplace on winter evenings. On one such occasion, Ed came by to visit with us and, seeing the popcorn, commented, "Ain't nuthin' better than a fresh popped batch of corn to walk in on." He proceeded between mouthfuls to delight the children with information of the old days that considerably enlarged their knowledge and appreciation. He showed them how to tie knots and explained to them how fires were made from prairie coal, or cow chips.

"In them days, we carried a bag of jerky, which is made by slicin' strips o' meat an' hangin' it in the sun to dry. It was sump'n to chew on an' was a prime comfort to th' stomach, huh? Sometimes they sprinkled it with salt an' red pepper. When this was softened up by boilin' a few hours, it made mighty good eatin' an' could shore season up a pot o' red beans." Ed said that in those days in this country, beef kept even in the summer. "We didn't have no refrigeration, but th' nights was allus cold, so we'd hang th' beef up in the coolest place we could find at night, then wrap it in canvas in th' day an' keep it in th' shade. Of course, it didn't take a cow crew long to eat a beef. Nuthin' ever spoiled aroun' a cow outfit."

The stories he told the children fascinated me as well. Ed virtually acted out his scenes. When he spoke of shooting coyotes, he would extend his left arm to represent a rifle, squint at an imaginary sight on his index finger, and draw a bead on a coyote. He had a rare talent for bringing the feel and flavor of the past to the minds of his audience. Little Burns would listen captivated and would unconsciously imitate each gesture and movement that Ed used to illustrate his narration.

He brought to life much of the social history of the past: what games the children played, how the young people amused themselves, and the hardships and sufferings endured by the women and early ranchers. Ed told of the loneliness and the pain and suffering of the early-day women: childbirth without care and under the most unsanitary conditions. Only a few had a midwife to attend them. Women were often left alone while their husbands were on cattle drives. At such times they had to hold the fort against attacks from Indians, painters (cougars), and wolves. Their domestic duties were extensive. Besides doing the cooking, the washing, and the housekeeping, they carded wool and worked outdoors. If any gardening was done, they did it. They also raised the chickens and the pigs. Milking was thought of as a woman's job. These women had little time for cosmetics, but they did use berries as rouge for their lips and cheeks.

Ed told about his grandmother's coming in from the garden one day to discover a painter crouched and ready to devour a child. When the painter saw her, it sprang out through the open window.

"Ranching is not a whole lot easier, but it's a whet more convenient than it used to be for ranch hands and ranch women." Ed laughed, and added, "A visit to the bathroom then was a trip out-of-doors, huh?" Once, as he watched me pulling the garden hose around, he observed, "Ma had to carry ever' bucket o' water she used on her plants. Her plants were mighty few. Some four-o-clocks an' two lilacs is all I kin remember, 'cept two honeysuckles on th' fence an' a trumpet vine on the outhouse. Ma had a little patch of Bermuda grass aroun' th' cistern where we got our drinkin' water that she was so proud of. All th' women in the country wanted a start of it."

Ed remembered Ivy Rader and commended the food she prepared when she cooked on the Forks during Dan Gardner's day. "It couldn't hardly a been beat," he declared. Another cook he told about was Miss Ida. "Miss Ida usta take th' bread to bed with 'er on cold nights to make it rise."

As Ed recounted these tales of the rigors endured by pioneer women, I realized that my experiences on the Pitchfork, compared with the perils of Ivy Rader and Mrs. Nolan, were a breeze. Problems that existed now had existed way back then. Ivy Rader's dreams and ambitions for her home and her children were about the same as mine, but she had her problems too, featherbeds torn up by goats and cornsalve linament, wool fat, kerosene, pliers, and wire-stretchers always on her clock shelf. Still, I had undergone some rather trying ordeals myself.

Old-time ranchers had endured many hardships too. Ed said the early cowman hated Indians, rattlesnakes, centipedes, and skunks, but that he'd rather "put up with all four than have one sheepman on th' outskirts of his ranch." The opinion of sheepmen has softened now. Some of the most prestigious cattlemen in the business are also running sheep.

Ed remembered a story his father told him, a story, like all his father's reminiscences, confirmed by good evidence, of brave marksmen who galloped beside the last wild buffalo to keep their camps free from Indians. He entertained the children by explaining to them what a Comanche moon was. "My father called ever' bright moon-light night a Comanche moon, because the Indians raided then."

Recalling the difficulty of travel in those days, Ed said, "The cowboys got inta town about onct a month ridin' their horses over prairie roads. They was lucky to git in onct a month on Satiddies, if they was caught up with their work." He remembered that "on rainy days we cleaned the bunkhouse, straightened up the shop, did some horseshoeing."

Speaking of the weather, Ed claimed that the sandstorms were worse in the old days because "there wasn't nuthin' to stop 'em. They almost drove th' women outa their minds, but th' men got to where they never noticed 'em." Snow was rarely seen on the ranch, but Ed said that when it came, the oldtimers "made the most of what snow there was. They went sleigh ridin' a heap an' after ended it up with a dance-frolic."

Other forms of amusement Ed told about were quiltings, which gave the women a chance to get together and socialize. The boys and girls had candy pullings. Mrs. Campbell, wife of the Matador manager, was the social arbiter of the county. She was famous for her three-day parties—"swahrays," she called them. Ed remembered that at the end of one of these prolonged parties, two cow-boys, heavy with drink, decided to play a joke on the guests. The mothers had put their babies on pallets in an upstairs room. While the babies were asleep, the pifflicated pair slipped in and shifted them around. Consternation prevailed when, upon reaching their homes, the parents discovered the bundle they carried did not con-tain their child. Ed shook with laughter. "They had a turrible time mammyin' up them babies."

After Ed's father died, there were obviously critical times for the little boy. "Until Ma married Uncle George," he said, "we had it hard, but he was th' best husband and th' best stepfather any per-son could have had. It was th' luckiest thing ever happened to us. I learned a lot from him an' Mr. Gardner. Both of 'em wanted me to grow up right, an' they took pains to learn me."

"Ed, did you bring this rain?" Veto Austin said as he came in the west door of the chuck house. "Why didn't you come sooner?" They swapped a few yarns before D put an end to the reminiscing.

"Looks like the shower's over. Let's get out to the office and mix a little medicine."

"I'm ready to get in harness." Ed jumped up from the bench. He hadn't unpacked his gear, so they went out together, D walking between Coy and Ed. It seemed to me that D's shoulders had straightened. For the first time in many months, I felt a gathering hope that things were going to get better for D. He had Coy, and he had Ed, "and they know this country like the backs of their hands," he'd told me.

Ed was to become such an essential part of the cow crew that his value could hardly be estimated. He was the first down to the chuck house in the morning to help the cook build a fire in the wood stove and put the coffee on. He was not only an outstanding ranch hand, but also a trusted source of information and pleasure. His enthusiasm for ranch work was contagious, and his sharp wit served as a damper to the cowhands when they were inclined to gripe or complain about conditions. "You orta quit if you don't like the setup," he would tell them.

From the beginning, everyone kidded Ed about his appetite. He ate as if each meal would be his last. "They allus have dinner," Coy told him that first morning at breakfast. Ed's capacity for work equaled his gusto for food. But he did not linger at the table. He was always ready when D said, "Boys, let's get at it."

17

Wartime Troubles

Everything in the house seemed to be falling to pieces, beat up, battered, and peeling. When anything got out of order or was broken it stayed that way. There was no such thing as buying another or replacing a part. The iron had gone bad. Every button on the gas stove was broken. We had to keep the pliers lying near to turn on the burners. Door knobs just didn't seem to care. One door wouldn't close. We had to keep a chair against it. A leg got broken on the divan requiring constant warnings to visitors. The egg beater had given up the ghost and the vacuum sweeper was having labor pains.

But the thing that caused D loss of sleep and temper was his bed springs. About six nights out of seven, sometime during the night those springs would fall. I'd hear the most horrible crash. I never seemed to get used to it. Always I thought a plane had nose-dived into the house or a cyclone had struck until I heard his groans and curses. I'd go in to help him lift the things back into place, to straighten his covers. From D's hurt, accusing look, you'd have thought I'd yanked those springs from under him. Sometimes it would startle me so, especially if I'd been sound asleep, that I'd scream out, "What was that noise?" This was exasperating beyond words to D. He'd say, "What do you suppose it was? What the hell could it be but this damned bed? I'm going to burn it. I'm going to—" I'd stuff a pillow in my mouth to keep from laughing. At these times I didn't go in to help. It wouldn't have been safe! Of course, the bed could have been fixed. Two screw eyes and some picture wire was all that was needed to pull the side pieces together to hold the slats. That is what was finally done. I couldn't do it by myself, but no one had the hour or so to spare then just to help me fix a bed.

Things that had seemed amiable enough in the morning went to pot before night. Furniture was antique in appearance and performance. Sitting down became a dangerous business. There was hardly a chair, be it porch, yard, or house, in which we could place complete confidence. Drawers wouldn't budge. Casters broke off just at the rollers.

Shortages began mounting. We used Kleenex, that is, as long as we could get it. I remember the day a visitor pulled a few yards of tissue from his pocket. It came out folded one square at a time and streamed to the floor to his consternation and embarrassment. "My wife put that in there. We can't get Kleenex now." "We can't either," D said, reaching in his pocket for his own wad of toilet paper.

One by one, but in quick succession, our five time pieces played out. D had complained in San Angelo, "Three antique clocks ticking away in this house, no two together, none of them accurate, and those damned chimes!" To me those chimes were music. There wasn't five minutes difference between those clocks. They were close enough to make bridge games, beauty parlor appointments, or a plane or train if you were an "ahead of the hounds" sort of person, as I am.

I would have loved one of those clocks ticking away now, for D's watch that he had worn so long, the gift his mother had given his father on their wedding day, had stopped, and a jeweler had told him it could not be repaired. Two of those antique clocks were smashed in that breakneck move to the ranch; the third simply stopped, being too lonely and too elderly to adapt to ranch life. My own watch was stolen. It was just an accident when I'd catch the time on the radio. So it was a sad thing when D's watch ticked its last.

We simply had to close our eyes to slow decay. If we looked in any direction we saw scratched wood, frayed slipcovers, chipped china, peeling paint inside and out. All the faucets leaked, and no washers to be had. The door bell did not work. The oven door warped, so while the lovely pine wall that I'd so lovingly picked became a golden brown, the biscuits remained white.

The battered perculator is a fine example of wartime disintegration; first the little glass top fell and broke (a cup could be used instead), then the handle came off. D suggested using a small stew pan instead. "Boiled coffee is best anyway, just to a boil." This was great until the day Ink fell with his pressure cooker and smashed the saucepan beyond use. Our next pan had a wooden handle that soon became wobbly, so you never knew in which direction it would turn or on which foot you'd spill the boiling coffee.

One of the window panes had a big hole in it, and the shade grew spotted and circled by the rain when the wind came from the south, and the floor underneath it suffered, too. Unavailable at any price were radio tubes, springs, universal joints, elbows, nipples, bushings, bolts, wire, wiring, nuts, and sockets, and the Lord knows what else. D grumbled, "It's enough to make a man old before his time."

D really is a penurious person. He felt it was useless for me to try to find replacements and unpatriotic to buy them if one could find them. "It is the wrong time to do anything drastic in the way of repair," D proclaimed. I don't know why D feels anything I'm considering has to be drastic, but sure enough, the few bright shiny handles, latches, and knobs that we replaced did look a little drastic on those beat-up pieces.

Something seemed always to be wrong with the ailing, rusted hot water heater. The only advantages appeared to be that a man could put his feet up anywhere and scratches no longer showed. My war was waged against wear and tear, sand and mud, flies and cockroaches, mice and men. Yet our home was still an oasis to guests who didn't view it with our jaundiced and candid view.

We consistently warned all guests not to forget any of their belongings, because we had no time to wrap and mail packages. So perhaps you'll be sympathetic to our wartime attitude in the following episode.

"One of them left his clock," I told D. "It's a Little Ben." I picked it up and held it to my ear. It was running! And it was right on the dot with the chuck-house bell that was clanging then.

"Let me see it," D put out his hand greedily. "On the nose!" Then plaintively, "They'll write back for this." He wound it lovingly. "I'll bet that's a good little clock." He walked into his room with it. I knew that he had placed it right beside his bed on the table with his flashlight, his bottle of Vicks, his gloves, reading light, and his car keys. Those were the Untouchables. He'd roar like a bull if any one of these was rearranged. He wanted them where he could lay his hand on any of these things in the middle of the night or when the lights were off. Well, that clock was mine. I'd found it, I mean I'd come upon it, well, it wasn't his. At least we could put it in the big bedroom where we both could see it. I hurried in to claim the treasure.

It was a joy to have Little Ben right there on the candle stand beside my bed next to my Untouchables, the Mentholatum, nail file, pencil caddy, hand lotion, and lipstick. Just to look in at any hour of the day and know the time, not to have to wait and listen for it on the radio, and how D blessed the alarm.

A few days later, D came in with a letter in his hand and an unhappy expression, "Well, I guess this is it." This was what? Wasn't that what people were saying when they said good-bye to good friends and good things? Were we leaving the Pitchfork then, after all? What else could cause the end-of-the-world look on D's face? I took the letter fearfully. It was addressed to me. Colonel J. K. Saunder's name was in the corner. Stricken, I understood. Our Little Ben! We had so come to depend on him, in my room in the daytime, on D's table at night. He had saved D many an hour's sleep. D had the faculty of waking at an appointed hour, but sleep under such conditions is a nervous, uncertain thing. Little Ben's clamor had been sure, no oversleeping from fatigue. I opened the offending missive: Thank you etc., etc., pleasant interlude in a wartime inspection trip, etc. . . . Hope we did not overstay our welcome . . . Sorry to have missed D. Darned good roast, steaks, and ham . . . etc. Thanks again. J. K.

They hadn't missed it! I mean, they hadn't mentioned it. Slowly the darkness of D's countenance lifted. A happier, brighter expression spread over his face. "Perhaps we should write him about it?" I put it in the form of a question. Just suggesting it was salve to my conscience. Never one to sidestep a tough issue, D said, "Perhaps—," neatly passing the buck back to me. His manner suggested that all this fuss made over a clock was excessive. He tried to be light, offhand. After all, he had more complicated issues. To name two: J. M. Hickman on the line about six hauling trucks for Sunday afternoon and engaging cattle cars to go north from Paducah.

It was a good half hour before he turned from the phone, but he hadn't been sidetracked from the main issue of the day. "They're in the army, Mayme," he said. "They can pick up another one at the PX for next to nothing." We enjoyed that clock with amazing unscrupulousness.

18

Ode to Cooks

Like all Gaul, our cooks and kitchens were divided into three categories. There's the chuck-house couple, the chuck-wagon cook, and there's, intermittently, the Big House couple. Cooks were the most temperamental and all-important personages on the ranch, and they knew it. Criticize one or suggest a change, and you have lost a helper. All cooks are prima donnas whether their food is edible or not. It takes a flow of compliments to keep one happy and on the job.

Good food is the basis for contented cowboys. At the chuck house we had hearty, no-fooling meals. We averaged one beef a week. Anything beyond beef, red beans, and potatoes was considered fancy. During the war years, with any kind of beef fetching a king's ransom, we occasionally tried serving other meats, fried chicken, ham, or even salmon croquettes. The men didn't like it and started making noises about it at once.

My most delicate problems arose when complaints came from the men about the food at the chuck house. Invariably this happened when a new couple took over the job there. The Austins were hard to follow. We heard comments for months and even years after they were transferred to the Purebred Camp. "I think she makes up a batch of biscuits onct a week and serves 'em to us cold and hard as rocks the other six days." "She never puts no onions on the table for the beans and the beans ain't half cooked. They're so hard they rattle in the bowl." "The butter tastes so old and strong it could walk. They don't churn mor'n onct a week." "Them cobblers and puddin's ain't fittin' to eat. Shure ain't like the Austins."

Ranch work is tough. Cowboy fare must be hearty. Vegetably speaking, they'll take beans, potatoes, and tomatoes. Beans are pretty much standard fare on any ranch. We soaked ours overnight and cooked them a long, long time. What boots are to a cowboy's raiment, beans are to his stomach. With lean salt pork or ham hocks they are mighty tasty. They want their steaks chicken-fried and drowned in ketchup or gravy. There must be ketchup. Roast will do in a pinch, but chicken-fried steak is what the cowboys love. Ed swore, "It's got vitamins A, B, C, and D, and the gravy's got the rest of the alphabet."

If the cook strayed too far away from anything other than pepper and salt in the seasoning department, I was sure to hear about it. "She puts perfume in her cakes," the boys told me if the cook had used almond or lemon flavoring. Only vanilla was acceptable. One complainer hotfooted it over from the chuck house to tell me, "That cake tasted just like sawdust." Mandy's comment to him was, "Ever et a bait of sawdust?" She had a dimension few people have. She made you think and she made you laugh.

Chuck-house food was not bad, but I couldn't call it good. Too many starches: beans, potatoes, corn, rice, bread. We wanted a better-balanced and more varied menu. To be sure, the boys didn't ask for it. In fact, they distrusted and for a while refused vegetables.

Before Coy came, they gave the impression they wouldn't be caught dead nibbling a carrot or cabbage slaw. It was amusing to see them popeyed at the sight of a he-man munching lettuce, turnip greens, cauliflower, and kale-on-the-leaf. Before too long there grew up an "I just think I'll try some" attitude, and eventually we served raw vegetable salads all the time.

With a good cook in the kitchen, the chuck house became the exuberant center of ranch activities. It was our common meeting ground, where everyone exchanged news, rumors, and gossip while gathered around the long table that seated thirty, and many times every place was filled.

All of us enjoyed the informality of the chuck-house meals. That table was accustomed to elbows. A cowboy sits where he can see outside and always wants elbow room for dunking. Table manners, or the lack of them, were not nearly so important as over at the Big House, so the children always chose the chuck house if given a choice of eating places. The boys ate not noiselessly and with great haste, and D ate just as fast as any of them, their jaws working at the same relentless rate.

Between the big dining room and the big kitchen was an eight-foot pass-through where sat the enormous crocks of iced tea and milk and the day's offering of desserts. Mouthwatering pies, left in their tins, with and without meringue, always several varieties, "So's if a feller don't fancy chocolate or lemon, he can have apple, coconut, or banana cream, egg custard or fruit pie" (But not all on any one day). In the fall, around the holidays, we'd be sure to have pumpkin or mincemeat, not to mention pecan and chess. While Mrs. Johnson was there, she started the popular custom of having a big tray of homemade ice cream for the cowboys to spoon onto their pie or cobbler. The boys saw to it that that custom didn't die with Mrs. Johnson's departure. All spoke admiringly of Mrs. Johnson.

The aroma of coffee permeated the chuck house and reached out tantalizingly. Some folk maintained, "We tried to drive past the gate on the highway, but the coffee smell pulled us back." Even before the chuck-house cooks were up, the early morning addicts, Roy Cross, Ed, and Tom, would be down building up the fire and getting the big pot to talking on the back of the stove.

The hour for breakfast or supper might vary according to the time of year or the kind of work that was being done on the ranch, but the chuck-house bell, which hung on the west porch, was rung every day at straight-up noon for dinner. You could set your watch by it. In fact, we largely regulated our lives by that chuck-house bell.

On the wall in the chuck-house dining room there were two telephones, one to the outside world—Spur, Lubbock, Fort Worth, Saint Louis, and other ports-of-call—the other a rural intercom, the camp phone, we called it. This line was the ranch newspaper. On it each noon D would talk to all the outlying camps, checking off his list and adding to it as the men told their various situations. Tommie Smith was sure to have some extravagant brags about his cow dogs that were good for a laugh, and there was the perennial request to Mr. Oliver for wood. D would make comments to the eaters between shouts on the phone, which functioned only a little better than two tin cans on a string. A typical one-sided noontime bulletin might sound something like this: "How much did it rain up there, Roy? Enough to plant on? . . . Water gaps out on Brushy? I'll send you a man if we can spare one. . . . Got any salt? You say you need a float-pan at Dugout Well? . . . Do we have to work Devil's Corner this week?"

An SOS from Veto would prompt an explanatory aside "That 54-heifer is calving, needs some help." Then "John Ballard says there's a bunch of worm cases in Croton."

Eternally there would be news of the windmills. "The wheel blew off the mill at Gibson. The Presley mill's uncoupled. . . . You say somebody left the gate open at Boxcar trap and the yearling got back into West Croton? . . . Floyd Smith's baby arrived last night! . . . God Almighty! They found a stray bull in North Shinnery where those heifer yearlings are. Make you want to pull your hair. . . . Coy, those boys are sitting on Long Canyon with a flat and no extra."

Just then one of the cowboys glanced out the window and yelled, "Looks like there is a fire back in the steer pasture." This was the all-out alert. The chuck house was cleared in a matter of minutes.

The chuck-house cook stove was one of those old square wood-burners that was cozy in wintertime but death itself in the summer. At all seasons, the cook was never far from her stove. The boys sat on the woodbox or stood around the stove with their heavy coffee mugs warming their hands on cold days. A string line was stretched across the corner where the dish towels dried. A cistern was built into the screened-in back porch, and there was an opening that served the wood box. In the summer, there were cots on this south porch and pot plants. Here the cooks could enjoy the breeze if they had a minute to spare. After the war, we had a huge refrigerator and deep freeze unit installed that took up half the milkhouse. We've hung quarters of beef in there.

Some of our merriest times took place at the chuck house, and some of our sweetest memories. It was from the long table of the chuck house that I first saw Ed. A stranger sitting at the table would think the men a sober-sided lot, but in reality the chuck house was a place of warmth and amity. Watching and listening to the cowboys was part of the fun of living there. From the first to the last of the meals I ate at the chuck house, the cowboy brand of wit entranced me. The same magic happened each time I found myself at that table.

We had to let guests in on the customary routine of the ranch.

Being on time for meals was of the greatest importance. The chuck-house couple had to rise at five in order to have breakfast ready by six. They were entitled to a few hours' rest in the middle of the day. They could not get out of the kitchen by one-thirty or two if people came straggling in for meals at all hours. Cooks at the Big House and the chuck house were necessarily distinctly separate breeds, of separate abilities and of separate worlds.

At our house, the help, when we had any, opened the kitchen door at seven. After lunch they would go to their room to rest an hour or so, then return to do some of the hundred things that keep a place going, washing woodwork and windows, waxing floors, polishing furniture and silver, occasionally cleaning the basement. Many times when we had guests the cook was in the kitchen until nine or ten at night.

Guests were never herded through a planned schedule. We loathed forced fun. Neither were our guests cramped by domestic perfectionism. The only inexorable law was to be on time for meals, or to let us know if plans had changed and they were not coming at all.

Every woman knows entertaining takes time anywhere, but on the ranch we often felt that precious time was being stolen that could have been spent on our jobs. Visitors found the Forks exciting. Our surroundings were not dull or drab, and the show was always on. We had a fun setting and a cast of characters that stimulated guests. If a cowboy rode or walked by you were sure to hear, "Oh look! There goes one." The cowboy is conscious of his appeal, and does his best not to disappoint. We entertained simply and constantly and had to be prepared for instant entertainment. We kept an emergency shelf, and when there was a free day, I spent it filling the deep freeze. We were always expecting the unexpected.

Ours was ever a varied group at table. Laughter and congeniality kept the atmosphere lively, and routine was never the usual order. Who might be working in the kitchen or who the guests might be were often unknown factors until we were seated, but mealtimes were happy times when the four of us were assembled plus maybe a guest or two. Funny events were always funnier when we had an audience to share them, like the evening new friends from Connecticut were dining with us. We had seen *House and Garden* pictures and movies of their ancestral home in New England with beautiful antiques and family retainers much in evidence (a footman behind every chair), so my best silver and linen were brought out for the first time in ages. Burns slid into his chair beside Anne, spied his napkin, placed his hands to mouth, and in the loudest stage whisper ever said, "Look, Anne, rag napkins!" Our diplomatic guest smiled, "Burns, it's been a long time since our home has known the pleasure of rag napkins."

I always sat at the foot of the dining room table with the kitchen immediately behind me. D sat at the head, so it was he who most often registered surprise or consternation at what was coming through the swinging door. His startled expressions have alerted me more than once to approaching catastrophe. Sometimes it was amusement in his wicked eyes. Such was the case when Rose, the Indian girl, appeared to serve dessert, wearing one of my dresses, and a very good dress, I might add. She explained that she had spilled beet juice down the front of her uniform and it was raining. "More better wear your dress than get wet going to my house." Perhaps, but if she had spilled crème brulé down the front of *that* dress, more better she leave.

Once during a near-formal meal, I saw D half rise from his seat, hands outstretched, with a bewildered, unbelieving look, then sink slowly and helplessly back into his chair. I turned to see Mrs. Martin, the one who had so successfully managed a tearoom, entering with plates, partially served in the kitchen, stacked from hand to shoulder. She had bumped the door open with the back part of her and closed it with a fast foot. Sashaying around the table, dropping a small curtsy, she placed each plate. No one really breathed until she had served the last guest and flashed a triumphant smirk at me as she marched through the swinging door.

Everyone, including D, was convulsed with laughter, everyone except the hostess. I felt a shudder of misgiving. Would Mrs. Martin remove in like manner? How could we hope to retain the services of this gem, the first to grace my kitchen in many months, yet save those Quimper plates, wedding gifts that could never be replaced? Suddenly I heard myself saying, "If you will excuse me, I'll have a word with Mrs. Martin." Later I recalled only snatches of that kitchen conversation in which I requested as diplomatically as possible that each setting be removed separately.

"Why?" Mrs. Martin asked indignantly. "What's wrong with the way I serve?" Eager to get back to our guests and to have the matter over, I made the unfortunate answer, "It is not correct." My concern was for our plates, but Mrs. Martin's face showed hurt, utter amazement, and disbelief. "Do you mean after all the time I takened to learn how to carry six plates at once, it ain't k'rect?" A pause, then, "I don't think I'm going to like this job." The next morning she was gone.

Perhaps I should say that my original interview with Mrs. Martin had excited the greatest hopes that I had indeed struck gold in this cook. When I asked if she served, she emphatically replied, "I reckon I do, I've been managing a tearoom." Then to my inquiry about uniforms, she snapped, "Of course." I was overcome with such perfection.

Had I been putting too much emphasis on table setting and serving? If so, that was soon remedied. When I had no help at all, when every step was mine, we ate buffet. After the children were with us, Anne and Burns learned to help considerably. We wanted no stuffiness in our table etiquette, but we wished the children to be considerate of others, careful in their speech, their appearance, and table manners. How little we cared for our own sakes, but how much for theirs. Perhaps I had added unnecessary worries by insisting that meals times, especially dinner, be just a bit less casual. Mrs. Martin was not the first who departed because of my standards. Even Mandy, who loved us, rebelled at my using a bell to summon her.

Aunt Fannie, the proper Waconian, might be shocked at some of the dizzying changes in dress and language in the past few years. She would never accept a barefoot wedding or tolerate the four-letter words used by some in mixed social conversation, but she would, I believe, approve wholeheartedly the changes I'd made to meet the situations confronting me in which the old rules of etiquette could not apply. She'd understand where I'd conformed to such new customs as dinner at noon, paper napkins, serving buffet, trays before the fire, cattle as perennial table topics, meals interrupted to answer the phone. (If a call was lucky enough to come through, we'd have to talk so loudly every word could be heard at the table. One must not be queasy if the call concerned a cow in trouble having a calf or a horse killed on the highway.)

Aunt Fannie thought eight the perfect number for a dinner or *convivium*. Hers were that. She was concerned first with her seating arrangement. It's vital, the decision of whose chairs belonged side by side. Of course, one must reckon with circumstances and reality, but Aunt Fannie mixed old and young with beautiful results. She did not hesitate to place David Warfield, the actor, beside her minister's wife.

In Aunt Fannie's smooth-running menage it was feasible to follow the Duchess of Windsor's dictum: "A souffle is a lamentable omission to a dinner party." Still, if one's help does not have a way with souffles, omit them. It would be impossible to keep one hot and fluffy for more than eight. Imagine Vanilla's, "Miz Burns, hit's done fell," as she neared the seventh guest. I recall Mandy's "Ain't nothin' worser'n somebody trying to and caint." I concur.

Snake-bit as we were in the help department, where food was concerned, we were luckier than most of the wartime world. We had steaks, ham, chicken, milk, eggs, and butter, plus D's smoked sausage and bacon. We did quite a little foraging right there on the Forks. There was wild game—turkey, dove, quail, fish, duck, geese—and we lived within picking distance of a clump of wild plums that made the most tantalizingly different jelly and preserves. D loved the little chili pequins that we grew, and he ate them with everything if the blue quail, mockingbirds, and wild turkeys left any on the plants. This hot little pepper was responsible for the much-discussed flavor of D's sausage. The boys said there were three grades to his sausage: hot, hotter and hot as hell. "The first is for Mayme and the children," D explained, "the second for the boys, and it takes a man to eat the third grade." It did indeed! Aside from being the best steak broiler in the United States, D admittedly could smoke the best meat.

We did our bit for beef consumption by serving steaks, roasts, and hamburgers. People expect beef when they visit a ranch and were disappointed if we did not serve it. So we had steaks, two-inch steaks. D broiled them himself according to individual likes.

"This place serves the best and the prettiest steaks in this state," George Sheppard advised the other two men, as we sat down to the table. D tried to look modest. Imagine, if you can, our dismay to see those gorgeous steaks cut into inch-square bits with a peculiar looking something over them. D's consternation was evident, but before he said a word, Lucy announced, "Ah po'ed flour and water gravy on 'em. Sho makes 'em good." D couldn't say anything. He was on the verge of apoplexy.

Now the cooking of a steak is a question on which friends have been known to divide. It has even set brother against brother, Republican against Republican, Democrat against Democrat. We like ours broiled and rare, but you know there are many worthy people who don't. Cattlemen love to enliven the dinner table conversation for the benefit of strangers with subtle remarks about the good red meat. "Cripple one and run it in, D," or "That's done just enough not to hook you," or "Slide it in, turn it over, and pull it out," or "I've seen 'em get well, hurt worse than that one." Some city folk found their appetites slightly impaired by such wit. I'm in their camp.

D returned from an inspection tour of another big ranch with the comment, "Their steaks were cooked to death, Mayme. The only thing I found well done on the whole place." Some maintain that Eve tempted Adam not with an apple, but with an Elberta peach. We contend it was a T-bone steak.

We used the out-of-doors every minute we could in our everyday life and in entertaining. Food has a special flavor cooked in the open air, but Texas weather is not to be relied upon, and we had to plan always against sudden plagues of flies or mosquitoes and be prepared to move inside in case of sand, wind, or a sudden shower.

"Come in and take pot-luck with us" is the warm and friendly invitation of the range. When we entertained at home in the country, there was no such thing as taking guests to the hotel or running to the corner grocery store for ice cream. But I soon learned folks considered a meal at the chuck house a real treat, and eating behind a wagon a never-to-be-forgotten experience, so I offered no apologies for not always serving them in our dining room. There are those who suppose a Texan fills his car from an oil well in the backyard and eats son-of-a-gun as his daily fare. Most Texans' lives are as far removed from the ranch scene as is the New Yorker's. Out-of-state visitors are sometimes amazed that the native Texans find a ranch as interesting as they themselves do. Unless one has close rancher friends, one may never have the opportunity to go beyond the wire fence. Ranchers do have something else to do besides conducting tours.

"There was a time," says a Marlboro cigarette ad, "when the only chuck wagon around was the long-eared kind, one mule carrying a chuck-box full of food." Then in 1866, Charles Goodnight took that chuckbox and put four mules in front of it, four wheels under it, and a cantankerous old cook to look after it. The chuck wagon became, as Tom Thornton said, home in the middle of nowhere.

The wagon was the cowboy's home about eight months of the year. It was the place where a man could hang his hat, swap a story or two, and fill his belly before turning in. A cowpuncher did all his sleeping in the open. "Beddin' out" is what he called it. In the spring, sometime around the first of April, the wagon pulled out and the bunkhouse was practically abandoned until June or July. Then along in September the cow crew went out again until Christmas or later. Naturally the wagon followed the work. One day it might be in Croton, the next on the north side or Steer Pasture or South Camp, wherever the weather or brush or circumstances permitted, and depending on whether the men were dipping, branding, or shipping.

Cowboys have nothing but contempt for a cook who is just a cook. Only a well-seasoned cowhand-turned-cook has the proper sense of timing to understand why they are hours late for a meal sometimes and will keep the food hot and ready. A wagon cook must be adept at improvising camp, throwing up a tarpaulin for shade in summer or rigging it up as a windbreak so he can cook in a norther or a driving rain. These simple and homely tasks require a certain amount of knowledge.

Coffee is the first thing on the fire at the cook's roll-out long before day, and throughout the day and night. If camp is not to be moved, the pot rests on the hot coals so that the hands can have a cup at the change of guard. Nothing else a cook can do will make the cowboys hold him in such high esteem as keeping the coffee hot and handy. The old-time wagon cook used to tell the tenderfoot his recipe for making cowboy coffee. With the greatest of secrecy he'd say, "Well now you take two pounds of Arbuckle, put in enough water to wet it down, boil for two hours, then throw in a hoss shoe. If the hoss shoe sinks, she ain't done." The cowman likes his coffee to kick up in the middle and pack double.

The wagon cook, especially if he has been an old cowhand like Tood Arthur, Chalma Reid, or Al Bingham, gives a real hiding to those boys who are late getting up for breakfast or are just loafing. "Orta got yore sleep last summer 'stead of galin' around."

I recall a wartime autumn. As usual they were two weeks late getting started. The country had been combed for hands to work through the fall roundup, but a wagon cook simply could not be found. D said, "Finding a good cook is always the biggest problem, and it's the most important factor in keeping a cow crew together and satisfied. They're scarce as hen's teeth and harder to get every year." Finally, just out of friendship for D, Chalma Reid came to help us "until you can get someone else." Chalma was badly crippled with arthritis and D hated to call on him.

Reid had a great feeling for people and a great respect for right, but loyalty was his most endearing characteristic. We on the ranch called him Reid, though his first name was Chalma. I once asked him why this was so. He answered, "Well, Mr. Burns and me have known each other a long time. I'm somewhat older than he is so he calls me Mr. Reid, and since he is my boss now I call him Mr. Burns."

Reid was not our only well-loved chuck-wagon cook; there was Coy Drennan, too. In their later years Coy and his wife Bessie filled in at the chuck house, and Coy went out with the wagon. When Tommie Smith came to the ranch, his son, Jimmy, was added to Coy's wagon crew. He was about Burns's age and size. As a rule they had fun together, but for the good of the outfit, Coy kept them separated most times. The boys were not yet nine.

In 1953, the election of Eisenhower over Stevenson for president was still a pretty hot topic. Since the Burnses were decidedly in the minority on the subject, we did not discuss it much, but at the wagon it often came up, along with the favorites, drouth and decline of cattle prices.

Jimmy Smith was led to remark, "It's all old Eisenhower's fault." "Do you mean," Burns asked, measuring his words carefully, "that you think President Eisenhower is the cause of cattle going down?" "I sure do," Jimmy answered. "And I guess you think he's the cause of this drouth, too?" "I wouldn't put it past him," Jimmy declared. Burns thrust his face within a few inches of Jimmy's and asked one more question, and a dangerous one. "Do you want to make something out of it?" Jimmy answered that he did and proved it with a well-aimed blow.

I don't know how many licks were exchanged, or how many connected, before Coy stopped them with a stern lecture. "I guess you boys don't know that we don't allow any fighting in this outfit. Generally, when there's a ruckus, we send both parties in for their checks. I'm willing to make an exception in your case if you boys can settle your differences, because I don't think you knew about this rule and because you're both good hands, and I need you." Coy went on, "I don't know what you boys will be when you grow up, and it don't make too much difference, but you'd just as well learn right now to respect the other fellow's opinion. It will help you get along with people further down the road. Shake on it, now, and let's get to work." They did.

That night Burns confided to me that he had not minded that Coy stopped the fight, because, he admitted, "Jimmy's arms are longer than mine." He fingered a tender place above his eye.

Coy's diplomacy and his plain good sense made him a popular cook. When he died, M. B. Parks and the Pitchfork cowboys wrote a poem to express their sorrow at his passing.

Our Cook is Gone

On April 7, 1970, we lost our chuck-wagon cook.
The Lord takes waddies, bosses, and hoods,
    but our cookie this time he took.
Everyone liked him for the things he did,
    like settin' grub on the chuck-wagon table.
He filled many a lank tummy and never was grumpy,

when sometimes he really wasn't able.
But there was always a welcome for a stranger or
    friend, and with a big ole Texas smile
He would say "come on in and get you a plate,"
    then sit and visit you awhile.
We'll miss the ole boy and the grub he fed us,
    with his big bronze face a grinnin'.
It won't be the same without going to the wagon
    and "Good morning, Coy Drennan."

Then, of course, there were the Big House cooks. There was a procession of them, the good, the bad, and the in-between. The year was half spent before Vanilla and Pinkie came from Paducah to help me. Late in November we got a collect call from Vanilla Small from Paducah. She announced that she had heard we were looking for a couple to help us. "We are!" I could hardly contain my elation. After a few questions about age, children, and what all, I asked, "When can you start?" She answered that there was nothing wrong with right now, and on they came. To say they were trained or expert help in any department would be the grossest exaggeration, but when you've been without anyone to do anything for months, two smiling faces look like heaven. We quickly found that at least these two were willing! Vanilla learned to prepare most of our food the way we liked it, and I was grateful for her willingness to work and do things my way.

When Ink and Dessie came to us, they were well recommended—by themselves. Ink assured me I had sure gotten a good man, and Dessie chimed in that I sure had a good cook, too. One day Ink asked me if I sang. "Only for my own amusement, Ink," I answered truthfully. He agreed with my assessment, nodding. Dessie and he would teach me sometime, he said; they sang at the True Vine Church. He even offered to sing for us some night when we had company.

One mellow summer night we were sitting on the terrace with some friends. A companionable lull had fallen on the group. Listening to the small night noises from the creek seemed more interesting than conversation, and I was soothed by the distant croaking of the frogs. I was almost asleep when from the servants' house came the notes of an old song, "Deep River," followed by "My Home

Is Over Jordan" and "Old Time Religion." Ink's voice rolled out low and rich. Vanilla carried the melody, a rhythmic moan compounded of longing and defeat. Dessie's voice rose silvery and clear on the night air.

One day I smelled a very peculiar odor and, upon investigation, I found that it was from peaches that were fermenting in the back of the servants' quarters. Ink was doing a brisk business with the boys. D sent him packing. He was an old rogue in more ways than one, but I liked him. He was so obviously what he was and so darned cute about it.

Into our unhappy midst one day walked Mr. and Mrs. Lon Holleyman. They had just called down from Crosbyton. "We hear that you need a couple for your chuck house. We'd like to come and talk to you about the job. I figure we can be there in about an hour if it's convenient with you." Mr. Holleyman was obviously ready and eager to work. "If we make a deal, we will stay. Our things are in our car and trailer. I think it's only fair," he went on, "to tell you that we're committed to another job, one that's not yet ready for us. It may be a month or six months before the building is ready." His voice sounded nice on the phone, but we'd had so many disappointments I didn't want to let myself in for another. Nevertheless, I suddenly felt cheerful. If even for a few weeks they would lend their services and training, it would give us a lift. We needed such heartening things to sustain us.

The day the Holleymans came to the ranch is pasted in the album of my memory in gold stars. They did their share in bringing about peace and happiness when we had almost come to the conclusion that there was no answer. It was noon when they arrived. We were getting ready to eat, so we invited them to join us. Looking almost too large for even our dining room table, Lon Holleyman sat down for lunch. His wife sat opposite him. His big mop of hair shot through with gray, he looked like a prosperous businessman as he told us about himself. He had been a cowman since he was eleven, when he bought his first cow with his own money. Of course, before then he had been a cowboy. He and his wife were now in the process of opening a liquor store, an accomplishment he did not much relish. "I have never touched it myself, and would rather not sell it to anyone else." But there was money to be made in it; they had a son to educate, and jobs for a sixty-two-year-old uneducated man were scarce.

When the meal was over, D and Mr. Holleyman got up from the table and went into the living room to talk. The big man moved with surprising grace for his bulk.

Mrs. Holleyman, in her innocence, thought I was just another woman, perhaps friendly, kindly, even sober and sane. I loved her from the very first minute she moved her chair over by mine and said, "Let the men make the deal. I want to get acquainted with the woman I'm to work with. I'm going to like you, Mrs. Burns. I hope you won't find it too hard to like me." I could feel something breaking up inside me. I finally managed to say, "Oh, I will—I do."

We fell to discussing foods. "I've cooked for a big family of boys and girls," she said. "Maybe if you'd tell me some of the things they especially like, I can please these men and boys. Is steak their favorite?"

"It definitely is, and they like it best chicken-fried." (This almost broke our hearts, for D and I are fiends for thick broiled ones.) "We are trying," I said timidly, "to get away from the habit of just opening a can of everything in the commissary each meal. We are working on the idea of green salads, when we can get them, instead of the cold potato standby each day. We'd like the boys to feel the ranch is as near their home as possible. So if you find that one is especially fond of a certain thing—"

"I'll make the effort to find out. And I'll learn their birthdays. Each one shall have a cake." Her motherly eyes twinkled. Oh, I hoped the boys would treat them nicely and not behave as though the Holleymans just weren't there.

"We'll try to make a place for ourselves," I heard Mr. Holleyman say, as he rose to his straight, broad-shouldered six-feet-two. One was conscious of his great size. "We're kinda new ourselves," D said, "and I don't know that we've made much of a place yet, but we're working on it. And with good people like you to help us, maybe we can make the grade together."

Nothing I can say would do justice to the warm humanity of this couple. Their friendliness and eagerness to please meant more to us than I can tell. When branding time came around, Mr. Holleyman said to D, "Could I help you out today? I haven't hung up my saddle yet." It took all hands and the cook at branding time. Floyd Smith had to leave his blacksmithing and his windmilling. His own work would pile up.

I no longer dreaded going to the chuck house. The food was delicious, and their greeting was always cheery and sincere. What a cozy feeling it was to know that we were wanted and enjoyed. After an overdose of indifference, we were ready and grateful for the love and attention of the Holleymans. A feeling of peace that we had not known for many months came over us. They are still in our perennial garden of friends.

19

Windy

"Windy's shot hisself!" The boy could hardly suppress his glee.

"Har, har, har," laughed Roe Corahn. "Wonder if old Windy thought about them damn lies he's told when that bullet plowed through his belly?"

"He's already a hero the way he's telling it out there," Jake added.

"We're all choked up about it," Slim said.

"Mr. Burns bawled ever' one of us out," Ed commented, "between belly laughs. Then he put on a firm face an' went out to see about Windy an' takened him to Spur to the doctor."

Windy hadn't been on the ranch long, but all the boys knew they didn't like him. They had adopted the name Coy gave him, "Windy," and they called him other names. There was no doubt that he was a man of questionable honor. For one thing he was an inveterate liar, for another he was too lazy to breathe.

Coy had sized him up pretty well when he said that Windy was the biggest liar ever come down the pike and that the chuck-house bell was the only thing could drown Windy out. After a longer acquaintance, Coy was to add, "To know Windy better is not to like him more."

I remember (all the time trying to forget) the day Windy came to the ranch. He barged right in to the chuck house and asked, "Is one of you all Mr. Burns?" D said he was. "Well, I want to talk with you after dinner is over," he said, taking a seat near the door. This position, although we didn't realize it at that time, probably indicated an uneasy conscience. He always sat where he could see the driveway. Not until after Windy was hired did the boys begin to suspect that he was at outs with the law. He couldn't keep the thought of sheriffs off his mind. Whenever someone drove up to the chuck house, Windy would ask, "That look like a sheriff to you?"

He soon earned a reputation for lying. He had a world outlook; there was nothing provincial about him. When he spoke of his

military experiences, he modestly reported himself present in every
theater of the war. He had told the stories so often that not only did
the new budding cowhands believe every word he said, but Windy
himself seemed convinced that he had been there. Name any outstanding battle or event; he was there, no matter how far apart
those battles were or what branch of the service fought them.
Bravely he would ride into the jaws of danger. "Did you get out
alive?" Slim would ask just in passing.

According to Windy, we were an extremely undistinguished
outfit. "Why the Bar Everythings and the Bar Sums in Wyoming
could—" It was no wonder that Windy didn't have a friend on the
ranch. Jake wanted to crawl him bad.

Until Mandy informed him that the lounge chairs were reserved for guests, Windy used to make himself at home on our
screened-in porch. When I came onto the porch, Windy would
raise his length, or rather half his length, from one of the porch
chairs. Though he was a great talker, especially about himself,
Windy couldn't talk standing up. He'd plop down on a chair in his
greasy coveralls. Mandy resented this. "He wouldn't recognize manners if they come up an' spit in his eye." Windy was not very
gallant.

But to hear him tell it, he was quite a ladykiller, and if his
stories were to be believed, a man-killer, too. There was no denying
his life contained some dark chapters, but this woman stalker had
failed to tree a single cat. His way with women caught up with him
eventually.

Though the doctor said Windy's wound was slight and should
not be painful, no one at the bunkhouse got a wink of sleep the
night he came back from the hospital. You could hear him groan in
the next county, they said.

From so much attention Windy had become so impressed with
his importance, he found it difficult to return to windmilling and
ordinary ranch tasks. Some unfeeling persons thought Windy was
using this melodramatic method to avoid work. He said he had not
yet recovered from the pneumonia that he claimed to have developed since coming home from the encounter with the .22.

Windy then developed new complications—a wife and two
children in California he had completely forgotten. The sheriff

came out to tell him. It was a low blow, and the sheriff wanted him. Well, we didn't. He could have him. We handed him over lock, stock, and six-gun.

Windy brazened it out. "I'd be a fool to stay on here," he told the men. "I can be making more'n twice as much in California." In general we agreed. But it was saddening to see Windy so completely windless.

20

Pleasures of the Pitchfork

The World of Our Creek

The creek was an unexpected delight that D had not mentioned. I saw it first in April, perhaps the luckiest time to see a Texas creek, for miles of mesquite are then just putting out their young leaves, and the aspen-like cottonwood shimmers a new and tender green. It was a chartreuse world that I beheld surrounding this pleasant meandering creek.

Little Wichita, alternately dry and rampageous, wound like a cowpath through the heart of the ranch. It was only a gravelly creek, not a river at all or even a stream except during unusually wet years or after a spring melt or a summer cloudburst. This creek that can rise so menacingly barely trickles during hot summer. There are times you see no water at all, but dig a hole in the sand with a spade or your hands and you will see that water seeps in almost immediately. Because of this moisture the cool, gray-green cottonwood, the lacy mesquite, tamarisk, and numerous tall grasses and reeds grow at its banks.

There was no time of the year when I did not look to the creek for contentment. I have seen it green, red, and yellow. I have seen it in all its moods that vary with the seasons. How delightful it was in the fall when the summer gave way to the flaming reds and gold of autumn. At this loveliest time of our year, I would roam the creek and the hillsides. In late October through November, when the big cottonwoods had turned gold and the entire creek bank was abloom with color, I would gather dried berries, gourds, the bronzed plumes of the bunch grass, the silver sage, liatris, mullein, buck brush, and turpentine weed. Though humbler than the offerings of spring, there is nothing softer yet more spectacular than the Michaelmas daisies or fall asters. The delight of bees and butterflies, these flowers were gathered by the armful and put into old jugs and pitchers. They lent themselves gracefully to arrangement and dried perfectly, fading only a bit to a lavender-blue from their original purple. Our roomy basement was an ideal place to hang these clusters upside down so they would not lose their color. In this season, the creek would sometimes be strewn with bluettes, sometimes aflame with autumn glory. Fallen leaves would gather at the corners of our fences, and I'd rake them up for compost heaps.

My bedroom overlooked this tree-lined creek with its shadows and sunlight and outcroppings of rock. Of all the places on the ranch, I knew and loved the creek best. It was mine, as the big bedroom and the screened porch were mine. From my window, I could view it at every time of the day and find it restful and interesting. I would sit for hours studying it. The chattering squirrels, the rabbits, the birds who made the creek their home no longer became frightened when I walked among them or sat quietly on the large fallen tree that served as my rest. Many times in the dusky shadows I sat there with a pillow and a book, careful that my feet were high enough not to disturb a rattler or watching ever and again for birds in the quail run. I still remember the little squirrel that stood on its hindlegs trying to get at the cracked grain I had brought in a bag. No wonder I wept when someone would take a gun and go to the creek to shoot the dove and quail that had come to trust man because of me. I felt that I had betrayed them.

Although I didn't ride or shoot and was not an avid bird watcher, I loved ranch life. My reasons were strictly personal, and my simple pleasures were those of a non–sport enthusiast. I could look up from my terrace and see nothing but treetops and blue sky. There were no neon signs glaring at me during the night, painting the skies with spurious, artificial splendor. Instead there was quiet, stillness, and clean unpolluted air. I could roam the creek and listen to its voices, the frogs and crickets tuning themselves for their nocturnal serenade. There were so many intangibles that I could not measure: the sunsets; watching a new colt get its legs; the wild turkey gobblers strutting, going through their courting ritual, or roosting on the dead trees at night; the tender green of willows; doves swooping in to water at the creek just at sunset; and the yapping of coyotes on wintry nights. Then there were the ranch celebrities, Coy, Ed, Tom, Riley, and the handsomest cowboys in the land, John Sullivan, Coy, Jimmy Pippin, and Jack Cook. They might come riding by at any minute. I was happy to be the lady who lived

on the porch of the Big House at the creek that I shared with squirrels, rabbits, and birds.

Visitors at the ranch were always delighted at the antics of the
wild turkeys. Our turkeys were true giants, weighing from eighteen
to thirty pounds, and they elicited more exclamations of pleasure
from tourists than any other attraction we had. The actions of the
wild turkeys measured the advance of spring. During the winter
the gobblers and the hens separated and occupied different parts
of the ranch. With the return of spring they came together again.
From our porch at sunset, D and I would watch the whole pomp
and pageantry of the gobbler's courtship as the stately bird paced
back and forth beside a feeding female. His chestnut tail spread like
a fan, his wings drooping until they touched the ground, he would
swell and strut, pausing only to utter a loud gobbling sound before
resuming his pacing.

The Williamses would not allow anyone to shoot the turkeys
on the ranch. But there is nothing more watchful than the wild turkey, whether hunters are abroad or not. The threat from coyotes
alone is enough to justify their uneasiness. Watching on a wintry
dawn, I had seen hungry coyotes lying in wait for them, while the
fearful birds still roosted on the dead cottonwood trees.

The children shared my enthusiasm for Little Wichita. It was
here on the creek that Anne and Burns whiled away the timeless
summer days of their childhood.

Potatoes

The pleasures of the Pitchfork were made up of many things, and
not the least of these was the incomparable luxury of freshly picked
vegetables. Once you've grown your own, you can't abide the market variety. Being salad eaters, we grew anything that could be
tossed in a wooden bowl—upland cress, New Zealand spinach,
chives, parsley. We revelled in herbs.

The real joy of growing things ourselves was that we could pick
them as young as we liked, crunchy, crisp radishes, baby onions,
thumb-sized beets, finger-length carrots, potatoes no bigger than
marbles, and okra in the bud. Mandy thought we used them slightly
immature. "Hit's a waste," she complained. Maturity meant one
thing to her, another to us, except in the case of roasting ears.

As everyone who has had the joy of going to the corn patch for his own roasting ears knows, there is a very short period when the ear is just right for eating. The kernels must not be too tender—those are blisters—and not too hard, for the corn will have lost its tastiness and flavor. The grains should be round and full, bursting with sweet milk that pours out when pierced by the thumbnail. I, like Mandy, "don't confidence them as goes into the patch pulling ears ever' whichaways." First you look for an ear topped by a coarse, dry, brown hair-like substance called the silk. You have to strip the shuck down just enough to see and puncture a grain before you can be sure. This perfect stage lasts just about an hour according to Mandy, and she's the one who had to "pull 'em 'cause Miz Burns'll be on the telephone and Jeet'd never git there in time."

Not many know how to prepare corn to be fried in a skillet. The secret lies in the cutting of the corn from the cob. One must have the corn shucked and silked. With a very sharp knife, just barely tip the grains from one end of the ear to the other. Come back the second time and cut just a bit more from the grains. Then scrape clear down to the cob for the sweet milk.

"Them beans ain't ready to crop," Mandy told me as I lifted a large water bucket from its nail on the service porch wall. She didn't see the kitchen fork in my hand or she would have had more to say on the subject of waste. Smokey, my erstwhile gardener's helper, was lurking outside the door. When he saw my bucket and the fork, he knew my intention and shadowed me out to the potato patch, protesting at every step that he knew nothing about digging potatoes.

It was a bright morning, early and keen. The scent of the spice bush filled the air, and the pleasant sounds of country noises were music to my ears. It's a grand, good thing to be going to the garden for one's own vegetables. Bare legs and sandaled feet give a wonderful feeling. One could never be happy in the city again after these country years. I'd always wanted to live in the country and wear sloppy clothes.

Digging for potatoes is what I like best of all gardening. The find of this harvest is hidden, revealed only by some yellowing leaves and telltale cracks in the brown earth beside the vine. Surely no miner digging for gold could feel a greater thrill when his pick turns up a nugget than I do when I hear that familiar scraping sound and my kitchen fork turns up a potato. What fun, earthing-up potatoes!

The odor of onions growing beside the fence stung my nostrils as I knelt to rob the hills of their succulent store. At last, my bucket filled with rosy potatoes, I straightened up (gardening is hard on the back) and wiped the perspiration from my face. From my kneeling position I saw the biggest, blackest, shiniest chauffeur-driven Cadillac I'd ever seen, and there just outside the fence a group of friends, on their way, of all places, to the Kentucky Derby. It was Effie Wilson, Lela Krueger, and Edwina Luther. They were standing there convulsed, first by my costume (the one D said was frightening away potential cattle buyers), and then by the earnestness of my digging. I thought wryly that for this first visit of my Lubbock friends I would like to have been suitably picturesque, the gracious lady of the manor, and instead here I was wearing a garden hat, swinging a basket of yellow squash, red beets, and purple turnips from my arm. I could only look hardy holding a pail of plebeian Irish potatoes.

Small wonder the chauffeur's nose lifted at his employer's hobnobbing with one of the ordinary unwashed. I tried to think of something witty, something gay and gallant to say, to indicate my complete emancipation from conventions, to show how quickly I had absorbed the cowboy viewpoint of wearing clothes to fit the job, to show that uppity chauffeur my fine detachment. But it's hard to be gallant with a scratching fork in your sweaty, grimy hand, and they were so dashing, so glittering, so full of repartee and the trip they were making and the money they would win on Citation and Coaltown.

I took them down to the house for cokes and coffee, and after half an hour of chatter they left me. As their shiny Cadillac flashed out of sight up the highway, my thoughts returned to earth and the charm of grabbling for potatoes. Just for a second I envied them. They were going to have a whole week of fun and rest. Rest—what would I give for just one day's rest? What did Lela mean by that stupid remark, "Mamie, you look and talk just exactly as you did the first time I ever saw you. You haven't changed a bit." Of all the silly things to say. That was twenty-one years ago. I knew I'd never been pretty, but surely I didn't look this old then. "Miz Burns." Smokey's keen black eyes divined my dejection. "Beauty fades, but ugly holds its own."

A Pleasuring Place

Mary Sarton would have said, "A whole day before me in which to think and be." Beautiful sentiment, but when I looked out my window that morning in early spring of '45, I thought, a whole day without guests, and D is in Dallas for the weekend. Limitless possibilities opened up to fill my leisure time. A second look brought into view the pile of big smooth rocks stacked against the office. I'd been adding to these for a long time. Ah! and double ah! It was as simple as that. So Mandy and I went on a beautifying binge. This was the first out-of-doors project Mandy had helped with. As a rule my outside activites brought forth some grumblings from Mandy about my health.

During those three days, Mandy and I, with Jack Gotcher's help with the heaviest rocks, built a flagstone terrace underneath the three big trees between the office and the house and planted flowering shrubs and perennials along the south wall and a *Vitex* beside the office steps. *Vitex* is one of the few plants that will live in the blazing sun from the west, and its lilac-blue spires and pungent odor have been a joy. On the east side of the waist-high rock wall grew a lilac, a spirea, and a crepe myrtle; below them we transplanted iris, both tall and low growing, to the most effective spots, taking them up in full bloom with such huge chunks of earth that they never suspected they had been moved. We wedged sedums and portulaca (yellow, lavender, and red) between the cracks of the rocks and filled in with sandy loam. The *Vitex*, *Buddleia*, and tamarisk I'd brought from San Angelo in 1942 made a splash of color and beauty on the east.

"I think this spot is going to give us lots of pleasure, Mandy," I said, as she gathered up the spade, trowel, broom, and wheelbarrow. "Gots lots of pleasurin' places you made already, but you don't take time out to use 'em," she stated flatly. "We are going to use this one," I said. "I'll shell peas and snap beans and talk through the window with Mr. Burns at his desk."

At noon on the last day, Jack stopped five men on their way to the chuck house and asked them to help us place our two old stone benches and table from the house in San Angelo. With the help of some iron bars and much heaving and groaning, the men settled them almost facing each other with their backs against trees. We pulled up great pots of shrimp-colored geraniums and blue plumbago and put them at the ends of the benches.

When all was finished, we had a protected corner of beauty that might have popped right out of the pages of *House and Garden.* Mandy was pleased as punch with the job. She stood back, looked at the results of our hard work, and said, "'Pears like it was twenty years a-growin'." Truly it had old-world charm, but how could you sustain the magic with D about? On his return from Dallas late that afternoon, he came from the office carrying the inevitable armful of papers, magazines, and mail into the house. Suddenly he saw us peacefully shelling peas, sitting on the benches enjoying the flowers, and he exclaimed, "What on earth has been going on here?"

"Just a pass-through to serve you and Jim refreshments. How about a coke right now?"

"Be right back." D rejoined me as Mandy came from the kitchen. One of the ranch's pleasantest pleasuring places was in business. Birds were tweetering all about us, bathing in the soft spray from the hose we were using to settle the new beds and the soil between the rocks.

Mandy's dour prediction did not come true; for once she proved wrong. It was a spot we came to use often in the months that followed—so convenient to drop down to visit with D, to sort out the mail, to sit while moving the hose from place to place. Often I'd have breakfast out there to see what was afoot. Sitting on those benches, I could look up from my reading and see all that was going on: watch the children on the creek or riding the hills, call to my help if she was in the kitchen or in her house, keep an eye on the yard man, listen for the phone, see Coy and Burns walking toward the corral, Coy's hand on Burns's shoulder one pal to another. Always I have thought with love of my pleasuring place; a friend said it was my "catbird seat." But monarch of all I surveyed I was not.

21

The Bunkhouse

When we were showing guests around headquarters, we waved in the direction of our biggest building with a casual "And that is the bunkhouse." There were two good reasons for this casualness. One never knew in what state of dress or undress the boys might be found. The bunkhouse was their home, the one place on the ranch where they had any privacy. We thought it only fair to keep women and visitors out.

The second reason involved our pride. Bunkhouses, as a rule, are not the show places of a ranch, but ours had managed to win for itself a particularly dirty reputation. The Williamses had never liked this building, a one-storied rambling bunkhouse would be more to their tastes. Virgil Parr had built it when he was manager. "That damn thing will burn up some day," Gates Williams and D Burns muttered darkly, but so far they have been disappointed. Nothing could be done about the exterior, but the Williamses, ever thoughtful of the needs of their people, furnished the one large community room where the boys congregated with solid, substantial stuff, including an enormous handmade pine table soon to be branded with cigarette burns, notched and initialed by the knives of the cowboys, marred with columns of jotted figures. The party to celebrate and launch the handsome room was a beer bust that resulted in the demolishing of most of the comfortable overstuffed pieces. The Williamses had hoped the men would take pride in the room and were justifiably distressed that the cowboys would smash up in one rollicking night all that had been planned for them.

One old-timer was moved to poetry because of the bunkhouse dirt. Ed Nolan thinks without a doubt that Buttermilk Gaines was author of the unfinished piece found in a yellowed writing tablet that had become twisted into some bed springs. Ed thinks further that the reason it had not been discovered in all this time was that "the mattress ain't been turned in thirty years."

This masterpiece of truth and poetry, with many erasures and words scratched through, reads, as best we can piece it together:

> This bunkhouse ain't as tidy
> As them bedrooms up in town;
> Because like ever' cowpoke
> We pyorely like the ground.
>
> Our boots they tote it in for us
> And scatter it about;
> So jest by never sweepin'
> We thinks we're sleepin' out.
>
> Well now, if females hit the range
> And seen the way we live,
> They'd think our habits mighty strange,
> But a damn we would not give.
>
> Our cook, Miz Ivy Rader,
> Keeps her kitchen clean and neat,
> But we'd burn this here bunkhouse
> Afore we'd . . .

The rest of the last line was not finished. I suggested that "change a sheet" was what he had intended saying, but Ed said, "Never used no sheets." Ed believes the writer had heard someone coming and had hastily shoved the tablet under his mattress. It looks as though even Buttermilk's vaunted toughness could not bear up under the humiliating stigma of "poet." His poem at any rate made up in broad mirth anything it lacked in old-school elegance.

No, our bunkhouse wasn't pretty sitting off there by itself. It looked as forlorn and formidable as a prison. I planted trees about it, but horses were soon dragging them around by their reins. I set pyracantha by the dozens by its walls. The sprangling orange-berried shrubs would have softened and brightened the place, but tobacco juice and urine are not conducive to plant growth. We put up bars to protect the shrubs and trees, but since a truck couldn't back right up to the cement porch to load on bed rolls and saddles, the iron bars were pushed down. The boys didn't want the bunkhouse prettied up, so there it sat, bare and gray, its twenty windows staring blankly. When there were no boys about, it could look very gloomy, but when lights and laughter were bursting from every window, it had a gay and friendly aspect. There were continuous and sometimes boisterous doings in that bunkhouse; the shenanigans, the horseplay, the monkey business that went on was far from dull. For a breach of range etiquette, a Kangaroo Court was often held. Then there was the sure and serious business of initiating new boys. There were water fights and foot-warmings (cowboy vernacular for the hot foot). There was sometimes high excitement, as when the boys found old so-and-so sleeping with his mouth open. It looked so much like a fly trap they baited his week-old whiskers with molasses. And the rattlesnake trick was sure to be played on a boy known to be scared to death of the things. A rope would be stretched under his blanket, and one of the boys would declare, "I seen a rattlesnake in here today long as my arm. Afore I could find any-thing to kill 'im with, th' durned thing crawled into thet closet an' got away. I couldn't find no hole no place. He couldn't a gone to th' basement, but he shore ain't in this room. I turned th' place upside down." As soon as the new boy stretched out on his pallet or bed-roll, they'd give the rope a little tug, then wait a second and give it another one. "Some of 'em woulda jumped outa th' window if we hadn't caught 'em," Ed said.

To do our bunkhouse justice, I steal a few sentences from C. L. Sonnichsen's *Cowboys and Cattle Kings:*

> Probably the most grandiose effort to civilize the cowpuncher by put-ting him in proper surroundings was made some years ago on the Pitchfork which belongs to Eugene and Gates Williams of St. Louis who come down in the quail season for fifteen or twenty days and let God and D Burns take care of it the rest of the time. The bunkhouse was a two-storied frame building painted a rebellious blue-grey and looking like an Odd Fellows' hall in the lumber district of Michigan. Inside, the walls are panelled in natural wood, which does not look so natural now. The halls have not been swept for a long time. On the second floor landing there is a sign "Trash Downstairs." Underneath is a trash can which was long ago filled to overflowing and is now disgorging copiously on the floor. The bathtub in the shower room needs a cleaning worse than West Texas needs rain. . . . The white elephant was never completely finished.

Miss Hobson, an exchange teacher from England, had read this tantalizing Sonnichsen account, and her curiosity was piqued. Her

Lubbock hostess, Mildred Boone, had been trying to arrange a visit to the ranch for months, since Miss Hobson was determined not to return to England without seeing that bunkhouse. After our noon-time visit to the chuck wagon (where Coy in his typically precise fashion categorized her as "the lady who sang when she talked"), we approached the bunkhouse "yoo-hooing" in warning. The coast being clear, we walked in, not into the expected masculine chaos, but rather into a totally tidy, scrubbed, and even dusted living room. The clean-up of the decade had somehow occurred. Miss Hobson promised not to go away and tell how orderly our bunk-house was for fear of ruining our reputation.

As a rule, the bunkhouse was altogether grim; Mandy is the only one who ever found it beautiful. She awakened me one foggy dawn to ask, "Ever seen the bunkhouse in a early morning mist? You'll not be knowin' it or rememberin' it the same," she told me as I stumbled out of bed and followed her sleepily. Could be I was carrying this thing of humoring Mandy too far, I thought. "Feather soft an' furry lookin'," she mused. "A body sees sich houses in th' clouds." In wonder, I gazed at the bunkhouse. It was beautiful. The dimly lit building against the foggy sky seemed touched with mystery; it looked older and as if it held secrets.

22

Croton Brakes

One sunny Sunday D said he wanted to show me some country I had not seen at close range. "It's the Croton Brakes," he told me, "but the boys call it Big Ugly." He went on to say that at times, because of the condition of our dividing fences, neighbors' cattle got into our pastures and ours got into theirs. "They have some fifty-section pastures in here. That's why the boys hate it. It's the devil to work, almost impossible to get cattle out of here. They nearly always come out with men and horses bunged up."

The car climbed the steep, rugged Croton hills. On the very highest hill, D stopped and pulled on his brakes. After getting out of the car, we had a clear and full picture of the rough terrain. "This is the most spectacular view of the whole country," he said, then added, "We ought to own this land." D and the Pitchfork were now one. "We need it for winter protection." The words I'd heard so often when we were driving along Croton's north boundary fence on Highway 82. "Any chance of buying it?" I asked. "Not much, I'm afraid, but the Williamses have given me permission to try."

John MacKenzie was executive manager of the Matador Ranch, of which this range was a part. Running north and south, Croton covered forty-three thousand acres. D intended to see Mr. Mac-Kenzie on his next visit to Denver. "I see in the papers that they are selling off a few scattered sections. I'm going to feel him out on the subject."

In a few weeks he did see Mr. MacKenzie, but the latter's response, while not entirely discouraging, was not hopeful. D said that they hadn't given such a proposition any thought, but Mr. MacKenzie had told him that the Pitchfork had been a good neighbor to them for about fifty years. If they decided to sell, we would have the refusal of it. D is a born optimist; he did not give up easily. Each time he saw John MacKenzie at stock shows or cattle conventions in Denver, he'd come home with some comment about their

discussions of the Croton deal. "I think we'll get that baby sometime. It would mean a lot of work and expense getting it in shape,
but it will be worth it."

"What does Croton mean?" I inquired. "Poison, I think," D
replied. I had already heard a lot about that word, *croton*. It was
tossed about considerably on the ranch. But until one of the boys
let me in on the secret, I was completely baffled. Whatever its exact
meaning in the beginning, the word has taken on varying meanings
through the years and can mean almost anything. *Croton* in its
original sense meant "poison." "An' boy, she's croton" means "she's
a pizen, a tough baby, hard to stay with." "That's croton" might
mean "it's cricket" or "it's fair." But when you hear "he's croton,"
you have to judge by the tone of the voice or the look in the
puncher's eye whether he's speaking of an okay gent or a yeller-
livered skunk. If the term is applied to a girl, you know she's just
what you're looking for.

It was several years before D was able to close the Croton deal.
Late in 1946, I was in Lubbock at a party where a fortune teller
presided over the destinies of guests assembled there. Eventually I
was persuaded to join the queue before her. "Concentrate. Think of
the thing nearest your heart," she instructed me. "I am," I replied
soulfully, if a bit skeptically.

"You are not interested in knowing if someone tall, dark, and
handsome with oodles of money is about to come into your life.
The man you are interested in loomed up beside you, boots and all,
about twenty—" she cocked an eye speculatingly, inquiringly "—or
thirty years ago. You are wanting to know if the job that means so
much to him will continue to make him happy, if he is going to be
a success in that work. The answer is yes." I was not going to be
duped. My hostess had obviously done her work nicely, and this
woman had a good memory. She continued, "And you are wanting
to know if the little daughter—" What mother and wife wouldn't
be wanting to know if all would go well with her husband and
daughter? "Unusual perception," I smiled. "And thank you."

"Tell your husband the deal will go through." "Is he on a deal?"
I laughed. "A very big deal," she answered quietly. "It involves a lot
of money and a lot of—" she hesitated.

"Are we going to strike oil?" I asked facetiously, but my mind had hopped to the land deal that D had recommended to the ranch owners. "It does not concern oil," she said unsmilingly. "No?" innocently.

"You know about it," she went on. "It's a big tract of land lying near you, I think it joins you. It's been under consideration a long time. The deal will be closed in February or March. It's in the making this minute. When you get home, you will find this is true." D Burns would scalp me! What was I doing here telling all I knew? I mean being told all I knew. Letting people read my mind? He had told me never to discuss the company business with anyone. I was scared limp, but I had to carry it off lightly for the sake of those two friends listening. "Is it a good deal? Will it make lots of money?" I asked jokingly. "It will be an advantageous deal," she said. "The land bought will be worth the money."

When I got back to the ranch, Gates Williams was there. "Gentlemen, I have good news," I addressed Gates and D. "Bunkhouse burning?" they asked in unison. I ignored their irreverent remark. "You are going to purchase Croton Brakes country in February or March." I told them of my fortune teller. "And you will have a message regarding it very soon."

"That came today!" they yelped. This was November, and we had heard nothing regarding the deal for months. Those two laughed "master," drank to me and the fortune teller, then shrewdly asked, "Did you find out what we should offer per acre?" "It doesn't make any difference," I told them. "You're going to get it. Madame Saunders said so. And she said it would be a good buy." "That's all we wanted to know." Their laughter hit the rafters.

But the contract was soon drawn up, around the first of February. And so part of the Matador country had improved; that much-slandered shirt-tailed outfit known as Croton Brakes or Big Ugly was now ours.

D, Coy, and Ed were just getting on top of their work when the Pitchfork bought Croton. Now a new responsibility awaited D. Drilling water wells, putting up windmills, building roads, fences, a dugout, and remodeling houses were started all over again. D was lucky he had the extra windmills stored in the shop. Those windmills were the first but not the only wartime scarcities Ray Grisham had provided for the Pitchfork.

It would not be easy whipping Croton into shape. It was a vast range of rugged but good cattle country, full of canyons and rocky knolls that would furnish excellent winter protection for cattle. Those rocky knolls, flecked with moss, provided not only shelter, but also soil and grass for forage. In addition, Croton possessed ample spaces where the eye could wander endlessly; it was open and free, with long, long pastures of waving grass that the wind constantly stirred. The living green of the cedars contrasted beautifully with the soft gray of the rocks. A feeling of freedom, of honesty, of openness pervaded the whole country.

Shortly after the purchase, ranch hands and brush-poppers from the Matador came to gather their cattle from Croton. Our boys were there to help. Many of these cows were in their teens; many had not been branded. One of the boys commented, "Some of them cows was old enough to vote." There was much sharp wit and enormous good humor sparkling back and forth between the Matador representatives and our hands. Ed would say, "We allus knowed you'd never git your country cleaned an' we'd hafta take it over to git it worked proper." And the response, "Well now, we're might proud to see you git it. Hit'll help a little outfit like yourn, an' a spread like ours'll never miss it."

Another problem was finding a good man to put in charge of Croton. Coy suggested John Ballard. The Ballards had driven up to see about the job while we were busy in the field. No one else had asked for the assignment. It took John and D less than thirty minutes to make a trade. While the men were talking, Mrs. Ballard came over to the car where I was sitting. I asked her if she had seen the Croton camphouse. She said that she had and that she felt it would be suitable for them. I told her that I hadn't yet seen the place but would be happy to help her with any remodeling that might be necessary.

In the meantime, D had hired about twenty-five Navajo Indians to build fences and roads. It did not take long to construct a new road to the Croton camphouse. D was bursting with pride after the completion of this engineering feat and wanted me to see it.

Some of our roads were terrible, uncomfortable to travel and actually dangerous. As we jostled over D's freshly finished road, I was reminded of the story Alice Duggan Gracy tells of the unusual experience of Willie Day Twichell, an early surveyor on the Plains. Thinking D would like the tale, I told him about it.

Late one evening, a short time after the Twichell surveying party had begun work on the lower division of the XIT Ranch, the cook ran out of flour. Their main provisions were at Yellowhouse, twenty-two miles away. Although Twichell had never been to Yellowhouse, he volunteered to go during the night and return in time for breakfast. He drove two Spanish mules hitched to a buckboard, one dun colored and the other black. There was no moon, so he had to keep his direction by the stars and a dim trail that he hoped his team could follow. As the mules jogged along, Twichell grew sleepy and dozed off. Suddenly the buckboard stopped short, almost throwing its passenger out. When he was fully awake, he could see the dun colored mule plainly against the sky, but the right-hand mule had just disappeared. Completely mystified, he took the stick he'd been using from time to time to prod the mules and poked all around where the animal should have been, but he could touch nothing. He got out of the buckboard on the side of the dun mule, followed along to his head, and crossed in front of him. Then he discovered what had happened. The black mule had dropped into a road run (a narrow, washed-out hole). The road run was deep enough to hide the beast entirely. Twichell led the mule out without difficulty and continued his journey. He returned to his outfit in time for breakfast.

If a mule could be lost in a big gully or ditch, so could a woman, I reasoned, leaning close to D and holding on for dear life to his arm to keep from being thrown out. I was glad we had not taken the old road, the one that was a "bugger." D had informed me that it used to go in behind the house and was pretty rough.

After a sharp turn, we came upon the camphouse quite suddenly. On a rocky hillside, it lay hidden by mesquite, cedar, a few chaparral, and cactus. It was located in an ideal Old West setting, but no amount of picturesqueness outside, not even a trumpet vine over the outhouse, could make up for the lack of conveniences within. The three-roomed, once-painted white house had no bathroom, no lights, no closets, no water except from the cistern on the back porch, and, of course, no telephone within ten miles. D said they intended remodeling the house when they could get to it.

When they could get to it. This was the saddest statement he could have made. Poor Mabel Ballard, my heart bled for her. All the way home I pondered how I might help. I remembered the big ugly storage tank below my bedroom window; it hadn't been moved yet. After five years they hadn't got to it. I gave D no peace until work was done on Mabel's house.

23

The Tradition of Hospitality

The Pitchfork's tradition of hospitality to the traveler was established during Mr. Gardner's day. Dan Gardner gave food, shelter, and heart to many a traveler who stopped hungry and despairing. "I say, I say, stay with us a few days. Rest your team and yourselves. Trap with the boys. It gets monotonous driving so constantly. We are enjoying your company; we need a change too."

After a few days' rest, of being fed and grazing in the pasture, the horses were ready to resume the trip. So was the cow tied at the back of the wagon. So was the family, greatly heartened by the hospitality found in Texas. It brightened the wayfarers' outlook and gave them a glowing picture to paint for their families back home.

Mrs. Deaton remembered that Mr. Gardner's hospitality sometimes worked out well two ways. A family named Ault with a boy ill of fever was here long enough for the man to help Uncle Charley Welcher with building a chuck house. He refused to accept pay for his carpentering, but Mr. Gardner started him back on his way with a well, strong team, a fresh young cow, a good supply of groceries, and these words: "I say, come back to see us sometime. I say, it won't be soon, because a man with a skill like yours will find plenty to do in this new country." That Mr. Ault did prosper was attested to by letters he wrote Mr. Gardner and by the pictures he sent of his box and strip house that grew a wing at a time as his family increased. Mrs. Deaton did not remember whether Mr. Gardner ever saw the Aults again, but I was to hear many other stories from the children and grandchildren of people who were befriended by Mr. Gardner in those hard days.

One story relates that on a chilly night in the early '8o's Mr. Gardner, his brother Med, and his brother-in-law Colonel Godwin had just gone to bed for the first time in their newly constructed dugout, when a feminine voice called, "Hello!" They admitted a frail woman who was driving a team of tired-looking horses. She told the three men that her husband and baby were in the back of the covered wagon. Her husband was ill, and more than a hundred miles lay between them and their destination. For days this little family was to know the comfort of the Pitchfork dugout, while Mr. Gardner and his kinsmen slept in the covered wagon.

Dan Gardner's ranch was not only a refuge for weary travelers. Settlers, ranchers, cowhands, and outlaws, everyone who passed that way, was welcome at the Pitchfork table. Neighbors went to him for advice or to borrow money, and he seldom turned them down. Because of his generous hospitality to neighbor and suspect alike, outlaws and marauders rarely bothered his spread. They gave the Pitchfork a wide berth. His door was literally open to anyone who needed him.

Sometimes he would drive fifty miles to what is now Crosbyton to see the Hank Smiths, his nearest friends and the first settlers in Crosby County. At the renowned Smith House, famous for its food and for "filling any order you could give," he held council and discussed problems of the frontier.

Mr. Gardner's kindness was not limited to people but extended to animals and plants as well. He would not allow his cowhands to abuse the horses or to ride or rope the milk cows and calves. A businessman once told me about the time a hen sauntered into his office while Mr. Gardner was entertaining a visitor. The hen anxiously eyed the intruder, but her business was so urgent that she hopped into the waste basket and began fussing about in preparation for laying an egg. Mr. Gardner calmingly patted the hen while he talked with his visitor. She settled down and quietly laid her egg. This accomplished, she complacently waddled out. She didn't even cackle until she had left the office. Such was the respect Mr. Gardner commanded from man, beast, and fowl.

Another illustration of his thoughtfulness was leaving a prickly-pear cactus that had been occupied for several years by a mockingbird family. Returning each spring, the mother bird would place her nest in the thorny plant where the neighborhood cats dared not bother her nestlings. Mrs. Deaton said that the cats would look, twitch their tails, and walk all around the cactus with their mouths watering, but the bird was not unduly disturbed.

Dan Gardner was also a lover of trees and the native Texas shrubbery. Unfortunately none of the pecan trees he planted and

tended with such care have survived. But the mesquites are everywhere. "Carin' for them mesquite was about the only mistake I ever
knowed the old gentlemen to make. Now they're takin' the country," Ed ruefully told me on one occasion. The mesquites were so
few in his day and so beautiful, it is not surprising that Mr. Gardner
felt impelled to protect every one of them. But those insolent mesquites are now coming up all over the place.

This tradition of Pitchfork hospitality remained. Mr. Gardner
would not have had it otherwise, and the Williamses had made it
clear to us that they wanted to keep it as nearly as possible as it had
been in those friendly days.

We set an awesome record for guests. I could mention a string
of names known all over the country. I could tell of cotillion lead-
ers, women of fashion who dressed from the great houses, and of
others primly buttoned into their calicos. One wore a bonnet.
There were smart Britishers, some of the nation's top industrialists,
some who were distinguished by birth or ability, and some who
lived by their wits. Some could have been proper Bostonians. We
entertained visitors of all brow-heights, even ill-smelling vagrants
at the chuck house. We rubbed shoulders with bankers, brokers,
writers, actors, hoboes, and sportsmen, some card-carrying members of the jet set. "We ain't partic'lar," Ed said. But a ranch tends
to cut people down to size. Our guest list read something like a
combination of "Who's Who" and "Who Ain't." They came from
as far away as South America and Australia, and as close as Guthrie.
With our employees, a curious variety—white, red, black, and
brown—consorted at the ranch table.

We did not find visitors unpleasant, just inconvenient at times.
Every person who came our way, every new experience, made our
lives mores interesting and valuable. Even those who bored us
served as conversation pieces. And, of course, we were bored sometimes. Who isn't?

Our first visitors were the Grobs from Saint Louis. We had
been at the ranch less than two weeks and were still pushing through
furniture and boxes of our household things in the big living room
to get to our quarters, when Mr. Eugene sent a wire requesting us to
entertain the bookkeeper for the Saint Louis Union Trust Company, the firm handling the Pitchfork account. Imagine my conster-

nation at this news. I had no help. The chuck-house refrigerator was out and my faithful Frigidaire, which I'd brought up from San Angelo and which had given us fifteen years perfect service without a whimper, now simply shuddered once, and that was it. The plumbing was acting up at the north end of the house where the guest rooms were. I had told myself I must get everything to rights, I must be ready for any eventuality, but visitors I was not ready for. How could I cope? We were within a few hours of their arrival, when I discovered there were no napkins. "There's not a fresh napkin on the place," I wailed to D.

"See here, Mayme," said D, shaking me by the shoulders, "this looks like a mighty good time for you to decide whether you can take this job chin up, or whether it's going to land you in an institution."

I went to take a bath. Not a drop of water emerged from those tappets, or whatever they were. Now, of all times, for the water to play out! This was too much. Never before had anything interfered with the basic business of bathing. It was the beginning of my career as a ranch woman. I was being given my first taste of the delights of country entertaining and the challenge ahead, and my first glimpse of D as a ranch husband.

Our visitors we lumped into categories in our minds. Our ranch family, our own families, and invited friends we thought of as welcome guests. There were not so many of these as there were business associates and tourists, and we had time to prepare for them. The Williamses were the most considerate people in the world. "How is the help situation?" they'd ask by phone before inviting guests for hunting or vacationing. It embarrassed me to death when I had to say I was without anyone in the kitchen. That was my department. I was allowed to pay whatever price I thought necessary. It would seem that I had the time to hunt around and find someone good and permanent, if I were interested. This was simply not true. It wasn't the labor but the loneliness that made ranch life intolerable for most of my helpers. Some kind of entertainment was mandatory, but they didn't enjoy reading and we could not provide picture shows; they talked incessantly of television, and all we had for them were radios.

Our social-minded friends were not encouraged to visit for

longer than the stop-by for a coke or cup of coffee on their way downstate or back. These were pleasant interludes, but if these friends expected entertainment, they'd stopped at the wrong place.

Then there were friends going downstate who stopped for the night to break their trip and to savour the odor of coffee and wood smoke that filled our house. Fearfully, I'd invite them in for breakfast or dinner, offering prayers that there would be a pound of cheese in the refrigerator and that the larder would not be empty. These travelers provided the good talk we relished.

Our visitors were generally willing to adjust to our local peculiarities, such as opening and closing gates, washing their own dishes at the chuck house, and getting up at 5 A.M. when we were eating over there. But there were some who would come, usually during the busiest time of the year or even during the war, expecting the ranch to have enough extra horses and saddles to accommodate any size party they might get together. They even thought that we should supply men to catch and saddle these animals, adjust stirrups, and to unsaddle them when the riding was over. They did not seem to understand that ranch people were busy human beings.

The popular picture of ranch folk not working just does not square with the facts. Most visitors saw only the color, a rider dashing by on horseback, cowboys tying their mounts in Mayo Park. They did not get the inside details. They were often surprised to see the boys unpistoled; one bunch, though, were just as surprised to find a cowboy with a gun. They saw only one side of the coin, the pretty side. There was also the other side, the work, the planning, the overseeing, the responsibility. I doubt that casual visitors to the ranch would at first glance have any idea of the work that went into giving it the peaceful, restful look they so admired. "How wonderful to live in this beautiful, peaceful place!" they exclaimed. "You hardly know there is a war." Yes, we knew about the war.

Among our visitors there were varying degrees of interest and different reactions to the ranch work. A group would go out in the morning to watch a roundup, a branding, or a drive. Whereas some would come in goggle-eyed at the danger, filled with admiration for the courage and daring of our cowboys, others were not enthusiastic. "I'm not going back this afternoon. I can't bear to see those animals roped, dragged, and thrown, and that hot iron put on them. Those men are so cruel." "It's not my dish," said another. "I had all I wanted of it in about three minutes." Some took an "I'm glad I've seen it, but once is enough" attitude. One woman said, "I couldn't eat a bite after seeing that." But some couldn't get enough. They wanted to sit on the corral fence, nose to nose with those cattle, and watch every minute they were there.

Women visitors were at once my comfort and my bane. It was a pleasure to have them and all the news they brought, to hear about all the things they had done and where they had been, but it was my stint to entertain them in the house or on the ranch. Men were so much easier to entertain then women. When D said that three men would be here for a day or so, I could think about serving good, solid food. I would not go into a dither or preparation or change. By men a house is accepted; by women it is examined. We on the ranch came to think of female visitors as works of the devil, designed to complicate our existence.

Always when branding or rodeo time came around, I would decide that no matter what, I would give them a miss. But invariably a newly arrived guest from Scotland, Australia, England, or Houston would confess that she had never been to a rodeo in her life and that it was her devout wish—And I would find myself saying that I would be delighted.

Women visitors asked incredibly stupid questions and made such inane remarks. Perhaps the nadir was reached when the jewel-bedecked opera singer begged D to continue his guided tour of the ranch despite his urgent insistence that he must see to the milk cows. She coyly suggested that D should give them the afternoon off. "Damn fool!" was D's recollection of her.

I decided to take a firm hand with my female share of the guests. "Would you like to help me gather the vegetables this morning? The blackeyed peas, squash, tomatoes, and okra are about to get away from me." I'd hand her a smock and some gloves, also a large basket. If she were allergic to vegetables growing in the garden, I'd say, "I wonder if you'd mind tidying up the living and dining rooms while I'm feeding the chickens? Here's a dustcloth, and the sweeper is right in this closet. You can empty the wastebaskets into the fireplace (if there was a fire going) or in the big receptacle on the back porch."

Most of them were delighted to help. The men were glad to bring in logs for the fireplace too, if they hadn't got off to the corral or gone with the boys to inspect the ranch. Having the guests do these little chores was of great assistance, when every step was mine, and kept the help from being so unhappy and complaining.

Travel-worn foreigners whose cars had broken down would come knocking at our door at all hours of the day and night. Servicemen, relaxing from the fears of the present uncertainty, would come to the ranch from Abilene and Lubbock to experience life that was simple and uncomplicated. Often representatives from magazines would call, asking us to receive visitors from overseas. Some visitors had heard about our dutch oven and sourdough cookery from friends, and had driven fifty miles out of their way to sample the chuck-house cooking. Visitors eating at the chuck house fell to like people possessed. They spent a good deal of time patting their stomachs contentedly. Our dining room rang with toasts and jokes. Our hospitality was strained to its limits. Finally, it reached the point where D and I would groan in inhospitable unison whenever a visitor appeared at the ranch. D said that it had never been his intention to run a dude outfit, but that if things got much worse in the visiting department, he'd have to put the guests to work and charge them for doing it.

Before we came to the Pitchfork, we had thought of guests, no matter how beloved or desired or entertaining, in terms of expense. Could we afford the theater, or tickets to the Cotton Bowl, or meals at swank hotels, or the caterer we'd need for the cocktail party? And now, as D said, our only expenses were our "smokin' tobacco an' drinkin' whiskey," but we had come to think of guests in terms of time to be spent on them, time we didn't have. How could I take the time from my duties that had to be performed every day? There were things that depended upon us for their very sustenance: cows to be milked, chickens to be fed, plants to be watered, garden vegetables to be gathered, and beans to be picked, snapped, cooked, and canned. It was not that our need for people and appetite for news and information had diminished; it was the lack of time.

There were those who thought our life strictly awful and I could not forgive them for this. "You poor thing, Mamie," they'd wail. "What do you do for entertainment? I should think you'd be bored to death, that you'd die of loneliness." Between tending chickens, pulling the hose around, cleaning those bathrooms, keeping carpenters busy, and sleeping a little, there was no time for loneliness. Now if they'd said, of exhaustion—

Sightseers roamed the grounds. I have looked up from a dirt-shoveling job to find a camera focused on me and not known the man behind it. "I hope you don't mind," he said in the nicest voice. "One of the men told me you were the manager's wife. It's so un-usual—I mean, I thought—my folks would so like to see—well, they've never been to Texas." They wanted the folks back home to see what a ranch woman really looked like. But even as I inwardly rebelled, I was inviting them in, offering silent prayers that the cake case would not be empty. Once they were beyond the stage of star-ing at my garden garb, I found they were not only interesting but interested in everything I had to tell and show them. I really en-joyed them. After a few hours my visitors had gone, but so had my day.

The minute tourists drive inside the gate or even lean on the fence of a ranch, they lose their old habits of mind and start think-ing, "Whoopee! A ranch!" Inexplicably a ranch doesn't strike them as serious; it isn't real, especially to the younger ones. We were caught up in a myth. It's a place to ride horses and to have fun, a place where all normal rules of behavior and customs are forgotten. They bounce out of their cars looking for horses and adventure. After a few years we resolved to take a firm stand on certain car-dinal sins committed on the ranch: leaving gates open, being late for meals, asking darn fool questions, and getting hurt or lost. Most of these could be avoided by one's simply not doing what he had been asked not to do. After all, visiting on a ranch did not mean anything goes, such as wearing dirty clothes, showing up for meals at any odd time, killing birds around the corral and feed lots. Quite the contrary. We had a very demanding schedule to follow. We couldn't take folks to the nearest eating place. People who couldn't or wouldn't comply with these basic rules were not encouraged to linger.

But a visitor we could not see often enough was Dan Thorn-ton. "Mayme," D would call as he opened the front door, "I feel a breath of air, sharper, fresher—" and Dan Thornton would be standing there. Dan was born and reared in this section and later became governor of Colorado.

While I live I shall remember the Nashes, a charming army couple who were friends of friends of ours. They came from New England and were entranced by everything western. They stopped by one day to say that Ellen's mother and dad were visiting them, that they had told some whoppers the night before about Texas and the Pitchfork in particular. They had said the Burnses were characters; the little woman was tough as saddle leather, wore a gun all the time, and wasn't afraid to use it. The Nashes had to hurry on to an appointment in Lubbock, but the parents were following on their heels and were so intrigued by the stories that they were going to stop to see these Burns creatures for themselves. Their name was Morris; they might arrive at any minute. Would we please get into some outlandish something and put on an act for them. "Please, please," Ellen begged, as they drove away, "Won't you?"

I ran quickly into D's office to tell him the plan. "Shall we?" I asked. D had no time, he told me, for any damned foolishness. D has a pale sense of humor. The thing appealed to me, but of course I wouldn't do it, and I'm sure I wouldn't have, but the beautiful gun that Sheriff George Humphrey had given D our first month on the ranch was lying right on the living-room table. D had been showing it to a friend only a few hours before, and the holster was beside it. I buckled it on just for fun, pulled on the greasiest old Stetson in D's closet, and took a squint in the mirror; tough as saddle leather, indeed. It would be a pity not to share the spectacle.

I started out to the office to show D, but I didn't make it. Their car was almost to the gate before I saw them. There was barely time to shoot an imaginary something in a tree before the car came to a stop. D, hearing the shot, rushed to the office door, beheld my raiment and the startled guests, and shook his head in disbelief, decided to leave the New Englanders to me, and slammed the door and went back to his work.

I put the gun in the holster, no point in overplaying my role, and greeting them with a wild "Yoo hoo!" ran to the car. They seemed almost frightened. I had meant to amuse, not terrify them. They were expecting characters. Well— "Howdy," I said in the roughest voice I could muster and thrust out my hand in ranch fashion. The dignified gray-haired woman gave me hers, looking slightly incredulous and asked, "Where could we find Mr. or Mrs. Burns?" "I'm Miz Burns. What can I do for you?" "We are the Maurice Obears from Phoenix," she said gently. "I believe Mr. Burns is expecting us."

"Obears," I echoed foolishly, realizing the name had some sort of meaning for me. These were not the Morrises. I felt a little faint. The earth started swimming under my feet. Summoning my faculties, which were needed, I dropped my gun and my pistolic manner. "Mrs. Obears," I said, "I'm not Mrs. Burns—I mean, I am Mrs. Burns, but I don't carry a gun—I mean—I'll get Mr. Burns" (the only sensible remark I'd made). I flew to the office.

"Who are the Maurice Obears?" I asked frantically. D raised his eyes over the edge of the time book. It range a bell for him, too. If only D could laugh at a joke that had backfired, but his stricken, "Oh my God, they're stockholders!" put the manager's wife into shock. D seemed on the verge of maybe apoplexy.

Surely the startled Obears suffered nothing more than momentary surprise. D was going to be furious forever. What would he say? What would he do? More important, what would Mr. Eugene Williams do? Could he afford to keep a manager whose wife was so lacking in dignity, common sense, or whatever?

This I pondered while D went to the car to welcome the Obears and to explain as best he could the situation. When I saw D taking their bags out of the car, I knew I had to rejoin them. Mrs. Obear was laughing with tears in her eyes. "My dear," she said, putting an arm around me, "I haven't had so much fun in years. I can't wait to tell my daughters about this."

"Just so no one tells Mr. Williams," I ventured. "If I know Gene Williams, or if he has any sense of humor, he'll enjoy this thoroughly." I was relieved at her reaction and her words, but not entirely. Prudence, decency, and kindness (not light things) were Mr. Eugene's outstanding qualities. But his sense of humor? Could it be stretched to find such a fiasco amusing? I was afraid such exuberance might be a little unsettling to Mr. Eugene.

What was fascinating about this seemingly unpatchable affair was that such a strong friendship resulted from it—the good times we had with the Obears in Phoenix. They had read in the newspapers that D was judging the Phoenix Stock Show and had contacted us at once to be their guests on some delightful occasions.

The list of military personnel who visited at the ranch during the war years was long and distinguished. For instance, there was Gates's guest, General Swerdrup, who brought with him to the ranch some elegant shirts, the kind performers like Gene Autry and entertainers like Rex Allen wear. Gates Williams had shown the general some of these beauties in a Western store window in Saint Louis and had remarked, "That's the kind of shirt we wear on the ranch." Taking him seriously, General Swerdrup had purchased a dozen at once. He discovered the next morning that his leg had been pulled. But when he came to the ranch he gamely wore them. He had to; he hadn't brought any others. Gates Williams said those shirts made Jack Meyers's shirts look subdued. The cowboys were impressed. One commented that the general "wore the durndest snappiest riggin'" ever he'd seen. When one of the cowboys admired a shirt General Swerdrup would pull it off right there in the pasture or at the chuck-house table and give it to him. By the time he left, every one of those fifty-dollar shirts was with the cowboys.

Terence Cuneo was one of the notables we hosted at the ranch. The British nobility's most famous portrait painter came to the Forks in June, 1960, to paint some of the real West before it was gone.

I had just returned from my cabin in Colorado, when D pitched me a batch of letters that had accumulated during my absence. Right on the very top was one that said, "I have just finished reading an article in the *Saturday Evening Post* about your ranch." The letter went on to say that he had made several trips to the United States and had visited a few dude ranches, but ours seemed like the real McCoy, and he wondered if it would be possible for him to spend a fortnight with us to get the feel of the West and to make his paintings more realistic. He enclosed a pamphlet dealing with his work. It included the coronation picture of Philip and Elizabeth. Even though there were fifty-two figures and the picture was quite small, we could easily distinguish such personages as the Queen Mother, Elizabeth, Philip, Margaret, Churchill, and Ramsay MacDonald.

"Are you going to let him come, D?" I inquired. "I've got no time to wet-nurse an artist, Mayme." I argued that our diplomatic relations with England were at low ebb and that this man was no fly-by-night, that his reception at the ranch might be looked upon with favor and might do something to ease international tensions. "Well, okay," D responded. "He's your baby. if you want him to come, write him and ask him."

I wrote immediately, and within a very short time, he was there. His arrival at the ranch created something of a sensation among the cowboys, and he appeared equally fascinated with them. His polished and very proper accent afforded quite a contrast to their West Texas drawl. Most of our traditions and our language came from England, but that was a long time ago. Mr. Cuneo found us pure Uncle Sam. Understanding us must have been as difficult for him as it was for us to translate his words into our lingo.

Very soon he became an obsessional subject of conversation. The boys rawhided him about his expressions—the *chuckinghouse* and the *bunkinghouse*. They questioned him about the meanings of *jolly* and *bloody*. He told us that the boys were giving him considerable hoo-haw at the chuck house. On one occasion when D returned from a cow butchering at the Navajo camp and reported it the "bloodiest mess" he'd ever encountered, he meant pure old American "bloody," but the word had taken on a different meaning to the men since Terence Cuneo's stay with us. "Must of been a bit of a battle," Tom said to me. Mr. Cuneo soaked up atmosphere and background at the chuck-house table. The boys did a bit of soaking up, too.

But Terence did not really get into the boys' good graces until the bronc-riding incident. D had given him a pickup to haul his gear in. One morning at the chuck house, he asked D if he could ride one of the horses. Asked if he wanted a Western or an English saddle, he said, "It makes no difference." The boys were full of anticipation. They saddled a bronc and brought him out for Mr. Cuneo to ride. All hands gathered. As soon as the Englishman was mounted, the bronc broke in two. But Mr. Cuneo was not in the least disturbed by its bucking. He just sat there and rode him. His prestige rose considerably. It did not, however, change Tom's mind about sitting for a portrait. Tom had worked up his own personal opinion about a likeness of his going to England to be sold on the block, as he put it, and had decided against it.

Our affection for Mr. Cuneo grew until his departure. Now, our most treasured possession is the painting he left us of the north wing of the Big House, the entrance to the home we loved for twenty-three years.

24

Armando

Armando was a wetback. His coming to us was a happening. I was on my way to Spur for groceries and supplies when I saw the small figure of a man with a large cotton sack over his frail shoulder walking on the highway. I felt I shouldn't stop, but he looked so helpless, buffeted by the wind, hair blowing in his eyes.

Though I remembered D's warning, "You're going to get killed picking up hitch-hikers," I stopped and backed up. He came running to the car. His eager, smiling face looked up at me. "Ride?" I asked. "*Sí,*" he answered. He got in beside me.

"You got a job?" I asked. He shook his head, but his eyes lighted in such a pleased way that I felt he had not understood my question and that the joke was on me. I realized that he could not "savvy Americano," but this was no time to take a chance; I'd try again. "You want a job?" He nodded eagerly with even more laughter in his eyes, and came out with a string of words that meant nothing to me. Surely no one could be so happy at being out of a job!

"You *caporal?*" he asked, and in case you don't know, *caporal* means Big Boss. I nodded. I knew I was stretching the truth, but after all he would be working with me when he came to the ranch, I hoped.

He tried to tell me he was a wetback, but my understanding of the English and the Spanish words he scrambled together was less than adequate. But his comprehension of my words and intentions was better than his English, for he jumped out of the car when we arrived at the grocery store and grabbed a shopping cart. Pushing it along as he watched me examine the vegetables, he spied a bin of avocadoes and picked one up gently. "You like?" he inquired. At my nod, he skillfully selected several of just the proper ripeness. "... *cuatro,* ... *seis,*" he counted. He handled them lovingly, careful not to leave a bruise. "*Muy bueno,*" he beamed. We were friends by the time my order was filled, and Armando was having no trouble in making himself understood.

The likes of Armando had not come my way before. His appetite for work was insatiable, a fact I soon discovered when I gave him his first assignment, washing the car. "*Ándele,*" Ed was later to call him after watching him dart from one chore to another. His was not a *mañana* tempo. Armando not only cleaned that station wagon; he practically wore it out with scrubbing and polishing.

My helpers had been by turns irritating, infuriating, amusing, and just sometimes helpful. Armando, though, was willing and anxious to please. He wanted to do the job as I wanted it done. Even fifteen-year-old boys would argue that they had better ideas than I. According to them, there were two methods, the right way and Mrs. Burns's way. But Armando worked because he liked it, and he liked me too. His dark eyes burned with satisfaction when he knew he had pleased me.

In his shy way he fitted himself contentedly into our lives. He was a picture in an old Stetson of D's. He wore it with more than a little dash, although he weighed only about 130 pounds in his sock feet and longhandled underwear.

"Ah, *Señora!*" he'd greet me in the morning. He'd always rise. Or, to D, "*Señor!*" It carried such a tone of respect. "Regards, *Vaquero!*" he'd say when D was in chaps and spurs, full cowboy regalia. It was apparent that Armando was an aspirant cowboy. On more than one occasion, he would announce his intention to buy boots on his next trip into town. But Armando never got his boots. He could never manage to do his shopping before he got drunk. "No boot," he'd tell me sadly when I looked questioningly at his feet. "Eight do-lar get in God-dam jail, twenty-five do-lar get out of jail. No boot."

He constantly showed his concern for me, never allowing me to lift heavy objects. Beside the job that he did so well, hardly a day passed that he did not show that he was partial to me by bringing me a fresh peach or a newly ripe tomato from the garden. He threw in as a *pilón* all these kindnesses.

By this time Armando was learning English rapidly, but I was not so successful with my Spanish. Although my day-to-day Span-

ish combined with gestures was sufficient for communication with
Armando, it was not good enough for anything else and even he
was sometimes baffled. In exchange for lessons in English, Armando said, "I tell you Spanish." He thought it might not be so
hard on him.

"*Sí,*" I replied. Armando was delighted. "You savvy," he said.
"You savvy *español?*" I shook my head. He had heard almost my
complete Spanish vocabulary. Studying Spanish from him gave me
a great advantage over D and the others in his affection. "You very
buena," he commented.

At times, however, his attempts at speech or understanding
English got us both into difficulties. One day I asked him to get the
wheelbarrow and a shovel to haul a load of fertilizer. "Wheelbarrow? Shovel?" He didn't know the words and had to be shown.
"Where we go?"

"To the corral."

"What we do?"

"We're going to get some fertilizer." I could see there was no
understanding in his blank look. "Manure," I emphasized. "You no
savvy fertilizer? Manure?"

"No. No *sé.*"

I ransacked my vocabulary, but there wasn't much more I could
say. I'd gone as far as I could in English, and my Spanish was definitely not up to it. I took him up to the cowpen, opened the gate,
and pointed to a well-seasoned pile in a corner. "See? Fertilizer, *manure.*" Armando, pleased at his great command of the language,
grinned in recognition. "Oh! *Sheet!*" he exclaimed.

Armando was my friend, no doubt about it, but men stick together. Observe my experience with him while we were building a
rock wall. "What the hell you do?" he asked when he came upon
me measuring sand and cement early one morning. He hovered at
my elbow and surveyed my tools. "We are going to build a rock
wall. I'm measuring sand and cement for the mortar," I explained.

"*Bueno,*" was his cheerful response. He wanted to help me in
everything I did. I sent him for rocks that lay just under the hill. In
no time at all, we had the foundation in place and were ready to
start on the second layer. Armando was strong as an ox, and from
laying stepping stones the week before, he had quickly learned how

to make a pick and iron bar work for him. Also, in no time at all, D Burns appeared. He came out of his car objecting to the whole project.

"I don't *want* that wall there!" he stormed, making gestures with both hands. He plainly indicated that he wanted it done away with. I pointed out that the shrubs I had planted there had been uprooted by the wind and that a wall would give us protection from wind, sand, and sun and provide us with much-needed privacy on our screened porch and the back garden.

"But look how much we've got done! The mortar is already setting up—"

"Why didn't you tell me you were starting a wall?" I hadn't told him, because D regarded my requests lightly, when he regarded them at all. I knew that he'd brush me off with, "All in time, Mayme; we have to do first things first." Cows, chickens, cedar poles, dirt-handling, and wall-building were not firsts to him. Armando's eyes kept darting from one of us to the other as we wrangled about the wall. I was afraid he might assault D for daring to wag his tongue at me in such a manner.

"That mortar hasn't had time to be very hard." D grabbed a grubbing hoe and started slashing right and left at the wall's foundation. Then after razing my two-hours' labor, he stalked away. I glanced expectantly toward Armando. To my astonishment, his eyes beamed congratulations to D. Even Armando shared the ranch man's antipathy to a woman's having her way. "You very *buena*," he told me. But he added, with his charismatic grin, "You no *caporal*. You *segunda*."

Armando liked the cowboys and emulated their mannerisms and modes of expression. Within a month after he had come to the ranch, he could say "Howdy" with the best of them. And like Mandy, he expressed profound indifference to the "lookers" who drove into the ranch. "Turista," he'd shrug to indicate his sublime unconcern at their presence. In the evenings, he would go up to the bunkhouse to be near the cowboys so that he could master their rich and varied language. Soon his English became more fluent, incorporating all that I had taught him with innumerable cuss words learned from the cowboys. Jake was his ideal. It was amazing the way he'd picked up Jake's lurid vocabulary.

"The hell and by God," he said one day sighting me atop the Rube Goldberg contraption I'd cobbled up to reach and decorate a certain above-my-head shelf. With anxious concern for my health, Armando said, "You no remember you fall in thees floor?" Yes, I remembered: a kitchen stool, box on top of stool, books on top of box. I remembered. The other had not worked so well, but I assured him nothing would happen this time. I was using a splendid new stepladder, much firmer, much taller than the old stool, with only very large, very flat magazines on it. My footing was solid, and I was being very careful. But somehow in climbing down, I missed the bottom step and landed on the floor again.

Armando went into a fine Spanish fury, "Damn and the hell," he shouted, glaring at me. "Make me very damn." He was angry with me, of course, but he kicked that stepladder, and with every abusive word of his vivid vocabulary told it what it was and where it could go. Not yet content, he stormed, "Son of beech!" His eyes lighted up. That was the word he'd been striving for. He kicked the stepladder across the floor and out onto the porch.

On rainy days he would often join the cowboys in pitching horseshoes or washers. They readily accepted him into their company. Windy was the only one who gave any signs of resenting Armando's presence in the bunkhouse. "Damned Mexican," Windy had growled when Armando sat down next to him at the table. Armando overheard the remark. "He not know what I call *heem,*" he told me with only the slightest suggestion of a smile. That was as close as Armando ever came toward being malicious.

Armando was too good to last, and he didn't. Although his quick intelligence, willingness, and ability endeared him to everyone on the ranch, for some compulsive reason the ever-smiling Armando could not resist alcohol whenever he went to town. Almost every weekend he would go to Spur, take a drink, and then go on drinking until he landed in jail. He was a different person when he touched liquor, but we never saw him under those circumstances. Sometimes he'd stay away from town for a weekend, but then his thirst would become intolerable, and the next week he would wind up in jail. D had repeatedly warned him about his drinking, and on numerous occasions had bailed him out after these excursions.

Armando's most spectacular binge took place in Paducah. Peace officers there told D that it took three of them to put Armando behind bars. Once inside the cell, he raised a splendid ruckus. He stripped himself of all his clothing except his socks and proceeded to whip every one of his cell mates. After this escapade, D called Armando into the office and told him that this was the last time such goings-on would be tolerated. Armando, as usual, was ashamed and sincerely penitent for his actions and promised, "No more, no more." And for six weeks he managed to keep his vow. He stayed at the ranch on weekends, but finally his need for alcohol overwhelmed his resolution.

We begged Armando not to go to Spur, for we knew he was now given to profanity as well as strong drink and would surely get into trouble. He did. It was a week before the ranch saw him again. D sent no one to pay his fine to get him out of jail. After serving his sentence, Armando came back to get his clothes. The small poke he carried away with him held no boots.

D and I were away from the ranch the afternoon he left. To this day, I cannot think of Armando without sadness, remembering his toothless little face, his hand over his heart, swearing, "No more, no more." It is unlikely that he reformed or that he long survived. We remember Armando with fondness and gratitude. He helped us through a rough, rough time. I am sorry to have missed him; I wish I might have said, "*Adios, amigo.*"

25

Pee Wee and the Old-Timers

A pleasant part of the Pitchfork job was greeting old hands who came back. In the spring of 1947 one knocked at our door. "Is this the Pitchfork Ranch?" he asked. His sparkling eyes were black as coals beneath a shock of iron-gray hair. I liked his good-humored smile. "It certainly is," I answered.

"Says so on the gate, but I can't believe it." He opened the screen door and held out his hand. "I'm Arthur 'PeeWee' Ryan." The name was not a new one to me. The old hands often talked of Pee Wee. He was "a mighty shore hand with a horse." But before I could tell him this he went on: "I worked on the Forks thirty years ago, and not many days have passed over my head that I haven't thought about it. I've come a thousand miles to see it again." He shook his head unbelievingly. "I never would've known it. I'd have passed right by it. But I'm glad," he smiled, "to find more, not less, than I remembered. You see," he told me confidentially, "I've made some pretty big brags about this ranch. My wife's out in the car, and if it wouldn't be imposing, we'd like to look around." He went to the car and brought her back with him to the porch. His arm was around her shoulder. "This is Gladys. Her hair," he laughed, "reminds me of a chestnut filly I once had. That's why I married her." There was still a touch of Texas on his tongue.

"Mrs. Burns, please don't pay any attention to Arthur," she warned me. "I can't believe I'm on the Pitchfork Ranch. This man has nearly killed me trying to get here in time to go to the wagon. We've been on the road since four o'clock this morning."

"Is the wagon still out?" he asked eagerly. "Any of the old hands here—anyone I'd know, you reckon?" His questions were pouring out.

"Ed Nolan's here—."

"Why, that son-of-a-gun." I told him they were working East

Long Canyon Pasture. I started to give him directions. "You have to go down the highway about three miles, and turn—"

"I reckon I'll find 'em," he said. He couldn't get to his car fast enough. And find them he did.

They were too busy winding up a hard day's work to pay much attention to a stranger who said he'd never seen a ranch closer than in a picture show. He went from one cowhand to another, getting in the way, standing in the wrong place, asking the sort of questions a greener would ask. He explained to D and Coy Drennan, wagon boss, that I had invited him to visit the cow crew. D wasn't too happy about that. He thought the matter called for firmness and made a mental note to speak to me about it. Finally, Pee Wee started questioning the boys about roping. How long would it take a fellow to learn how to catch a cow? He had a ten-year-old boy at home he'd certainly like to impress. Would they show him how it was done? D told me later that he'd never seen the men more disgusted. Ed never looked toward him. But someone finally showed him how to hold the rope. He carried the loop in his hand, and when the chance presented itself, he used the *hooley ann* on Ed, jerking his feet from under him and flattening him on the ground. Nobody figured the rope was swung by an amateur, but only Ed could recognize one of the best ropers the Pitchfork had ever known. "Pee Wee Ryan, you !!!*." (No one had a more picturesque vocabulary than Ed.) "What the hell you doin' here afoot, huh?" They slapped each other affectionately. That night, Pee Wee said, "Putting the *hooley ann* on Ed today was about the happiest loop I ever throwed."

Happily it had started raining, and the bunch from the wagon came in to the chuck house for supper. There were thirty of us gathered around the long table. All eyes and ears were for Pee Wee. He was a big man with a singularly gentle voice and an extraordinary gift for storytelling. He brought the early days to life with words that stirred memories for the old Pitchfork hands and made the rest of us somehow melancholy, yet proud to be a part of the show. He talked of the times of feuds, of high feelings and taking sides. Ed's face became grave. It reminded him too keenly of the day they'd found his father dead, dead with a bullet in his heart, of the changes that had taken place on the ranch. Some of them were maybe for the better. Some of them were—well, he wasn't sure. "I was wonderin' today what he'd think of this free-wheelin' outfit." He meant Mr. Gardner, of course. "His dugout was right down there. I can see him just as plain, sittin' there in his chair, with books stacked all around him. Nobody was ever allowed to move one, not even to dust 'em. An' I can just hear him saying, "Oh, I say, I say, boys—.""

"Reckon he coulda said anything without startin' off 'I say, I say'?" Ed asked.

"Never heard 'im. Used it ever' time he spoke, startin' an' in the middle of a sentence too. Sometimes even at the end of a sentence."

"Funny thing about it, though," Ed recalled. "Nobody ever got tired hearin' him say it. Seemed like they allus listened fer it, like it was part of 'im. They'da been disappointed an' knowed he wasn't feelin' right if he hadn't a said it."

"A grand ol' man," Pee Wee said. And that's the way Dan Gardner was known all over the state, as the Grand Old Man of the Pitchfork.

"Who is Mr. Gardner, Baba?" Cuppie wanted to know.

"He was the manager of the Pitchfork, darling. The Pitchfork's first manager. He was here forty-eight years," D explained.

"Where is he now?"

"He's dead, darling," I answered, but Ed broke in.

"Leastwise they buried him, but he ain't dead, honey. Not by a long ways." The children listened, wide-eyed and reverent. To the younger cowboys, these tales were sagas from a far world, peopled with heroes with hell-flint in their guns and with courage and daring in their hearts.

"How old were you, Ed, when you started drivin' for 'im? I remember you were jest a shaver. When we'd see the buckboard comin', first off it'd look like the team was a-runnin' loose, but we figured you were hangin' onto th' lines even before we saw you, or Mr. Gardner wouldn't a been sittin' so calm an' content."

Ed wanted to know where Pee Wee had "been keepin' hisself" after he left the Forks. "Nobody ever heard from you."

Pee Wee replied that he'd bought him a little shop in California and was now a barber. He added, "For a spell I joined a one-horse outfit in Colorado, but it seemed piddlin' after the Pitchfork, so I left. I had jest enough money to go to a barber school." Pee Wee had not quite a Texas drawl but was so peculiarly Texan.

"This here was th' ropin'est, ridin'est, bronc-bustin'est ranny ever hit the Forks," Ed told the other cowhands at the table. "Usta give the wisdom-bringers a fit too, huh?" Ed accused.

"Married one of 'em," Pee Wee admitted. "Hadn't you noticed my grammar?"

"Knowed they was somep'n wrong with you, but I jest figgered you'd been away from civilization so long," Ed winked at Gladys. She was loving all this.

"That's about right," Pee Wee grunted, "but I can pick 'er up agin quicker'n you kin spit and holler howdy," he boasted. "That is," in feigned meekness, "unless the schoolmarm here objects." He indicated Gladys.

"Cowboy," was her answer, "let th' hair go with th' hide. But don't get your spurs tangled up." She raised her coffee cup, as if in a toast.

"Powder River!" yelled Bainey Smith. There were cheers and whistles, as merry laughter rang out. She'd won the hearts of the Pitchfork gang. Pee Wee saw it and was glad.

"That's the way she roped me in. 'Come an' get it,' she called out at a lodge supper. I hadn't heard that in seven months. I looked around to see who said it, an' she's laughin right into my eyes. She was as good lookin' then as she is now. 'Want to eat at our table?' she ast. 'Columbus took a chanct,' I said. Soon as I tasted her cookin' I said, 'Now, I got a half-interest in a barber shop.' She give me that 'take-it-easy' look, an' I caught on. I never was dumb about anything but talkin', but she gimme a date too, an' it wasn't a month till my horse an' buggy was a'standin' at her gate every night. It didn't take me long to pop th' question, seein' as my mind had been made up. She looked at me plumb pitiful. 'Oh, Arthur,' she said, an' busted out cryin'. Well, I never felt so helpless or so unnecessary. I coulda swore they was lovelight in her eyes right then, but—."

Gladys laughingly begged, "Oh, Arthur, don't tell all of that." The big man paused and looked at her for just a moment. It seemed there were just the two of them in the room. His story had given rise to a flood of memories—tender, amusing—then he went on.

"Well, it fin'ly come out, little at a time. She said she'd come to think a heap o' me, that she wasn't afraid I'd starve her to death, an' that she'd be proud to be my wife, if it warn't fer my *grammar*. I wondered what was wrong with my grammar. I'd been doin' all right fer thirty years with it, hadn't nobody complained before. Then I remembered there was some terms she used that sounded plumb peculiar. Bein' as I was in no frame o' mind to argy, I said, 'Why, honey, you could learn me.' She sorta winced like I hit her over the head with a bridle, an' said, 'No, Arthur, that wouldn't work. You'd resent my corrections, and it would bring heartaches and bitterness between us. I've thought it all out, and—'

"'I've thought it out too,' I said. 'Give me a six months' course in that grammar. I'll bet you'll be struck dumb by my improvement an' th' way I love my teacher.'"

"Do you have to tell everything you know?" Gladys interjected.

"Well sir, I was a glutton fer learnin'. I'd a stayed in after classes if she'd a let me."

"Arthur!" Gladys scolded.

"Well now, I done plumb noble. I never said 'heerd' agin after she told me it was 'heard.' Never said 'takened' mor'n two or three times. But it looked like I was bound to say 'had went.' I worked on it all day. Never was two words more mouthed over. I'd practice on my customers. I'd say, 'Now if you *had gone* to that other barber shop, you would *have gone* to the wrong place.' I'd say, 'If you *had gone* to the picture show, you'd a seen a good show.' I even put a sign in my window: *Had gone* to lunch. I showed such talent fer grammar that in six months she was Mrs. Ryan, an' we was on our way to visit her folks. I was nearly bustin' with happiness an' improvement. 'Honey,' I said, 'I'm glad you had th' nerve to tell me what you did. I wouldn't a wanted you to be ashamed o' me ever. Why, if we had went to see your people six months ago—' She busted out cryin' agin, 'Oh, Arthur, you've said it again! I'll *die* if you say *had went* at Mama's.' I'd a cut my throat if I'd a had my razor. 'Honey,' I said, 'Don't you worry another minute. I won't say *had went* at your Mama's. I jest won't talk about goin' nowheres.'"

While Ed and Pee Wee were reminiscing about the old days, I

noticed the children. Burns's eyes shone with pride over the valor of these tough oldtimers.

The next morning D and I called as many old Pitchfork hands as we could locate to invite them to the ranch. They arrived that evening. We hoped that Pee Wee and Gladys would enjoy their three days with us, and we knew that Pee Wee would be pleased to see some of his friends of the past. We mustered up quite a few of the oldtimers, men like Allen Deaton, Uncle George Watson, Red-mud Lambert, and Press Goen.

Some grand tales were told around the chuck-house table that day, and some grand arguments followed. A story credited to one outfit by a narrator would be claimed by another for his old spread. There were yarns of cowboys, ranchers, rustlers, and settlers. Squatters, the oldtimers called the latter. Their contempt for the squatters was still alive. We were entertained.

One old fellow named Lige, who'd just been waiting to get the floor, took over. "That was in 1884. Mr. Gardner was put out by all the talk over the XIT. They couldn't nobody think of nuthin' else. It was the damndest outfit in the world, I reckon, an' ever' feller that come by had a bigger tale to tell than th' last. Word was goin' around that they was needin' five hunnerd men an' was payin' thirty-five dollars a month." (A princely sum in those days.) "It was rumored that Barbecue Campbell of the Matador would soon follow suit. All over th' country cowhands was rollin' their suggins an' lightin' out fer the Big Spread. Us Pitchfork hands was flirtin' with th' idear, but like a good cuttin' horse, Mr. Gardner was allus one jump ahead of us. 'I say, I say, boys, you might try it a fall.'" This unexpected suggestion made the boys leery that Mr. Gardner might be willing to part with some of them. So the XIT became less interesting, except as a subject for idle gossip.

Ed said, "They never knowed Barbecue Campbell if they thought he'd put wages up. My pa was a eyewitness to th' way he operated." It would be impossible to repeat with fidelity these yarns. They made good listening and lived up to the adage that Texans like and tell their stories tall.

One oldtimer told of an itinerant photographer who brought his darkroom wagon to the Forks and followed the roundup outfit for a week or two. Day after day he photographed the delighted cowboys. He took their pictures while they were eating at the chuck wagon, riding, roping, and branding, or while they were on the corral fence, leaning against posts, in cowboy rigging, and in newly-bought blue serges. "He struck our beauty about ever' way imaginable," Ed said, "sittin' still an' in motion. Got to where th' boys was posin' continual, an' one of 'em takened about as hard a fall as ever I seen a feller git, eye'n th' camera 'stead of watchin' his horse's ears." It was easy picking for the photographer. Mr. Gardner, always hospitable and ever mindful of his men's enjoyment, let the picture man bunk with the boys and eat at the chuck house. He advanced them funds to purchase their likenesses. It was an innocent enough way to spend their money, and spend it he knew they would, come pay day. It is said Mr. Gardner himself posed a time or two.

The Pitchfork has long been praised for its excellent food. Men who speak of nothing else on the ranch remember its long tables of good things to eat. This the traveling photographer also noted and was loathe to leave. Even Mr. Gardner's "I say, I say, you still here?" when they met in the mornings failed to send him on his way. Ed said it was not only the man's sponging that got Mr. Gardner's dander up, for the old fellow said, "Blast it, I don't believe the bounder thinks we've got sense enough to know we're being worked." So with his customary directness, his stern gaze upon the nonpaying boarder and with no thought for the pun he was making, Mr. Gardner said, "I say, I say, you've struck our likenesses enough. Why don't you strike the road?" Ed let us see Dan Gardner as a man who stood his ground, let us hear his voice and his words to one who had overstayed his welcome.

Ed started picking at Pee Wee again. "He's set th' hair on many a Pitchfork horse." He continued, "He's the feller tamed ol' Gangster. Huh? Remember him don'cha?" Rosy Deaton said, "I've heard that story all my life."

Pee Wee said, "I ain't likely to be fergittin' him. But I ain't right shore who done the tamin'. He throwed me an' ever'body else," he remembered with chagrin.

"You rode him longer'n any other, cowhand."

"Yeah. Some durned edjicated fool with nuthin' to do but count said I rode him seventeen bucks. I've got a faint recollection of some o' them bucks but thet number *eighteen,* the one that set me straddle of thet corral fence, is the one I remembered the longest."

"That's one he never told me," Gladys chimed in.

"The story went like this," Ed began. "Gangster was brought in while Pee Wee here—we allus called him Pee Wee or Runt 'cause he hardly ever weighed over two hundred pounds—was visitin' his folks. Ever' cowhand on the ranch had tried to ride Gangster 'thout no noticeable success. We had more boys a-limpin' an' with arms in slings at one time then we'd ever had before. Now we all held Pee Wee top peeler, he even thought so hisself," Ed grinned, "with the Pitchfork Kid runnin' second. Th' Kid hadn't takened his turn at Gangster neither on account of he'd been helpin' th' SMS's. Some thought that the kid could ride 'im, an' that Pee Wee could ride 'im shore. Others was willin' to bet neither one of 'em could stay with 'im. When Pee Wee come in and heerd th' talk, he jest reached fer his suspenders an' said modest-like, 'I'll ride 'im or bust a leg.' Bein' a slack Sunday, we all went down to th' corral to see th' fun. Word had got 'round that th' Kid an' Pee Wee was gonna gentle Gangster, an' they's a right smart crowd gathered fer th' show, among 'em th' schoolteacher from Guthrie that Pee Wee was settin' up to. And thet city dude that come out from Fort Worth about onct a month to see her was a-settin' by her warm side. He wasn't regrettin' their presence none. He waved th' Kid to ride first. His actions said plain as day he was a-savin' th' best fer th' last. Huh?" Ed grinned. "Well, sir, that Kid didn't last no time. One big buck an' that's all she wrote. Pee Wee got a squint o' this brand of buckin', an' his face got plumb serious. 'What's a-matter, cowhand?' somebody asked him. 'Jest a-wonderin' how I'm gonna look ridin' in th' rodeo with a busted leg,' he moaned."

"I wasn't feelin' so good," our visitor admitted.

"How did he make out, Ed?" Gladys asked.

"I remember it like it was yesterday," Pee Wee recalled. "I remember th' riggin' I had on. Bought it offa the Kid. He'd been to K.C. an' decked hisself out right special. I thought I looked purty good."

Ed could hardly wait to break in. "You did. You looked good till you got on Gangster. He was at his best," Ed choked over the memory. He was at his best, too, as a teller of tales, and he knew it. We begged him to go on. He had opened a page from a half-forgotten history.

Pee Wee grinned at the memory of the incident. "I left enough hide on that corral fence to make a pair o' chaps."

"He shore showed some fancy footwork," according to Ed. "That busted up his case with th' knowledge-bringer too," Ed shook his head. "He shore buggered up a good peeler." Ed went on to say that Pee Wee was the terror of his boyhood. "I tried to imitate his ever' move. I durned near got killed a time or two tryin'."

The oldtimers continued drivin' trail, as they called reminiscing on the Pitchfork. There were still a few around who remembered when the Pitchfork was young without a single windmill and no fences—Al Bingham, Ed, and Mr. Deaton. Pee Wee recalled when he was here there was only the north and south pastures. "They drove cattle over th' very spot where th' bunkhouse is now." They spoke of the wild buffalo hunters. "It took a lot o' gun to kill a buffalo." Then followed a long conversation about J. Wright Mooar, early-day buffalo hunter. "He used what he called a Big 50. They said it'd shoot today and kill tomorrow. He killed the white albino buffalo." Al Bingham remembered that Buttermilk Gaines's father had been a scout and a noted trailer. Butter used to tell how he and his father had hunted the wild cow and bull for beef, lying on the edge of the timber in the early dawn, waiting for the cattle to come back to their thicket daytime cover. He said they never fed or watered except in the darkness of the night.

Buttermilk made his share of history and headlines on the Pitchfork. He was a mixture of showmanship and daring and given to impulsive bets and extravagant statements. All of the old-time hands boasted of his strength, his skill, and his way with a story. We have no counterpart of the fiery Butter. They had a hundred anecdotes of Butter in his prime, tales of his generosity, of his rages, his strength, and his courage. Al Bingham recalled, "Butter uster entertain us by tellin' of scrapes he'd got into an' about his father. He had a wit that snapped an' crackled through his conversation an' convulsed the cowpokes." There was a spectacular story that Buttermilk told about a friend of his who, in the presence of a bull, had got down from his horse to open a gate, although Butter had warned him repeatedly that longhorn bulls didn't like men on foot. The bull came in a charge, tore out the entrails of his horse, and would have killed the man if there had not been a big tree nearby and if he had not been a fast climber. As it was, the bull kept that man in the tree all day.

Although many a selfless and generous act was attributed to Buttermilk, he purely loved to fight. "He'd fight at th' drop of a Stetson," Al remembered. "His fav'rite way o' pickin' a fight was to come up to a feller an' tell 'im he didn't like his looks, or maybe th' color of his horse." Al went on to regale us with another of his countless anecdotes about Butter.

"One hot Sunday mornin' Buttermilk seen a feller drivin' a big bunch o' sheep to his windmill tank for water. Now, Buttermilk never had no more love fer sheep 'n any other cowman, an' this feller jest bargin' in without askin' shore got his taller. He grabbed up his six-shooter. 'Wife,' he said, 'I'm a-gonna run that yeller-livered poachin' sheepherdin' son-of-a-gun clean outta this coun-try, but I'm a-gonna skeer th' livin' daylights outta him first.'

"Mor'na hour went by, an' Miz Gaines begin to wonder what had happened. She could see sheep a-grazin' ever'wheres, but she couldn't see no men. Her dinner was gittin' cold. Buttermilk was a great hand to be on time fer grub, an' well, that feller mighta hurt Buttermilk, she reckoned. So after a spell, she put on her bonnet an' started down to th' windmill. She come up on Buttermilk an' this here sheepherder a settin' on the fer side of th' tank dam with a big jug betwixt 'em. They was talkin' an' laughin' fit to kill. Butter-milk stood up. 'Wife, this here's as fine a gentleman as ever I met, an' I've ast 'im to stay th' winter with us—sheep 'n all.' They tell me she lit into 'im good an' proper—an' boy, she was croton." We all laughed and, full of amusement at these reminiscences, we begged for more.

"That ain't th' reason she left him though," Ed put in. "She left 'im on account un th' time him an' Peely busted thet poker game over at Stinkin' Creek. They's comin' home purty late an' purty drunk an' decides they could cut off a few miles by swimmin' th' river. Well, when Buttermilk gits home an' starts undressin', he dis-covers his roll of bills is wet. He takes 'em out to th' back yard an' strings 'em all on a bobwire fence an' leaves 'em dry till mornin'. Leastwise that was his aim, Buttermilk allus said. An' ef thet by-God sandstorm hadn't of come, she wouldn't a went."

Though he wasn't a Pitchfork regular, Buttermilk achieved legendary status. Probably the most notable story told about him was the following. Butter was helping out at roundup time on the Forks. All the cowboys were going in their several directions. Buttermilk was assigned to work the Willow section. When he failed to show up at the appointed time with his quota of cattle, everybody wondered what had happened to him. "It ain't like Butter to be late with his part." Finally, when he arrived with only a handful of cattle, he was white as a sheet. "Where in hell you been?" he was asked. He told them he'd been at a birthin'. And he had remained to officiate. "Well, how'd it come out?" they wanted to know. "Is ever'thing all right?" "Th' kid's all right. She showed me how to tie off th' cord. But that woman's gonna die. I couldn't make her eat her afterbirth."

This episode is such a shocker that some may doubt its truth. But an incident occurred a few years ago that gives this story vitality and credibility. A Mexican, Juan Martínez, came by the ranch and declared that he had been born on the ranch, that a cowboy had helped his mother through her ordeal. We failed to connect his startling declaration with the afterbirth account then. Juan was sixty when he was here. This would place the date of his birth during Butter's day and time. These yarns, true or not, now belong irrevocably to Buttermilk.

It was pleasant consorting with the old hands, hearing them tell of the men and women who had lived here before us and who had gone up the trails, those trails paved in concrete today. These oldtimers had come to revisit old haunts, to relive the old days, and to talk over their lusty pasts. And a lucky handful of Pitchfork people were hearing some old stories to treasure.

We listened to some pretty crude remarks, humorous and earthy—they were about artificial insemination—and talk suggesting a new branding method was hooted. "There'll never be nuthin' like th' hot arn." Theirs was the great generation of the cowboy. "Ain't none o' these young buttons a match fer th' Pitchfork Kid or Buttermilk," they claimed. A young hand, Jim Ghost it was, presumed to insert, "It ain't our fault we was born thirty years too late." One of the oldsters promptly responded, "Well, we're mighty sorry fer you."

Here was the Pitchfork as it was in the time when Dan Gardner forbade his boys to marry, in the time when he was king and had argued against Press Goen's taking a wife, "I say, I say, see here now, Press—I say, you can't leave me without a foreman." "You got Hawley Bryant, Mr. Gardner. What's wrong with him? He can run things," Press defended. "I say, I say, why, he doesn't know the range. He's only been here eleven years."

To these oldsters, the things they saw on the ranch that day, or the day before, might have amused or angered them at the time, but it was not of real importance. Whatever belonged to Dan Gardner's day and time belonged to them. Looking at our modern buildings, they recalled the old days when the half-dugouts called chosies, furnished shelter for men and their families. A privy in the house would not have been condoned. Now electric lights were glowing in the darkness where once oil lamps or lanterns would have shown through chinks in the houses.

"Them was happy days, but we never knowed it. No, sir, we never knowed it. 'Pears a feller's like that. Never knows he's happy till a thing's a time gone and it's too late." Said one old hand, and tears welled in his eyes, as he referred to the Forks, "It's th' last time I'll see 'er, but it was worth th' trip. It gives a man a thing to think on." It gave us all a chance to measure our days against those of Dan Gardner, the Pitchfork Kid, and Ivy Turner Rader. Mr. Gardner would find the Pitchfork much changed. Even Pee Wee shook his head at the difference in the cattle. Instead of the slow-moving long-legged, spindly creatures he remembered, these were short-legged, deep-bodied cows. (D can and will tell you every step that has gone into their development in recent years. "We got seventy young bulls from the TO's," he'd begin.) If the minds of the old-timers and present hands alike were centered on the past, at least one person in the chuck house was bent on the future. D called a halt to the evening's reminiscences by saying, "Well, folks, I'm gonna have to leave it with you. Tomorrow is another day."

Next day when Ed was driving a few of the oldtimers over the ranch, Pee Wee said, "If Mr. Gardner could have been with us

today, he'd of reco'nized th' hills an' hollers an' all th' natural landmarks, but he'd a blinked hard at those camps. He'd a thought well
of th' place bein' so modern. He was a purty forward-lookin' man
hisself. A bold planner an' thinker fer his time. But I'm afraid somebody would of been in fer a chowsin' when we got to headquarters
an' he missed his grove o' mesquite trees. Mr. Gardner wouldn't let
a tree or plant of any kind be cut down. This usta be a reg'lar wilderness around here. We nearly had to crawl to git from one buildin' to
another. Th' old man would of hit th' ground talkin'. 'I say, I say,
boys, what's become of my mesquites?'"

"Yeah," Ed admitted, "they's been a lotta changes made since
his time." Then he added, "But I don't think he'd find much dif-
f'rence in th' principles of th' ranch now."

After seeing the new improvements—the camps, the pig operation, the mixed-feed plant—and, among other things, watching a
branding and dehorning, they returned to headquarters. Pointing
in the direction of the commissary, Pee Wee exclaimed, "I thought
th' dugout was here!" Ed explained that the commissary had been
built over the old dugout. They walked down the hill to take a
look. "That cain't be th' dugout?" Pee Wee asked in astonishment.
Ed assured him that it was the same place where the men had slept
and put their saddles in the old days. "We use it now as a storm
cellar an' storage fer th' commissary." Pee Wee shook his head.
"Shore seems little. I allus thought it was the biggest dugout in the
world." It brought sadly to mind how things are reduced by time.

They went on over to the chuck house to eat lunch. Other
oldtimers were already there. Some had spent the night at the
bunkhouse. Some had driven home and had returned. Some had
just arrived. Some of the oldtimers who had surveyed the new de-
velopments at the ranch that morning had felt their age as they observed the youngsters "goin' to th' ground with 'em," but there was
a bit of condescension toward some of the new, up-to-the-minute
gadgets and methods that had been introduced. "Featherbeddin' it,
ain't they?" one of the oldsters cracked. "And the mesquite are
takin' your country." Some of the boys described their honored
trappings of the past. "Shore make better saddles now." The oldsters agreed that they were somewhat better.

Ed rose to the defense. "There's lotsa places on this ranch where a feller can still throw a loop 'thout gettin' it hung on a mesquite." He made no bones about liking present arrangements better than those of the past. "I ain't hankerin' to work a hunderd-section pasture. You fellers couldn't a got here today, couldn't a got across th' creek 'thout that bridge, an' you couldn't a got down from th' gate, huh?" He put two helpings of ice cream on his cobbler. "An' this grub. Dried apples, raisins, an' lick was th' only sweet'nin' we ever had then. Well, maybe sometimes a vinegar pie. Wife says a vinegar pie's a poor man's lemon pie."

It was a Roman holiday. Mandy and Jeet were there at the chuck house too. Mandy was miffed when the old-timers belittled the cowboys of today. "Whereat's one tougher'n Ed?" she muttered. But the old-timers, undaunted, went on with their stories of longhorns, cattle rustlers, and he-men of yore. There were stories of yellow summers, bleached bones, and rattling carcasses. We got an earful of real ranch lore listening to them tell of those tougher-than-tough heroes of the old Forks. Here and hereabouts roamed the Pitchfork Kid, perhaps the wildest figure of those wild days. His real name was Billy Partlow, but because of his prowess with a rope and a horse, he soon gained the title of Pitchfork Kid. His was a name that popped up often and, according to Ed, the Kid wasn't all legend, though many stories have been written and told about him. Some of the most colorful chapters in the history of the Pitchfork were about him and Buttermilk. But the ones I believe that come nearest the truth are the versions related by Mrs. Deaton and Ed. According to Ed, Dan Gardner had found the Kid, then a little waif in Saint Louis, had started a conversation, and had made friends with him in the station where the tyke was polishing Mr. Gardner's shoes. Discovering that he was homeless, Mr. Gardner brought him to the Pitchfork. Ed concluded, "Mr. Gardner was th' only person who ever tried to influence him fer good an' who gave 'im teachin' an' encouragement."

"Men was more lawless before 1880," an old-timer informed us. "Hit was trail-drivin' times an' Indian times. A man had to be quick with a gun."

"Men wasn't as bad then as some lets on," Lee Riddle qualified.

"Lots of old-time cowboys never killed a man. Disappointed, ain't ye?" His eyes twinkled as he looked at me.

"Why, I am," I said jokingly. "I thought they slayed folks coming and going."

"Been readin' stories," he said. Then, reflectively, "Now we had rustlers. Still do. An' folks ain't never minded drillin' a cattle thief. Ever' cowboy could use a gun, all right," the old fellow told me, "but they warn't gunmen. Not by no means."

"I mind th' time Pink Higgins spent th' night here," Mr. Deaton recalled. "He'd been followin' some cattle thieves into New Mexico. They'd killed a man, an' Pink found 'im bled to death on th' range."

"Yeah, I remember that story," Pee Wee inserted. "They laid him in a shallow grave." He paused. We saw the picture. Many men in pioneering days had been killed out on the plains by lightning, stampedes, drowning, falling from a horse, or a gunshot wound, far from home and friends, far from any settlement where a grave could have been dug properly. Buried without ceremony in a shallow grave.

"Pink Higgins. There was a man fer you," Al Bingham recalled. Then for the benefit of those of us who might not know: "He was protection man fer th' SMS in the early 1900s." His story, as Al told it, sounded like a true Western, and it was. Pink Higgins, remembered now as the good bad man, had begun his life much as any other boy of that time. Reared in a pioneer home of God-fearing parents, he grew up straight and strong, honest and fearless. Because of his honesty and courage, he had the moral support of both rangers and state police. He was not afraid to tell any man on earth what he thought of him. The West took this straight-shooting, eagle-eyed, rustler-slaying young man to its heart. And the Spur Ranch put him on its payroll as a protection man. "He allus set with his back to th' wall facin' th' door. Nobody ever caught him sittin' on his gun hand."

Then someone told of the Higgins-Watson feud. As a little girl I had listened to accounts of Pink Higgins and this feud. As the narrator told how Higgins had almost single-handedly wiped out the band of cattle thieves led by Watson, I noticed that Bainey Smith listened attentively. When the tale ended, he quietly said,

"Pink Higgins was my grandfather." Bainey then proceeded to give an account of Pink's last gunfight.

It was forty years ago that Pink Higgins drew his trusty gun and laid low his last enemy, Bill Standifer. Both Standifer and Higgins had notches on their guns. Some said that Pink had eighteen. But his friends declared that he had never killed a man unless he needed killing or else in self-defense. Standifer was not without mettle. He had sent word to Pink that he was coming to get him. Pink was at home when the message was delivered. Rising from his seat, Pink had quietly gone outside and mounted. He was going to meet Standifer on his way. Pink didn't want the shooting to take place at his home.

As he rode off, Pink's little daughters watched from the rooftop of his home to report to their mother what was happening. Mrs. Higgins, a gentle woman, was worried. She knew Pink was galloping out to meet a man who had sworn to get him. She had hoped this sort of thing was over for him, but the messenger had said that Bill was on his way. The girls were excited and terrified. A man was riding to his death. But they weren't afraid for Papa. They knew who was going to get killed. At last Mother got her report. "I don't see anybody but Papa, an' he's comin' this way in a lope." Pink Higgins had just killed his fifteenth man. Or was it his nineteenth? "Standifer wasn't no coward. He went down with both guns a-blazin'." Whether Pink Higgins was right, and some of the men thought he wasn't, the records show that he wasn't tried.

This rapt audience sat until about three in the afternoon. Such lengthy sessions were for rainy days and for after sunset. As the talk drew to a close, Pee Wee asked about Press Goen. I told him that Press hadn't been able to come to the reunion because of his health. He was confined to his bed now, but I added that Press's son had invited Pee Wee to come down to see him. So after lunch, while the others were riding over the ranch and talking horse, Pee Wee and I drove the short distance to the Goen home just out of Dickens.

When we drove up to the house, we were met by Mrs. Goen and Press's son Guy. They took us inside to see Press. The two old cowboys were glad to see each other. When they embraced, I was much moved at their elation and affection.

"Nice place you got here," Pee Wee commented. "And a fine

wife and son. With a setup like this, I'm mighty glad you didn't listen to Mr. Gardner when he tried to talk you outa marryin'."

"So am I," Press admitted. "But that's th' only time I didn't foller th' old fellow's advice. He was right about purt near ever'-thing else."

"They'll never be another'n like him. I'm proud I come along in his time," Pee Wee asserted.

"Finest man I ever knowed. Spunky too," Press recalled. "He was a real man, a good boss, an' a mighty good neighbor. I allus pulled my team outa th' road to favor 'im when we met anywheres on th' ranch. He'd stop his car to get out an' thank me. He was a grand old man." Press Goen was the man who knew Dan Gardner best, and as we sat by his bed, the old Pitchfork foreman took great pleasure in remembering and relating stories of Mr. Gardner. We didn't stay long for fear of tiring Press Goen, but it was a red-letter visit for the two old Pitchfork hands.

That evening in the chuck house, the oldtimers again searched their memories for stories of the Pitchfork's early years. Everyone talked of Press Goen. Strong, rough men with faces reddened by the Texas wind and sun, they unfolded their charming stories. They had told these stories many times. Knowing that storytelling is an art, they had polished their tales until they sparkled and shone. Somebody hauled out the old yarn about the cook who had put too much salt in his bread, and attributed it to his or his friend's outfit. They were very loyal to their old outfits, friends, and ranch bosses. We heard the names of men who were great in the cow business, names they had been brought up to revere. Dan Gardner and Press Goen were among the magic names from the old Pitchfork. Naturally, mention of one ancient notable would bring up memories of others: Barbecue Campbell, A. J. Swenson, Bob Hastings, Burk Burnett, Billy Pressley, Hawley Bryant, and Mr. Hobart. Parson Slaughter's name was one of those that excited veneration. It's a long time since Parson Slaughter, who had fought Indians, branded mavericks, and preached with a pistol in his belt, laid the foundations for the great empire that had become the far-famed Lazy S. I relished hearing about him especially, for his grandson, John Lott, who operates the spread now, and his family are dear friends of ours.

I heard them tell how it feels to stand guard at night. As they spoke of the things that pass through a fellow's mind when he sits his horse through those long hours, I recalled Pops's story of Jeff Smith, wagon boss for the Matador in the eighties. I couldn't resist telling of that stormy night when a group of Matador men were standing guard in the rain. The cowboys were fearfully silent as the weather raged. "You don't hear much cussin' around a cow outfit when it's thunderin' an' lightnin'," Pops always pointed out when he told the story. But Jeff, noted for his Lear-like invectives (Pops said he "cussed by note"), was undaunted. "Shoot 'im agin, you GD SOB!" he roared, as a crackling peal of thunder rent the air. Lightning split a tree not more than twenty-five feet in front of him. Jeff had a change of heart. He rode off, singing reverently, "What a friend we have in Jesus!"

Old glories of the ranch were recounted and old happenings rehashed. If there was a pang of regret for her colorful past from the oldtimers, D was equally concerned for her future. He had a respect for the old and an interest in the new. He believed in preserving the best of both eras. He knew of the difficulties of the past and respected the oldtimers for their grit and stamina.

26

Stamford Cowboy Reunion

The rodeo is one of the cowman's oldest forms of entertainment. But no other rodeo in the world is quite like the Stamford Reunion, which is held each year on the first four days of July at the Fair and Rodeo Grounds at Stamfod, Texas. What a show it is, if the creaking of saddle leather and the clip-clop of horses' hooves appeal to you. During our years on the Pitchfork we were always seeking typical divertissements to entertain and edify our Eastern and foreign visitors. Those lucky enough to experience the Stamford Reunion never forgot it. Hundreds of cowboys demonstrate their skills of roping, riding, bulldogging, bareback and bronc riding, in the cutting horse events and barrel racing.

In 1942 on the Fourth of July, the little town of Stamford paid homage to one of its favorite sons, Rudolph Swenson, Everyone at the ranch had attended this celebration, for the hands had all admired and loved Rudolph when he was manager at the Forks. It was his tragic death that had led to our coming to the Pitchfork.

A group of local businessmen organized the first Stamford Reunion in 1930. Now it is the largest amateur rodeo in the world, drawing riders and performers from Texas and all over the country. The official name is the Texas Cowboy Reunion. The town's entire population, high and low, take part in the celebration. Annually, all the roads leading to Stamford are alive with people. They come from ranches and farms, from the small neighboring towns and, in more recent years, from all over the United States. Once they reach the rodeo grounds, the crowd is mostly on foot or horseback.

The Stamford Reunion had been discontinued during the war years. For the 1947 celebration, which was the first reunion after the war, D told the Pitchfork hands that we'd just close up shop and everybody could go to Stamford. We would take the wagon and the horses, even Baby Bay and Keeno, the children's prize horses. The kiddos loved the idea. Ink, of course, liked it too. He'd have four days of uninterrupted fishing, no trek to a rodeo for him.

Anne McGuire, my sister Willie's daughter, was to be our representative at the affair. She would ride Dally Welte. The boys, who called Anne "Little Pitchfork," did a lot of shinin' around. They were proud of her and felt that the Pitchfork was a cinch to win the prize on looks. They were right. She got the most points in that department.

During the week before the rodeo, the Forks was buzzing with excitement. The ranch plunged into preparations for the competitions. The boys gave Anne's rigging a final going over. The children, full of anticipation, wondered what Keeno and Baby Bay would think of this new experience. They had lived all their lives on the Forks. They knew the creek, the corral, and their own pasture. They knew the joy of running and playing and kicking up their heels with their friends. They knew trucks and cars and people. But little Cuppie was worried about them. "But Baba, they'll be frightened by the music and the flags and things and the funny-lookin' kind of people that you always see in town."

When the first of July rolled around, it was a big day for the Pitchfork. The boys were ready to cut a four-day swathe through Stamford. The wagon was loaded and the ranch entourage was underway. The children could hardly wait for the rodeo after having seen Baba out there instructing "Annaguire" on how to ride the barrels.

It was a sight to see the grand entrance, where the old hands, cowboys, ranchmen, children, and entire families, all heralded by a high-stepping band, paraded past the stands and exuberant spectators. The atmosphere was fraught with excitement, expectation, thrills, and danger. Here was the first performance of a square dance on horseback. Here was bull-dogging, bronc-busting, calf-roping, and the cutting horse competition. There were the ubiquitous clowns who, with their antics, had saved the life of many a cowboy (the ambulance doesn't stand at the arena entrance for nothing). There was the sound of revelry by night when the square dance was in progress. And there were celebrities, like Will Rogers, observing from the stands.

It was a successful day for the Forks. Even Windy gained recognition of a sort. He was voted the bigggest liar of the outfits camped at the reunion. The boys looked at Windy with new respect. "You'd a-thought he liked th' spread th' way he poured it on," one of them commented. "He always wanted to be knowed for somethin'." Windy had exaggerated somewhat the prowess of Pitchfork hands while he deprecated the accomplishments of the other ranches' men. "Coy could outrope that feller sound asleep." He carried the proceedings too far, though, when he made the rash statement that any Pitchfork boy could lick any three from another ranch. Three Bar X men pounced on him. They smeared the ground with him pretty well. Windy knew when he's been smeared. He hadn't noticed Slim and Jake walking up either then, so he said, "I regard this here as the highest honor I had since I won the—" he saw Slim— "mesquite cluster," he finished. On his return to the ranch he described the encounter: "Hit taken three Bar X's to handle one Pitchfork."

Above the hum of activities and the clank of spurs, we waited for Anne McGuire. The crowd was laughing and sizzling in the July heat. We cheered and groaned when Anne came in riding Dally Welte. She was carrying a flag. We wondered how Dally would react to a flag. The question before the grandstand, at least the Pitchfork section, was whether she could stay on the horse, wave her hat, smile, and keep her seat at one and the same time. She did for awhile. Suddenly her hat flew off, but when she bent down to pick it up she made a sweeping salute to the crowd. The gesture brought a roar of applause from the stands, especially from the Pitchfork section.

All the big outfits sent their chuck wagons and wagon cooks. Picnic tables groaned under mouth-watering food: barbecue, son-of-a-gun stew, potato salad, cabbage slaw, stuffed eggs, fresh corn on the cob, baked beans, fried pies, a variety of cakes and ice cream with iced tea, soda pop, beer, and hot coffee to drink. The Pitchfork menu always included sourdough bread and pumpkin bread, for which our cook was famous.

Roy Mayo, known to us as Slug, was something of a power on the Pitchfork, and he knew it. He was our "hood," which meant that he kept the fires going at the chuck wagon, hauled water, looked after the team and harness, and did such a variety of jobs that he simply called himself the assistant to the cook. In a society of individuals, he was one of the more unusual. The highlight of Slug's career came at the reunion that same year.

Nearly every cowboy regards his ranch as something special, but Slug's pride in the Pitchfork and his loyalty to D was touching. Sometimes his loyalty almost overreached itself. He was an ardent admirer of General Patton, having served under him in the Second World War. He fondly reminisced about Patton and praised the Pitchfork whenever he could get an audience. Everyone from North Camp to Croton agreed that we had found our permanent assistant cook.

Hoods have come and gone on the ranch, but Slug remains our all-time favorite. His courtesy and consideration for visitors was an unusual trait not often found among cowboys. Many tourists at the Forks had never seen a cow or calf except in the movies. "Shore a job to milk," Slug would explain to them as he opened a can of Carnation. They were in for a lot of information and conversation when Slug was appointed to take them on a ranch tour.

In 1947 he couldn't have been happier than he was there at the Pitchfork wagon in Stamford talking to two reporters about "his spread." He had an enthralled audience with their pencils poised, hanging on his every word. They were not talking to Coy or D Burns. They were talking to him, Slug Mayo. It was the first time he had ever been interviewed. He was making the most of it. Slug wasn't smiling as he answered their questions, but one knew he was mighty pleased. The Pitchfork was his ranch, Mr. Burns was his boss, and cowboying was his game. He was giving his all. Reporters might not pass his way again. An interested bystander, a friend of ours, gave D this account.

"Where is the Pitchfork Ranch?" the reporter asked innocently enough. "You don't know where the Pitchfork is?" came from an incredulous Slug. "No," the reporter answered. He knew he had gotten off to a bad start and tried to make amends by saying he'd heard a lot about it, but just didn't know quite where it was. "How big is the Pitchfork?" was his next question. "It's a big son-of-a-gun," and Slug told it big. "Why, even the boys that've worked there for years ain't seen all of it." "I guess you'd have to use planes to work a ranch that big?" was his final query. "Naw," Slug avowed.

"We work cattle jest like they done fifty years ago, and that's the way me an' Mr. Burns aims to keep it."

Later that same evening, Slug and his sidekick, Riley Thacker, were having a few drinks at a beer joint just outside the town. Several local men plied him with further questions about the ranch. Slug's responses left them impressed with the dimensions of the Pitchfork (about four times its actual size). "I didn't re'lize the Pitchfork was *thet* big," one fellow stated. "I reckon it must be as big as the King Ranch?" Naw" Slug said, "it ain't as big, but it's jest a better outfit. A heap better managed, got better hands, an'—" Riley interrupted, "Come on, Slug. We better git outa here, afore you sell 'em the ranch, an' we'll both be out of a job."

27

Byrd Cochran

The day had been bleak and depressing. With bodies bent to the force of the wind we made our way to the chuck house, arms held before our faces as shields against the biting cold. The crowd in the dining room was smaller than usual, as most of our crew was working late putting out feed, shifting some poor cows to the brakes for protection. The radio had been issuing livestock warnings for twenty-four hours. Already our light system was out of commission, and lamps burned dimly in the long room. It was disappointing to find so few in for supper. I had counted on the banter of the cowboys to lift the somber mood that had been with me all day.

At first, we did not see our visitor, but as we took our places at the table, he rose and introduced himself. "I'm Byrd Cochran," he said. "I came down to see my boy, but figgered I'd best spend the night here at headquarters after it got so bad." His voice was low pitched, but vibrant. He could have been fifty or seventy; he could have been a lawyer, an actor or a preacher, this small white-haired father of Dee Cochran's. His face held our interest.

"Worst weather we've seen in a hell of a spell," the chore man said. Then, mingling with the gale-like wind that beat at the window panes, we heard the unbelievable words: "It was just such another day as this that I was buried." A feeling of fey ran through the half-lit room. Nobody blinked an eye; expectancy filled the air. The speaker was not a headless ghost, but his statement was just as spooky and unbelievable. Each person felt Byrd Cochran spoke to him. Now a dozen pair of eyes turned in startled amazement "Buried?" someone had the temerity to ask. "Six foot deep," our guest answered quietly. The evening was not destined to be a dull one. "But when?" "Where?" "Why?" We had found our tongues. We plied him with questions. It was a strange tale he had to tell, and he told it simply but fully aware that his listeners were spellbound.

"I got into some trouble years ago. It wasn't of my makin' or to my likin', but I had to shoot my way out." He had the frankest, bluest eyes I had ever seen and a voice so soft that it didn't seem possible that presently he could be saying, "I shot him once through the neck and twice through the heart."

It gave us an eerie feeling to be talking with one who had risen from the grave. Jeet, his chin propped in his hand, elbows resting on the table, turned ashy gray. The words were ominous to him. He'd had a week-long premonition that something was going to happen. He had told us of the presentiment. Mandy had thought the trouble lay in his liver, but Jeet knew his signs, and this was the fateful moment. Like one in a trance, he waited for the voice to continue.

As the story was drawn slowly out, we heard that Byrd Cochran had once surprised a bunch of cattle rustlers butchering a neighbor's cow over in New Mexico. "This neighbor was a widow and our friend, and she looked to me for help. It would've been a bad place to have my gun stick, for I had to kill two of them before it was over, but I fired in self-defense. The minute they saw me ride up, they started shootin' at me from ever' direction. The Bible says, 'Thou shalt not kill.'" he quoted reverently, "an' I never taken a life unless I had to. Another man's life don't make an easy piller at night.

"A third man was killed during that mix-up," he said, "but not by my gun. I got the blame for it, though, and his widow offered a $10,000 reward for my body." He told us that a warrant was issued for his arrest and that four good men had gone his bond. But ten thousand dollars was a lot of money in those times, and he knew that somebody would plug him for that bundle if he stayed in New Mexico. So he brought his wife, ill of tuberculosis, and their babies back to Aspermont, Texas, where they had once lived and still owned a farm. But he knew he had to go back and stand trial some day, and he knew his chances of coming out alive were very slim.

No words of mine can give you the picture of this frail, intense man as he sat at that table telling us his story. His life had been one of almost constant drama; a friend had written a book about it, *The Little Rooster;* the state of Texas had sent him to the penitentiary. But let me give you this story as nearly as I can in his own words.

"I never was afraid of any man for myself," he said. You felt that this was true as you looked into his fearless, unblinking eyes. "But I couldn't stand the thought of my children loose on the world. I was tellin' this to Charley, the man my place was rented to. He was my friend. He knew me well and all about my trouble in New Mexico and that I had to go in just four days to stand my trial.

"While we were sittin' there talkin', it come to him that there was a way out without hurtin' nobody, a way fer me not to go back, but we had to act quick. Our plan would release my bondsmen and save me from certain death. Charley and his wife Rosie would help, and Rosie's sister and her husband would help too. They knew a kind of paste that could make a feller look like he was dead. When the four of them come to my house that night, and we told Wife what we were aimin' to do, she said she didn't have long to be in this world, and she didn't want to have anything like that on her conscience. She didn't think it was honest. We argued with her for hours, but she wouldn't give in, so my friends went on home, but I asked them to leave those powders. I knew I could mix 'em up and put them on myself. When they were gone, I took Wife's hand and told her, 'You haven't got but a few months to live. When I go to New Mexico and get killed, what will become of our children?' We had five. The baby was seven months old, and our oldest child was just ten. It was about eleven o'clock at night when she give in. She went to the phone and called the doctor. 'Byrd's mighty sick. Can you come right away?'

"He didn't live far, and we knew he'd be there in no time. I took off all my clothes and stood on the porch naked until he drove the car into the yard; then I run and jumped into th' bed. Wife had put about six quilts on it, and I started groaning and talking like I was out of my head. It wasn't hard. My teeth was chatterin' so you couldn't understand me, for it was the coldest night we'd had in many a year.

"The doctor felt me all over and tried to take my temper'ture, but when he'd turn around, I'd spit th' thermometer out of my mouth. I wouldn't swallow the medicine or the whiskey he tried to force down me. He told Wife, 'I don't think Byrd will make it through the night; he's already gettin' cold. I've got a baby case ten miles from here, and I have to go. If he's alive in the morning, call me and I'll come by.'

"Before daylight next morning, Wife called Charley and Rosie and told them over the party line telephone that I was dead. They came, bless their hearts, just as soon as they could, and Rosie's sister and her husband was with 'em. I had already put the dope on my face and neck and even my hands. They said they felt like they was talkin' to a ghost when I opened the door and asked them in. We had to work fast, as we knew a call at six o'clock in the morning would have every ear on the party line glued to the phone for the news, and some of 'em would be showin' up soon.

"The men had to see about a coffin and gettin' the grave dug and arrangements made for the funeral, the preacher and all. They'd say they was having the burial that same day on account of Wife's health. The women started paddin' up a ironing board they could use to lay me out on, and I laid on that coolin' board from six till eleven, when the casket came. Sure enough, neighbors started droppin' in; three women came and pulled up the sheet and kissed me. Their tears fell on my face. I was scared to death them tears was going to cause that concoction to run. I was proud that two of them women kissed me, proud that they thought that much of me, but I never cared much for Mrs. Caperton kissin' and cryin' over me. It tickled me though and I come near to laughin', because she waited until ever'body else was out of the room before she kissed me. I allus thought she was half sweet on me.

"One thing though, I was sorry about. A feller come that I thought a heap of, an' he was feelin' mighty bad about me being gone. I wanted to tell him I was all right, but his wife was a great one to talk, so I jest had to let him stand there thinking I was dead. Man, it was cold layin' there so still. I had on some heavy wool underwear or I'd a froze.

"But just to show you, Sister," he looked straight into my eyes, "that what we was doin' was not contrary to th' Lord's will, th' only casket that could be bought thereabouts was big enough for a three-hunderd pound man, so it give me lots of air and plenty of room to turn around in. The women got a chance, as soon as the casket was brought, to close the door to the room I was in and put two inner tubes pumped full of air under the lining, one on each side of the casket where I could reach the valve stem. I might not be sittin' here talkin' to you right now, if it hadn't been for Rosie, bless her heart. She put some matches under the lid of the coffin to let the air in and jest fastened one latch on it. Cold as it was I didn't need to let any air out of them tubes until they had me covered up with dirt. It was so snowy and thick cloudy that it took 'em well nigh till night to get the grave dug. My friends shoveled like mad to get the job finished and so did the rest of the men. They were freezin' and wanted to go home. All this time I was layin' in the casket waitin' for 'em to bury me. They held services at the house, so when they took the casket with me in it to the cemetery, they just had a short prayer and a song and was gone. It sure gave me an eerie feelin' to be layin' under that dirt.

"My helpers had gone to th' cemetery gate with the rest of the fun'ral crowd; they was sixty-three people at the grave. Then one of 'em said: 'We left our shovels. You all go on home. It's jest a piece to Miz Cochran's; we're going back fer a minute.' Wife was too sick to go to the burial.

"Well, they come back and hid out by some brush until it was dark enough for 'em not to be seen. The worst thing against us was a house about a hunderd an' fifty yards away, but that's why I say the Lord was with us; cold as it was, nobody ever come out of it. Well, as soon as they dared, they come back to the grave an' started diggin' me up. I heard a spade hit th' boards of th' casket box, an' it was a good sound. I was beginnin' to sweat, but I still had air in them tubes, and I'd been under th' ground an hour an' twenty minutes. We went back to the house after makin' sure nobody was around, an' I hid out while Charley went to Post and bought me a car. I was anxious to get to New Mexico and let my bondsmen know that I was alive. Word had been wired to the sheriff there that I was dead. As soon as I could, I headed west. I went straight to the Big Man's house, hid my car in some thickets, and walked in the door. They were eating supper. Big Man was sittin' at th' head of the table an' saw me when I came in. He dropped his cup in his plate, an' set there buggin' his eyes lookin' at me. Th' others turned around, saw me, and jest froze, never moved a hand or nuthin'. Soon's they realized I was still alive, them buggers like to have beat me to death, they was so proud to see me.

"Next, I lit out for Kansas and worked there under another name till after Christmas. Then on the first of February, I went to see my brother. His mouth come open, but he never said nuthin' for sev'ral minutes, then he said, 'You look like Byrd, but Byrd's dead.'

"'No, I'm not dead,' I said, but what did that bugger do but jump into his car and left out. When he came back, he filled me in on my family. Said that they were in need of funds and that relatives had been keepin' them up. An insurance representative had seen Wife about my life insurance policy, but she wouldn't accept the money because she didn't believe in insurance. 'Besides that money will not bring Byrd back.' Fin'ly though, relatives persuaded her to collect th' insurance."

Byrd Cochran was getting near the end of his story. The children had sat bug-eyed listening to his stirring tale. Burns listened with hushed fascination. "I'm not a-scared—much." He leaned closer to me. Like a man fighting a spell, Jeet had struggled against looking at Byrd, but he had lost, and not only his glazed eyes, but his whole body had turned toward the ominous stranger with the intense blue eyes.

Byrd went on to inform us that on March 28 he had visited his family and had convinced his wife to turn over five thousand dollars of the insurance money to him. He wanted to buy a little place near Menard in the sheep country. He reminded her that she hadn't very long to live, and the children would be needing a place after she had passed away. It was not long after his purchase and after her death that Byrd Cochran was recognized on the streets of San Angelo by an acquaintance who informed Aspermont Sheriff Bingham of the encounter, Mr. Bingham said, "I don't see how that could be. I was a pallbearer at his funeral, I saw him lying in his casket." Because of these facts no investigation was made. But the informant knew that he had talked with Byrd Cochran and so took his story to the insurance agency. Immediately the insurance company took steps to ascertain the truth, and Sheriff Bingham with two black men went out to the cemetery to do some digging. The casket yielded no corpse.

It was past midnight when Byrd Cochran came to the end of his story. On the way home, little Cuppie said, "That was a shuddery story Mr. Cochran told, wasn't it?"

"He gave us quite an evening," D admitted as he stood before the fire when we were back at the house. We agreed that our friend had a penchant for the melodramatic and that the staring mesmeric quality about his eyes (I never saw him blink them) contributed considerably to his effectiveness as a narrator. Like the Ancient Mariner, he had held us with his glittering eye.

Suddenly I remembered something that had happened in my childhood. "D," I said, "I remember Governor Pat Neff sitting in our home telling my father the story of Cochran's trial. Little did I dream that one day I'd see this man, as Burns would say, 'in person.'" He had told his story extremely well, leaving none of us in doubt of his heroism in face of danger and his gallantry toward womankind. But Byrd Cochran's story, as he told it to us, was sometimes at variance with the newspaper accounts at the time and with the considered judgments of a jury. He did, however, tell us that the state of Texas had sent him to the penitentiary for two years.

Later it occurred to me that this gothic episode would go well into my journal. So I lost no time asking his permission to use it. Here it is: "this is to sertafy that I B. J. Cockran have given Mrs Dee Burns my Permishan to use my Name and the Storry of My Burrial—B J Cochran."

28

Little Tex

Every time I think of this story and start to write it, something takes place in my chest—a tightening, a hurting—and before me a blond young man with the frankest smile appears, just as he did that morning as I sat shelling peas on the screened porch. Then tears blur my eyes and blind me as I relive the awful moment that I last saw him.

I will tell you of Tex. That is not his real name, but he really exists and for a time worked on the ranch. Tex, our little pug-nosed beloved Tex, is no longer with us. He became ill and had to go home, but the memory of him is one of the bright spots of those dark days.

He came to the ranch through an employment agency and gave D a real turn by not asking what his salary would be. "Pay me what you feel like I'm worth to you," he said. "And put me wherever you need me most." He'd been accustomed to "I don't want nuthin' but a ridin' job" or "I could make that much sittin' down" from fifteen-year-olds who had never sat a horse or men too old to get on one. When D had recovered from the shock, he put Tex on the Caterpillar.

It was about this time that I fell heir to the cooking job at the chuck house. The cook just walked over one Sunday morning about ten o'clock and said, "I'm checkin' it to you." He was already packed. We'd had to send a truck two hundred miles to go get his household goods when he came to the ranch, but now he had every stick of furniture and his family on or in that Ford. (He came back about a year later and asked for a job, but he didn't get on. D's funny that way.)

We had twenty-two mouths to feed, and it was right in the middle of one of the hottest summers Texas had known for years. I sent out an SOS. Frances came and helped for ten days. When she was ready for the hospital, my sister and "Ann-aguire" came to my rescue.

We'd get up at five in the morning, gather corn, okra, lettuce, cucumbers, tomatoes, onions, squash, and beets while it was cool, scald, pick, and dress ten to twenty chickens, and make bread and some sort of dessert, generally bread pudding, cobblers, or custard. We tried to cook enough in the middle of the day so we wouldn't have to fire up the big range (so cozy in winter but like an inferno in the summer) in the evening too.

After supper when the blazing sun had gone down, we'd go once more to the garden, this time to gather snap beans and black-eyed peas for the next day's meal, and no matter how long and hard the day Tex had put in, he'd join us there, nor would he leave until the last bean was snapped or pea shelled. Sometimes it would be eleven o'clock before we'd finish. Sitting here under the stars, on the screened porch, was the only pleasant part of our day. Before saying goodnight, Tex would move the hose once more. I'd keep the water running on the parched plants until about one.

For about a year Tex dutifully and loyally helped us on the ranch. It surprised us that a hand so capable, able-bodied, strong, and willing to work was not in the army, but Tex was 4-F. Once when I complained, eyes streaming, that wind and sun gave me sniffs and sneezes, Tex said, "I'd as leave be dead." He inordinately valued his health, perhaps because he sensed the precarious state of his mental grasp. Ed, recognizing his worth, said that Little Tex had "a lot of untaught sense, a lot of smart."

But one week after a trip to Spur, Tex came in with a friend he had met. D put him on, but with indifferent results. Tex's friend was not much help.

Next weekend Tex and his buddy went to town but did not return for work on Monday morning. Soon the sheriff called, saying that the two were being held as suspects in a picture-show robbery. They were in the Dickens jail. Surely it was not true that Tex, whom we had loved and counted on, was behind bars, no longer trusted by his fellows, no longer free to go and come at will, to stretch on the grass, or to walk in the bright sunshine. Concrete walls and steel were not meant for Tex. D was away. The sheriff called again, saying that Tex was asking for me, and, against Coy's better judgment, I went to see him.

The old two-storied jail at Dickens is an appealing, even

pleasant-looking structure. Mellowed by time and covered with ivy, it seems almost inviting. The fact that the sheriff's family lived under its roof made it seem even friendlier. I went inside. The sheriff advised me to be wary, told me that the man behind bars was not quite right, and directed me to the cell where Tex was imprisoned.

Looking out between those gray iron bars were two hungry, burning eyes instead of the placid, candid blue ones I expected to see. The door creaked. There was a cough. His eyes—I noticed nothing but his eyes—were animal's eyes now. That he would be a danger to those about him, I could not forget. He kept his hat on, and he threw pieces of coal across the room as he walked back and forth, back and forth, talking with me. His face had the look of a hurt lost child.

He heard my words. He answered them, but he was beyond their influence. The face I was looking into was mad. I had heard that mad man scream when I approached the little box of a cell.

I returned to the ranch, much unsettled and filled with a nameless horror at Tex's transformation. Mandy was sympathetic. She too was fond of Tex. "If only there were something we could do," I grieved. "Let's pray, Miz Burns," she suggested. Mandy prayed wherever she was, whatever she was doing. "Let's jest ask God to keep him in mind."

Not too many days afterward, a face appeared in the door, a face needing a shave and smeared with coal dust. It was Tex standing there in the doorway. Floyd stepped back behind him and spun his index finger in the direction of his head. According to Floyd, who had been with him earlier that day, Tex had been muttering indecencies, he who would never utter an unseemly word. Tex put an envelop in my hand; it was addressed to me. The sheets inside it were covered with words, but they had no meaning. Little Tex was quite mad.

In his right hand he held two twenty-dollar bills and a five. And giving them to me in a lucid moment, he said, "I came to pay you, Mrs. Burns, and to thank you for letting me have this money. And to say good-bye. You all have been mighty good to me, and I won't forget you."

We have not seen him since. It was reported that he left the country, taking with him a girl from Dickens whom he had been courting. Later we heard that he had been arrested in Fort Worth for vagrancy. The last information—apart from undecipherable letters that he sent us, scrawled in wild and whirling words—was that Tex had been put in a mental institution in Wichita Falls.

29

Jake and Slim and Others

Bank Night

One of the most momentous events that has happened on the ranch (at least it has brought on the most discussion) was when Jake won the five hundred dollars on Bank Night at the picture show. "I aim to collect half of that or take it outta his hide," Slim threatened. The reason it mattered so much to Slim was because of the last time Jake had won big.

"Jake can't write, but he slings the goldurndest X in the country," said the banker at Paducah, who claims Jake has had an account with him since the rodeo where he'd lost his roll from an all-night poker game. In that game Jake so expertly cleaned the waddies of their winnings in the rodeo events that next morning they all had to borrow money from him to buy their breakfast. "At the regular rate of interest," Jake said.

This bankerish streak in Jake did not endear him to his fellow workers. Cowpokes are a generous breed, blowing their pay as Slim did one Saturday at the circus for twenty dollars' worth of peanuts or lending it to a pal with equal indifference. "He's so by-God stingy he won't eat enough lessen he's wropped around a chuck wagon," Slim said of Jake, "and he can outfumble any human bein' you ever seen at a pitcher show winder." So the guffaws were loud and long when Slim, coming up on Jake fondling his poker-winning greenbacks, grabbed the entire roll of bills out of his hands and, yelling like a banshee, threw them high into the air.

"Why you son of a —," the astonished Jake began. "What'd you want with money?" Slim drawled as he sauntered off, "you don't never use none." Slim maintains until this day that it was entirely by accident that so many Pitchfork hands were standing around to gather up the five, ten, and twenty dollar bills, but no one is convinced, least of all Jake.

But just a few weeks later there were groans aplenty when word got around that Jake had hit the jack pot on Bank Night. "A five-hundred dollar bill," one ranny lamented, "God a'mighty, he'll shore be hard to git along with now. Interest'll go up." But Jake took riches in his stride. When D congratulated him on his good fortune, he just shifted his tobacco from one cheek to the other and said, "Wal, hit all goes to prove ya cain't keep a good man down, but I ain't a gonna let hit make no fool out of me, Mr. Burns. I'm gonna keep right on a-workin'."

Christmas Drawing

"Jest leave me outta the drawin'," Jake said when the box with the names of every person on the ranch in it was set before him. This meant Jake would buy no gift for the Christmas tree, and there would be no gift on it for him.

Jake had taken part in the exchange of gifts until now. We knew what had happened. Last Christmas, strangely enough, the tight-fisted Jake and the tight-fisted Windy had drawn each other's names. The boys said, "Justice couldn't a been done no better." They said, "Hit'll be a draw between them two, who can spend the least. Both of 'em is tight as a pair of Levis."

We had set a price limit on the gift purchase, a modest two-fifty. But Jake and Windy had been accustomed to spending a shy twentieth of this amount. Jake drew my name the third Christmas we were here. He went all out for me—blew himself, the others declared, and I was impressed—a lawn handkerchief with a cluster of pink and blue flowers in the corner, with the nineteen cent price tag conspicuously left on.

It was supposed to be a carefully guarded secret whose name one drew. But one way or another it always leaked out. Once little Burns shrieked, "I'll tell everybody but Coy whose name I got."

And word got around in no time that Jake would spend his dime on Windy and Windy would buck off his money on Jake. The ranch accepted the news joyfully. Windy and Jake took it abysmally. "I ain't expectin' much," Jake said. "I'll go down for the eggnog," was Windy's comment.

Between them it was agreed that a pint of liquor would be a mighty fine and useful thing for each to present the other. They'd be needin' it anyhow, and they wouldn't be out nuthin' on Christmas gifts.

It was known that two squarish packages, tagged for Jake and Windy, were placed under the tree well in advance of the big occasion. They had been discussed, shaken, and their contents speculated upon at each meal. The shimmering tree stood in one corner of the chuck house dining room, packages on and around it. The boys said, "I guess this here's from Teeny, Jake." They said it Thursday night, but at the tree Friday evening those two packages were missing.

"Jake's worried considerable about them boxes," Coy said. "He halfway believed Windy got 'em hisself. Then he remembered that all of us boys wakened up with a headache Friday morning 'ceptin' him and Windy."

Jake was grumpy about it, as if he just couldn't enjoy Christmas jokes, and was in a mood to trust neither his enemies nor his friends. Slim was capable of mischievous intentions, he believed, and he'd believe anything of Tom Dowdy where two pints of liquor were involved. "That there was Three Feathers Whiskey, an' it don't grow on bushes," Jake complained. "You'd better change to Four Roses, hit does. And let them chickens alone," he was advised. Jake was so sobered by the loss of his liquor and the effect on his pocketbook that he didn't smile all during Christmas. The boys said, "When Jake smiles, you know the joke's on the other feller."

"Aw, you'd gripe if they was goin' to hang you with a new rope," Slim told him. Then, his voice indulgent, "Jest take the price of that whiskey offa that two hundred and fifty you owe me. I can afford to lose it better'n you can, I reckon." At the mention of the two hundred and fifty dollars Jake's face became graver still. He'd never been sure whether Slim was in earnest about wanting half of that Bank Night money. "Just because he'd paid my way in to the show doesn't mean he—hell, that lucky number was on my ticket. That money belongs to me!"

Jake was surprised when his name was called and a package was handed him from the tree. He looked at the card it bore and sidled up to Slim to ask him who it was from. He wouldn't have asked anyone else for the world, admitting that he couldn't read. Slim's lips formed the words "the Burns."

Jake just stood there and turned the wallet over in his hands, feeling the leather. Finally he put it in his pocket, after smoothing out a wrinkled dollar bill and carefully tucking it inside. He took it out and looked at it a time or two before he walked over to where we were standing and asked, "You put my name in the drawing? That how come you give me this hyar?"

"Why no, Jake," I answered. "We just wanted you to have a gift on the tree." He didn't say "much obliged" or "hit's sure nice" as most of the others would have done. He said, "That's what I figgered." He said it gruffly to hide what he felt. It was one of the nicest thank you's I have ever had. His real thanks was in his eyes.

The Lady Barber

One day a visitor announced that our neighboring town had a lady barber. The cowboys perked up—a lady barber! They hadn't noticed how careless they had been about their toilet, went around rubbing their chins. "Shore need a shave," they'd say. The boys became customers at once, took to shaving more often, all but Jake. No by-God woman'd shave him or cut his hair, he vowed, scowling. The boys reported the barber a beauty, a palomino, and as sweet-stepping a filly as ever was. Her prices were a little above average, but her work was well worth it. Jake said Veto could still cut hair. He knew the value of a dollar too well, he let it be known, and he wasn't one to toss his money about reckless, he added practically. But that was before Jake had seen her. The very next Saturday the boys discovered Jake lying in the barber chair, a steaming turkish towel covering his face. Slim, who had also learned the value of the dollar, placed one in the hand of the fair barber, waved her into the curtain at the back of the shop, and took over at Jake's head.

Slim ran his fingers softly over Jake's face, gave him gentle little pats, waved a delirious smelling pomade above his nose. Jake was not given to flirtations with young ladies. He did not reach for the hand that was carressing his cheek. He lay perfectly motionless while the towel was removed. But Slim said, "I've missed a gilt-edged bet if he wasn't purring inside. Anyways, I couldn't stand that silly look he had on his face no longer, so I lets go— He'd let go and slapped Jake almost out of that barber chair. Feeling was not so good between them for a while after that. Jake was still mad when they got back to the ranch.

"I'm a notion to throw ever'thing in this room that don't belong to me out in that hall," he fumed. Slim took this calmly, even hopefully. "Lay that two hundred and fifty bucks right on top of them things," he suggested. Jake wasn't that mad. But his manner implied that if folks just left him moderately alone, it might be healthier for everybody. Jake said something always happened when he went anywhere with Slim, usually to him. Jake was a poor sport where money was involved, and he couldn't take a joke. But when there was work to be done, he carried his end of the load.

Cookie

For a time Jake had substituted as cook at the wagon. Tood Arthur was sick and had to be away for a few days. Jake didn't mind the work. Besides he was getting a few dollars extra. (A good wagon cook makes more than the average cowhand.) But he dreaded the ribbing that he knew he'd have to take from Slim and the rest. It began the very first day. The boys all tipped their hats as they started for their horses. "Good-bye, Miss," they said politely, and "Good-bye, Cookie," they called back. They all came in early for dinner. They had almost broken their necks to be ahead of time.

"Ain't chuck done yet?" they asked. "I've got belly cramps." They went straight to the coffee. "Saaay, Cookie—you don't call this coffee. It's weaker'n rainwater and cold as hell." Jake didn't have the beans ready. It takes hours to cook red beans and the boys hadn't been gone any time. "No beans?" they bellered. "Why this here's worse'n the Sixes." Some of the 6666 Ranch boys were help-ing that day.

"Boys," Ed asked, "have you met Miss Lucy?" Jake's face was as red as the coals of his fire, but he never looked up. As the punchers were leaving the wagon and Jake was bending over the pot to get some coffee, Slim dropped a kiss on the back of his neck and added throbbingly, "Good-bye, sweetheart." Jake grabbed that coffee pot and without a word slung everything in it, grounds and all, over his shoulder and right into Slim's face. Never had anyone acted so rashly where Slim was concerned. A sudden quiet fell on the noisy crowd. No one moved until they saw Slim's slow grin. Then Jack Meyers yelled, "If you'd a kept your coffee hot, you'd a scalded a skunk right there." Slim's shirt was dampened, but not his humor.

One foot in the stirrup, he called out as he rode away, "And cook my beans upside down. I'd rather have the hee-cups."

"Mr. Burns," Jake said, unsmiling, and those were the first words he had uttered. "I ain't taken' no more offa Slim." Jake was in a fury. D knew that Jake meant just what he said. When he followed them to the pasture, D warned Slim and the boys that they would be cooking for themselves if they didn't let up on Jake.

That night Slim did everything he knew to get Jake in a good humor. Though never amiable or given to much joking, Jake was pleased at his companions' hearty enjoyment of his tunes. He sang on all occasions. Slim said, "If they ain't no occasion comes up, why Jake jest makes him one." He was especially pleased, as a rule, when Slim asked for "Thet Lonesome Trail," but this night Jake pretended not to hear when Slim called, "Now my song." He was finally lured out of his silence by requests from the other boys. His plaintive style went straight to their hearts, and he sang all the songs that the cowboys loved. Finally came Slim's favorite. As the last notes of the yodel died away, Slim said, "You've got to sing that song at my funeral, cowhand." The words hung in the stillness, but only for a moment.

Then Jake snapped, "Hit'd be a pleasure." The boys roared. Slim's roar was loudest of all. With the flattery of their laughter in his ears, Jake's good nature was restored. He had outwitted Slim, the champion. He had won their approval—and Slim's.

A Knight off the Range

"Say, Jim, they's a wisdom-bringer over at Dumont's you orta drop yore rope on. She's purty as a speckled pup," Slim joked.

"Been thinkin 'bout hangin' my hat up over at Johnson's," answered Jim with a sly grin. It was well known that Slim had his eye on Jenny Jo Johnson, so this started things rolling.

"Oh yeah, meant to tell ya, Slim, I seen a saddle-warmer over there a Sunday chinnin' up to that gal," Veto put in.

"Gettin' ready to get his horns clipped," was Slim's sardonic reply.

"I heared they was in town Monday, huntin' parlor attire."

"Jest loose head," answered Slim, "that gal's a fool about me. He ain't got a look-in."

"I'll tell you who shore 'nuff is sweet on Slim, an' that's Teeny Widener." Teeny weighed in at two hundred; she had long been claimed as a Pitchfork girl (always as the other fellow's). "She's Jake's gal," countered Slim. "Couldn't horn in on him." Jake really had been seen sitting on the Widener's porch several Sunday afternoons. "But he don't aim to marry nobody lessen Ida's clothes'll fit 'em." Slim continued. Ida was Jake's dead wife, and he had every stitch of her clothes in a trunk in his room. "Ever' pocket handkerchief," Slim declared. Whether he'd kept them out of sentiment or with an eye to future economy was a matter of conjecture among the boys.

About this time Jake came into the chuck house. "Yeah, he's purty hard to sleep with lately, too," Slim began as soon as he was sure of Jake's attention. "Las' night he throwed both arms around me, a strangle hold, an' sez, 'Got my brand on you, Bunny, and that's somethin' won't come off in the wash.'"

"Effen I loved a liar," said Jake, "which I don't, yo're the one I'd be a huggin'."

"Ain't nothin' as I can see wrong with that little sorrel-top filly of Jim Braden's."

"She can shore shake a ankle at a shindig."

"Nuthin' wrong 'ceptin' yo're liable to git a smoke built under yore hoofs, and Jim keeps a dawg, too."

"That's the trouble with gals that's got ancestors," put in Jack, "Now me, I goes in fer orphans." A roar greeted this remark, and the jibes went round the table. There was a story behind the laughs. Jack turned every color.

"Danged if he don't," whooped Slim. "Spoke outta turn that time, didn'cha cowboy?" asked Ed. "I never woulda said that," from Veto. "Ain't heerd that word since last March at Cowtown," another spoke up, slapping his sides.

The boys swore that Jack had spied a pretty girl standing alone beside the ticket window at the Fat Stock show and inquired coyly, "Do yore mama know yo're out, Little One?" Her plaintive, "Mister, I'm an orphan," went straight to his heart and his hand went straight to his pocket. "Make it a couple" he said, "O.K. by you?" "Suits me," she nodded.

Slim said, "He acted like the rest of us was ever'where but

present, grabbed him an armful of pillers, programs, peanuts, an' crackerjacks and sez, 'Come on, Bunny, this here's our night to howl.' Old Jack was spreadin' a big loop an' feelin' like a top roper after a fancy ketch, he shore was sage-hennin', an' then a shadder feel between 'em, a six-foot shadder, ringy as a pawin' bull an' shootin' questions faster'n anybody could answer. Some of 'em was plain upsettin'. Like when he ast who Jack was. Of course the girl didn't know Jack's name yet, and Jack didn't know it hisself, either, fer a minute er more, the atmosphere was gettin' so thick.

"Jack knowed right off he'd seen this mug before, but where he couldn't recollect. Jack got a little riled hisself and asked, 'Come to think of it, who're you?'

"Now somethin' in the way that feller raised his arm made Jack think of the prize fight we'd seen th' night before an' it come to 'im jest in time who he was.

"'Well now,' this feller answered slow like, 'I might be 'er pappy and I might be 'er brother; it jest happens I ain't neither, but I got a legal right to set by 'er.'

"Jack whipped off 'is John B., made a low bow, provin' hisself a true knight o' the range, and said, 'Have my seat while you're doin' it. Come to think of it, hit looks purty uncomfortable to me, used to settin' in a saddle as I am. Ever out around the Pitchfork, why drop in.'

"He'd shore had the spokes takened out of his wheel. We finally decides to git 'im outta his misery. 'Hey Pitchfork,' I yelled, an' he ambled over to where we's standin', lookin' like a sheep-killin' dawg. 'They's a likely lookin' bunch of fillies settin' up there with nobody ridin' herd on'em—an' not a orphan in the bunch!'"

Slim and Jenny Jo

Supper was simply a mass attack on Slim. He had a date with Jenny Jo again. A date for the dance at Spur that meant things were looking up for Slim. Those dances at the Spur Inn were important events. Ed revealed that Slim had bathed four times that day, and borrowed twenty dollars, Jake said. The boys said the dive smelled like a barber shop, he'd doused himself with everything up there and had used nine kinds of hair oil. They sniffed him as they passed back and forth for coffee. Slim waited happy and impatient for seven o'clock. Coy said he'd about wore his watch out lookin' at it.

"Telephone, Slim," Veto trilled. He made his voice high and clear and dripping with sweetness; that voice was reserved for bunny calls. "Your 'please don't leave me, never grieve me' is on the line." "Maybe she's expectin' a headache," some one suggested. "Wants me to come earlier." Slim swaggered to the phone, picked up the receiver, and winked at us as we closed the door and started to our own house.

"They're a great bunch," D said. I knew he was thinking, as I was, how happily different things were from a year ago.

But Slim walked over after a bit to say he would take the trip to Wichita Falls that D had planned to make the next morning. "I'll leave while it's early," he said, "and I'll be around tonight if you need a fire in the furnace. The weather man says it's gonna be cold." "But, aren't you going—taking Jenny Jo to the dance?" D asked before he had time to think. "She's found a better pardner." Slim tried to laugh but failed. His face told us plainly that he was sick inside.

Slim's hurt caught at my throat. Jenny Jo didn't have to do this to Slim. They'd been through it all before. She had made her decision. Or rather Slim had made it, for the choice had been his, after all. Jenny Jo had told him that she had rather live in town. She favored an easier mode of living than a cowboy's wife would likely have to share. Now, if Slim would get a job, and she'd put it up to him that way, say, in Paducah, or Spur— Slim said to me regarding his decision, and colored when he said it, "I thought more of her than I did of cowboying, I reckon. But she couldn't a thought much of me as a city feller—not fer long."

Mandy said, "Slim coulda beat that city slicker's time. He ain't carin' over-much." She was afraid that he was.

So Slim had closed her from his mind until the night he ran into Jenny Jo and Bob Luckner at the rodeo. "Come go to the dance with us," Jenny invited and held out her hand. Slim said no reluctantly. Then said it stronger in an easy uncaring way, "No, I aim to ride tonight." And he wasn't too down-hearted, the boys gloated, over seeing them two together to win everything in the rodeo events. But Slim did go to the dance.

Each of us remember the circumstances under which we heard the news of Jenny's marriage. Later we were wont to describe in detail just where we were and what we were doing and how we felt when we knew. D told me at six o'clock the next morning as he handed me the cup of coffee that he'd brought from the chuck house. "Jenny Jo married that Luckner boy last night." His face was grave. "Does Slim know?" I asked. But D was gone. Something knotted up inside me and I hoped that I'd never see Jenny Jo Johnson again as long as I lived.

When I took the cup of untouched cold coffee in to pour it in the sink, Mandy was sitting on the kitchen stool peeling potatoes and onions for hash. There was no easy way to tell her. "Hit's beyond reason she should favor him above Slim." Mandy wiped her eyes on the corner of her apron. "Them onions is that strong," she said.

Mandy walked straight to Jeet. "She takened that other feller. Married him last night." Jeet finished spraying the rose bush before he spoke. He spit a stream of tobacco juice over his shoulder. "Mighta married him but she never choiced him."

One and all, I think, our anger flared out against Jenny Jo. When the boy had blurted out the information at breakfast, Jake said, "Damn her soul to hell!" and pounded on the table.

Slim must have heard when he came through Guthrie that Jenny Jo was married. No one on the Pitchfork ever mentioned her name to him again. But Slim knew. And he knew we knew. His forced gaiety at mealtime, the absence of his whistle as he went about his work, the relentless way in which he drove himself—and he stopped by our porch more often in the evenings.

But he did not share our resentment toward Jenny Jo. A month or so later, he came bringing Jenny Jo and Bob into the chuck house. "You coulda knocked me over with a feather," Mrs. Clary said. Slim had met the Luckners up on the highway and had invited them down to lunch.

Snipe Hunt

"Ever been on a snipe hunt?" Slim asked the new boy. The men at the table exchanged pleased glances. Hoary with age is the snipe hunting game. It works only once, but there are still folks who haven't heard of it. The men love to get hold of one who hasn't heard.

The boy shook his head. His mouth was full of food. "Bunch of us goin' tonight," Slim said, without looking up. "If you can find a tow-sack that ain't got a hole in it, you can go with us." He'd liked the 'possum hunt the night before, so the unsuspecting one answered, "Don't care if I do."

The men held a long discussion on snipes. Some liked snipes if they were cooked long enough; others couldn't stomach 'em. Jack Meyers said that last tanking crew had just about cleaned the Pitchfork out of snipes, but Coy had seen a bunch in Brushy the day before and somebody else had eaten some at Veto's, fat as butter. Ed said, "Nights are in our favor anyways. Nights got to be black as pitch before they'll run." So the old chestnut was in the fire again. They would start the hunt at seven.

Now there are variations on the snipe-hunting game, but the way it's worked on the Pitchfork, and the way it worked that night, is like this. The men, a few with tow-sacks to catch the snipes, the others as drivers, started out together. Soon the leader, Jake this time, scattered the hunters. The fall guy (our little punk) was sent in the direction of a big tree where snipes were known to roost. He was to sit still as death against the tree, making himself as much a part of its trunk as possible. The rest of the men went back to the bunkhouse, of course, as soon as the punk was on his way. All but one of them. In this case, Slim, who raced ahead, perched in the limbs of the designated tree and started a soft "hoo-hoo." When the stealthy hunter, with his bag held just as his drivers instructed him to hold it, squatted beneath the tree, Slim was supposed to drop down upon him screaming and clawing like a panther. "Some fellows have been knowed to clear half a acre of mesquite," Coy said, "when the guy falls outta the tree."

But Slim didn't fall out. He sat in that tree and "hoo-hooed," getting louder all the time, but the punk didn't show up. Jake had dealt Slim one from the bottom of the deck. He, the new boy, and the rest of the gang were sitting by a warm fire back at the bunkhouse, laughing so hard they could hardly hear Slim's "hoo-hoo." "But along about one o'clock in the morning," Jake said, and it was quite a story the way he told it, "Slim got madder and madder and louder and louder. We could hear him just as plain. He was settin' in that tree yellin' "Hoo! Hoo! Goddamit! Hoo Hoo!"

The Big Jump

Mandy stuck her head in at the door. "They's been a accident, Miz Burns, and Slim's mortally ghormed up. They want you should take him to the hospital." Mandy was just excited. She was alarmed. Nothing could hurt Slim, really hurt him. Not Slim. He was too vital, too— I hurried.

The men were standing solemn-faced around the car. As we drove away they raised their hats, the cowman's salute to an act of courage.

"Mr. Burns is in Spur. Mrs. Street's trying to locate him," Coy said from his seat beside me. Jake was kneeling in the back, his eyes fastened on Slim's face. Each time I looked at Slim he smiled, the little crinkles appeared at the corners of his eyes, but he did not try to speak.

I remembered the day I had seen a new face at the chuck-house table, how Slim had answered my smile. I tried to answer his now, but my lips stiffened at the sight of his face against the seat covers. How could Slim's brown face be so colorless? I wondered if we would ever make it to Spur. Thirty miles had never seemed so long. (Not Slim. Oh, not Slim!) I kept asking myself the same questions over and over. Could anything be done for Slim? Could Mrs. Street find D? Would he be waiting for us? D could do something. D could always do something.

"Could you go faster, Miz Burns?" Jake murmured in my ear. Dare I go faster than ninety? The steering wheel under my hand had an alarming vibration. My mind was a broken record, praying and chanting crazily, "Get us there old Buick, get us there, get us there."

D was waiting. Nurses, doctors hurrying through the halls. We huddled together, hoping against hope. At last the doctor coming toward us, shaking his head kindly, sadly. "Only a matter of minutes," he said. "I gave him something. He is not in pain." We followed Jake into the room to stand silently by his bed.

Slim seemed to see D for the first time, gave him a long, searching look. "Is this the Big Jump, Mr. Burns?" he asked, coolly, unafraid. "It might be, Slim," D answered with characteristic frankness. "Then," from Slim, "where's my pardner?" Jake stepped to his side. Slim grinned. The old mischievous twinkle came into his eyes. "Keep your coffee hot, Cookie, don't forget . . . to keep . . . your . . . coffee—"

That night one of the boys told us how it happened. "Somebody said, 'Looky yonder,' an' we seen Red Lightin' make a lunge. The new hand was thowed higher'n a kite, an' when he come down he layed still. We never knowed how bad he's hurt, but in a flash Slim's ridin' hell fer leather after the pickup to haul the boy to headquarters.

"I never seen Slim go down, jest heered Jake say 'God a'mighty!' His horse had stepped in a prairie dog hole an' Slim was under 'im. He tried to get up, but jest stumbled an' fell. When Jake gets to 'im, Slim sez, 'Better go after that pickup, pardner, looks like I ain't man enough.' When we was gettin' 'im into the car, he tried to make little of 'is hurt 'Next time I forks a horse I'll go around dog town.' There wasn't one could answer 'im, fer ever' man of us knowed by that hand on 'is chest and th' rattle in 'is throat that ol' Slim had took 'is last ride."

The funeral was Jake's planning. "We don't want no paw an' beller made out of this here. Slim was a cowhand an' a Texan, an' I ain't gonna have nobody changin' 'im now." Jake was right. Any ostentation, any credit given him for virtues he did not possess, would have been distasteful to Slim.

"We'll have jest one song, an' I'll sing hit, named 'The Lonesome Trail,'" Jake decided. "Hardly appropriate for a funeral," the director objected. "'Propriate to us as knowed 'im," Jake replied, "an' this here's a Pitchfork funeral, so we're wantin' any flowers that's sent in put on one six-foot pitchfork an' layed on 'is box."

Some felt the services should be in the church and that Slim should be buried in Spur. His grave would be tended more carefully, they argued, and the little cemetery on the hill at Dickens was so bare and lonely-looking. But Jake said, "Slim never takened much stock in church houses, the out-of-doors was more to his likin'." So we gathered beside a twisted mesquite where his coffin rested and

Slim lay, part of the sky, the sun, the grass with the wind playing on it, part of the hill in the little Dickens cemetery that overlooked the ranch.

A feeling of unreality held me; the words of the minister were lost. Small, unimportant details stood sharp and arresting. Western men with hats off, that streak of white forehead between their eyebrows and their hair, a mockingbird's piercing cry from a nearby chaparral bush, and Jenny Jo standing alone, apart from the group, her face blanched and stricken. It would not be long until her child would be born.

Mandy's glance followed mine. "Crying inside, like as not," she murmured. Then with quiet pride, "No church could a held 'em. Slim wouldn't be lonesome wherever." And then Mandy, who had shed no tears as yet for Slim, cried for Jenny Jo. A long life of living with it had taught her what it meant to give up one she had truly loved.

Jake's clear, deep-throated voice was more beautiful than I had ever heard it. He stood beside the casket of his friend, strummed his guitar, and without a break sang "The Lonesome Trail." One could almost hear the heartbeat of the Pitchfork cowhands. When the time drew near for Slim's "Powder River, let 'er buck," I think we almost expected to hear him say it, but none of us were prepared for that scalp-tingling moment when Jake threw back his head and gave, just as Slim loved it, that yelping of the coyotes and the baying of the hounds.

Next morning D found Jake sitting on the office steps. "I guess I'll shove on, Mr. Burns." This was a great surprise. Jake had been on the Pitchfork a long time; the ranch was his only home. He was a good hand, steady, reliable.

"Has anything happened, Jake, or is it because of Slim?" "Shore hit's Slim, Mr. Burns. Ain't nobody done nuthin' to me." "Slim won't be there, Jake, wherever you go." "That's jest hit. I won't be seein' 'im ever' time I turn around."

"There are sadder things than death, Jake." D put a hand on his shoulder. "Think of old Knife Buckley back in the penitentiary, Tex in the asylum, and Red eaten up with cancer. Slim spent his days in the life he loved and ended them in his saddle. He went the way he would have wanted to go." "'Out like a light,'" Jake said,

"I've heerd 'im say hit." He stood shamelessly wiping his eyes with the back of his hand, but he seemed to draw comfort from his own words. "An' he died in Texas."

"Somethin' else, Mr. Burns, how much has all this set you back?"

"All of what, Jake?"

"Th' buryin' an' ever'thing. You put 'im away nice. Hit musta cost a heap."

"Oh that's all taken care of, Jake. The Pitchfork was proud to do that for Slim."

"I aim t' take care of that. I mean, Slim's a taken care of it hisself." He pulled the five-hundred dollar bill from his pocket and swallowed hard. "Half of this was hissen. He writ th' name down."

"I'm sorry you feel you have to leave us Jake. We're goin' to miss you and Slim. We didn't have two better men. I hardly know what I'll do without you, and the ranch has never needed you more."

Jake looked up with quick interest. "Why, Mr. Burns—why, ef I'm needed—why—God a'mighty—why didn't you say so?"

30

The Forks, Then and Now

"That bathroom will be right here when you get back," D argued, holding the old suede jacket for me to put on. He'd made up his mind that I was going along that morning on the jaunt he was taking. And when D makes up his mind—

I rinsed the Dutch Cleanser off my hands, "That's just the trouble," I complained, "it will be right here and so will those cattle buyers; they might bring their wives. I should stay."

"We have four bathrooms, darling," D mimicked in that half airy, half simpering tone he always uses when he's quoting me.

This piques me no end; I may be airy, but I'm no simperer. "And every one of them could stand a good cleaning right now. I wish I could nail up about three."

"Why, Mrs. B," in mock surprise, "aren't you the little woman who was so pleased to have four bathrooms?"

"Was the little woman," I amended.

"I'll help you with 'em when we get back," he offered generously. D really means to help, too, when he says those things, but something always happens that he doesn't get back in time.

"I want to show you the tanks we're building. I think they're going to be the answer to our water problems. We're going by the Purebred Camp, too. You'll have a fit, Mayme, there's a little white-face under every bush."

I loved going with D, being carried along by his enthusiasm. It seemed to me that nothing could give a woman so grand a feeling as seeing the man she loves doing the work nearest his heart. This job was simply tailored to D's talents, and the management of the Pitchfork to him was a sacred cause. Marie Williams said he looked and sounded as though he were preaching when he talked of it. He was talking of it now.

"You can never have too much water on a ranch, Mayme." He'd made some new locations for wells that had proved to be good ones. He was jubilant over getting water in pastures where cattle had been walking a long way for a drink. A lot of pounds can be walked off that way, he says.

He showed me the forty-foot steel tubs he was using to replace the old concrete ones as they wore out, and the overflow tanks down below the big tubs against those stretches of still, hot, dry days that are sure to come in the summer when there is no wind to turn the mills. He'd made twenty- to thirty-acre clearings around each watering place. He was putting up steel-geared windmills, too, as the old wooden ones fell apart. Their wheels would turn in a lighter or higher wind than the old-fashioned varieties, D said, though it was true, as some argued, that the wooden mills would pump more gallons to the hour.

I had heard many discussions pro and con this subject at the chuck-house table. Some of them waxed warm. The boys were all for "them steel babies." Mr. Deaton, the windmiller who had been on the ranch for twenty-seven years, preferred the older type. He was no longer young and, like so many of his age, clung to the methods of other days. Steel windmills were a departure from those days. He resented every shining foot of them. "I never intend hittin' a tap on one of 'em," he declared stoutly. D thinks the chief advantage of these mills is that there is practically no upkeep, they have to be oiled only once a year, not once a week.

It is fifteen miles to the Purebred Camp. Fifteen miles of gully-jumping, winding road, and five wire gaps. "Going to remedy this and mighty quick," D said, struggling with the wire loop that seemed determined not to go over the post. "I'm going to put a cattle guard in here."

None of this "all in time" business about *your* affairs, I jeered, but not aloud. "Well, it would save a helluva lot of time," he answered defensively. Ouija had nudged him again. "I know," I answered dutifully.

I hoped that I could tell whose babies were whose when we reached the Purebred Camp. D is always provoked if I don't recognize each animal by name. D had said the new bulls certainly marked their get. These were their first calves, and D was tickled to death with them. "Just little blocks of meat," he beamed. "Little coupons," I added, smugly rangewise. Our wartime ration-burdened friends called them red points. One of those coupons came running toward the gate, tail over his back, butting at everything in sight, piching and tossing his little hind end into the air.

"That's a Forney!" I exclaimed. Then, less surely, "Isn't he?" "Right you are," D said, and his proud look named me Woman of the Year. Time to quit, I thought.

The new bulls were Real Onward, grand champion of the Nebraska Cornhuskers Futurity Sale, and Real Evan Mischief, who stood next to him in class at the same show. More money had gone into their purchase than had formerly been paid for seed stock by the Pitchfork. D felt it his responsibility that they give a good account of themselves. The calves were part of a perfect pastoral scene. To me they were adorable, cute as buttons, but D was seeing them full grown with sturdy backs and straight strong legs, the extra pounds of meat bred into those hindquarters justifying the high cost of their breeding.

He explained that next year he'd use Real Onward on Ike Domino heifers. "That cross ought to put two good ends on some real calves. R. J. Kinzer says old Ike has one of the best heads of Hereford breed and Real Onward's rump—" D becomes lyrical.

Next we saw the bright new pens with wings and cutting gates that he and Coy had planned. "We can work just twice as many cattle in the same length of time as with the old setup," he said. Familiar words. For weeks I'd heard D and Coy preening themselves because of their foresight in building these pens. They had not only provided quicker working methods, they said. These pens were safer. Fewer cattle were injured in loading chutes than ever before, and fewer hides were damaged. They had also effected great savings in shipping time. As we drove on, I couldn't help smiling at this complacency. One would almost think those two had invented cutting gates.

"Got to stop in here a few minutes." D turned into a lane that took us to a gray, weatherbeaten house. "This old fellow wants to swap me a good milch cow for one of those young bulls in the commercial herd. He called over this morning and talked to me about it."

"I thought you didn't sell Pitchfork cattle in the state," I reminded him.

"This is an exception," D answered with an amused smile. "I'm here right now because the last thing he said before he hung up was, 'And see here, young feller, mind you get on over here while I'm in the notion to trade.' He was a friend of Mr. Gardner's. I've heard he's quite a character," D went on. "This will be my first meeting with him. I'm looking forward to it, and I'm prepared to be out-traded pretty badly."

I was looking forward to knowing him, too, by now. I crawled out of the car and went to the door with D. Out of a story book, I thought, as he answered our knock and looked long into our faces. "Why bless me, I'll bet you're them young people from the Forks," he said, and threw the door open wide for us to enter. How pleasant to be placed in this category. Everything is comparative, I thought.

"Drag up some cheers and set down. I ain't so good at handlin' 'em no more." Mr. Merrill indicated the rockers with a wave of his hand. "So you're the new boss of the Forks. I been wantin' to meet you. Hit's a big job."

"There's the real boss," D's old joke, nodding toward me.

"The Forks ain't never had no woman boss," Mr. Merrill answered bluntly. I was delighted. D was getting a dose of the medicine he usually gave me. He'd meant to be funny and had been taken dead serious. "Hit takes a man, an' a good one, to hold down that job. Dan Gardner never allowed—" I glanced at D; he was beginning to squirm.

"'D'you want me, Mr. Mer'l?" Another old fellow came in at the back door, trying to adjust his eyes to the darkened room.

"Yeah, Jeff, take Mr. Burns here down thar and show him that Jersey cow. Mind you show him the right one. Got no more sense'n a jack rabbit," Mr. Merrill grumbled, as Jeff moved to obey, "but he's got 'is two legs."

I rose to go. "It's good to know you," I began.

"Set down," commanded Mr. Merrill, "that ain't business fer a woman. Besides, I want a word with you." D flashed a triumphant grin over his shoulder as he followed Jeff out the door, leaving the monkey on my back.

"Ain't nuthin' can ruin a ranch quicker'n a pants-wearin' woman." Mr. Merrill went stright to the attack. I'd not say a word, I decided. D Burns had started this thing; he could get out of it the best way he could. But D really wasn't the one under fire. The old man fell silent, regarding me thoughtfully. His eyes softened, his voice did too. "You don't look like a woman that'd try to wear the breeches," he said kindly. There was an impish twinkle in his shrewd eyes as he looked over his glasses at my Levi's. "I mean bossin' breeches," he hesitated. "Them's the ones I'm talkin' about."

"I know what you mean, Mr. Merrill. There's just one pair of bossin' breeches on the Pitchfork," I assured him, "and D Burns wears them."

Relief showed plainly on his face. "I'm proud to hear you say that, daughter, real proud. Dan Gardner'd turn over in his grave at the thought of a woman bossin' the Forks. Why, he never allowed women on the ranch hardly. A boy knowed if he went off and got married, he'd done fired hisself. He said women was troublemakers." And there's a lot to be said for his point of view, I thought, as the old man went on. "Of course he had a woman there to do the cookin' an' house work. He knowed women was all right in their place—and he kept 'em in their place. He never let one get the bit in her teeth."

I knew of this eccentricity of Mr. Gardner's, how he discouraged his boys from taking wives. Walter Chalk, who was his assistant for sixteen years, tells a tale about it. The tale is of Joe Rader, a Pitchfork cowhand, who loved both his job on the ranch and a girl named Ivy.

Now Joe so far forgot himself as to get married one Sunday, and then he spent agonizing days trying to break the news to Mr. Gardner. "Mr. Gardner," he'd commence, "I'd like to talk to you." "Oh, I say, Joe, we're mighty busy this morning," would likely be the old gentleman's comment. Or, falteringly, Joe would venture, "You know Ivy Turner, Mr. Gardner?" Mr. Gardner would silence him with, "And I say, Joe, I know her mother too." Then at last, poor Joe: "Ivy's a good girl, Mr. Gardner, she's a good cook, and—" "Eh, what?" Mr. Gardner's chuck-house help was far from being satisfactory at that particular time. "I say, I say, Joe, come into the office. Now what's all this about Ivy?" And so, the word *woman* to Mr. Gardner being synonymous with cook, Joe kept his job and his wife too. Ivy cooked on the Forks for many years.

The belief that ranch women should have no interest or authority outside the kitchen was not exactly new to me. For two years, now, the Pitchfork had been trying to get this idea across, but the notion still seemed quaint. I could not resist. "Times have changed, Mr. Merrill, women nowadays—"

"Yeah, times have changed, but women ain't."

With the unchanged tactics of unchanging woman, I shifted to safer ground. I spoke of Dan Gardner, that gallant old gentleman who had ruled the Pitchfork without fear or favor for forty-eight years. "According to legend, Mr. Gardner must have been a very stern individual. I've heard when he was here the boys had to slip off under the hill to play a game of checkers."

He puckered his forehead in remembrance. "Legend? Never heard of 'im." Then his faded eyes blazed, "And I knowed ever' man that was there in Dan Gardner's day."

"Legend," I said— I started to explain. "Wasn't there long," he burst in, "or I'd a knowed 'im.

"They warn't no kindlier, sociabler man to found nowheres," this snowy-maned, eighty-six-year-old contemporary of Mr. Gardner loyally defended his friend. "Now he was firm, had to be them days. Any reckless rider endangerin' his life or th' lives of th' other fellers was fired. They was no job on the Forks fer a fussy er overbearin' man. He hated the guts of dishonesty, an' any slicker that was dealin' from th' bottom never layed around there long. Dan Gardner'd walk right up in 'is face, 'I say, I say, by George, you've been here long enough.'

"He was a understandin' man, though, an' 'is kind heart caused 'im to feel fer the feller that had got off the track. He was allus fer givin' a young button another chance, but," Dan Gardner's old friend chuckled, "he allus thought folks from the Indian Territory'd bear watchin'. I mind a time he ast his foreman, Press Goen, 'I say, I say, Press, who's this young button I been seein' 'round here the last few weeks?'

"'That's a boy from the Indian Territory, Mr. Gardner, he come up here broke, him and 'is horse both hungry. Thought I'd keep 'im 'round till the wagon pulled out and put 'im to wranglin' horses.'

"Mr. Gardner shook 'is head like he knowed the worst already. 'I say, I say, Press, that's a damn bad place fer a boy to be from.'

"He had a fine education, too; him an' ol' man Bates was the knowin' men of these parts, an' he used what he knowed to help all of us. Ever' man in this community went to him fer advice; he was as good as any lawyer—he never lost a case in court 'cause he knowed he was right 'fore he got inta court."

Mr. Merrill paused, his tired old voice trailed off, but a reminiscent look in his eyes told me he hadn't finished. These old-timers loved to talk about Dan Gardner. Give any man who had been his neighbor or had worked for him a chance and he'd keep you for hours while he sang the praise of that grand old frontiersman. Mr. Merrill leaned forward from his wheelchair, laid a gentle hand on my arm. "Yuh never knowed him, did you?"

"No, it was not my good fortune."

"Never seen 'im?"

"No."

"Wal, you may think I'm quare, but they's sartin words as brings up pitchers in my mind, and one of them words is 'gentleman.' I ain't never made out to be one, but my Ma set great store by 'em. She was allus a showin' me pitchers outta books when I was a little shaver. She'd say, 'Now, Johnnie, this here's a gentleman, and that word means jest what it says. Gentle means ya ain't wild, it means yo're quiet and perlite-like, an' of course you know what a man is. Leastwise you orta, 'cause yore Pappy was a man—a real man. He never taken no insults offen nobody, an' never offered none neither. Now put th' true meanin' of them two words together, with a slice of book larnin' to polish 'em up, and you got a gentleman. An', son, if I live—' But she died when I was eight.

"An' when I seen Mr. Dan Gardner, I knowed I was lookin' at my idear of a gentleman. I ain't right shore I ever seen nary nuther one that jest plumb measured up. I put the question to him onct, I said, 'Dan, what's yore idear of a gentleman?'

"An' he said, 'Why I say, I say, John, a gentleman's a man, irrespective of condition.' So I reckoned as how bein' a man was the most important part of the thing to him. An' whatever was good enough fer Dan Gardner was good enough fer me."

"Did you tell him why you wanted his definition?" I asked.

"Wal, no," he answered. "He never ast, an' I reckon it'd a hacked me if he had of.

"Jim Bates, now, was a diffurnt kind of man. He was at the Forks a lot. Him and Mr. Gardner was friends, but he was a infidel.

Onct when it was turrible dry, we hadn't had no rain for months—
we never had no windmills then neither—we was scrapin' th' creek
fer water. Cows was bawlin' an' slobberin', their tongues a-hangin'
out, an' this here feller Bates starts cussin' the Almighty.

"You never heerd nothin' like it, an' it ain't fittin' I should tell
you, but one of th' men said, 'Mr. Bates, I'd be afeerd to use sich
words. I'd be afeerd th' Lord'd strike me down.'

"'Why, Christ a-mighty,' he lets out, 'if that ol' bald-headed
son-of-a-bitch can sit up there and let them cattle starve for water, I
ain't carin' what I sez about 'Im. They're His cows, ain't they?"

"Hit looked like to us, sore troubled as we was about our cows,
that he had a argyment all right, but in jest eight hours Jim Bates
was pressin' a dyin' piller there in Mr. Gardner's dugout an' talkin'
mighty kind about God." The old man gazed thoughtfully out the
window and added softly, "I wonder if it done 'im any good.

"I uster jest set an' listen to them two talk. Of course, they was
lots they said I never understood, but they was a heap I did.

"Tamers of th' wilderness, Mr. Gardner called us, an' I guess
that's what we was. Anyways, men was hardier then. Women was
hardier too. Why, when I hear these young gals allus talkin' 'bout
bein' tahrd an' traipsin' off to these here hospitals for operations, I
mind how Het done th' cookin', warshin', and' ahrnin', carded the
wool to make all of our clothes, milked th' cows, tended th' garden
an' th' babies at th' same time. An' all the other women done the
same. Most of 'em lent a hand with the feedin' up an' farm work,
too, but I never wanted Het to strain 'erself.

"Why a woman we knowed had a fallin' of 'er womb. Hit come
right out into the world an' dried up. But she warn't runnin' to no
doctor, no sirree. She just takened th' scissors an' cut it off.

"Funniest thing ever happen, I reckon, come right off here in
this room. Ivy Rader was cookin' at the Forks then, hit's a good
twelve mile from here, an' she uster ride all the way over here a
horseback to quilt. Het had th' only quiltin' frames around here
close an' all the women used 'em. They'd come onct a month an'
quilt first fer one an' then fer tuther.

"Well, Ivy never missed a meetin', not even when she was carryin' th' little 'un. Hit was kind of a joke with th' women folks. This
day I'm talkin' 'bout, her young'un was nine days old, so of course,

they knowed she couldn't make it. They was settin' down to their sewin', an' talkin' 'bout how she was gonna hate to miss th' quiltin', when in walks Ivy, big as life. She laid th' baby on th' bed, retch in 'er pocket for 'er thimble, an' 'lowed, 'Hardest job ever I done, lopin' ol' Billie an' lettin' the' baby suck at th' same time.' Yessum, women was hardier then." Mr. Merrill's eyes were quite wet with laughing "Women was hardier."

But Mr. Merrill's story was unfinished. I had failed to ask what caused Mr. Bates's death. So at my first opportunity, I rushed to Ed to see if he remembered the incident. He did, and added: "They was some as thought a bait of green apples he'd jest et give him *cholera morbus*. But most of us figgered them apples never had nuthin' to do with it."

He wondered where I had heard about Bates. I told him of my meeting with an eccentric old man and of his earthy stories. "Do you know the old gentleman, this Mr. Merrill?" I inquired. "That man murdered my father," Ed answered bluntly. I was aghast at this statement. But Ed continued, "I never pass his place without thinking I orta made him pay for all the heartaches he give Maw and us kids. Maw allus begged me to let it alone, that nuthin' I could do would bring Pa back, and I'd jest be in trouble." Ed searched his memory, his face strained with anxiety as he recalled his father. "It ain't a thing I like to talk about or remember."

It's a good many years ago now that Ed told me this account of his father's murder. The feud and its grim ending was over grass-land. It was in the time of the open range. I have since collected from old accounts certain details, but how, after half a century, can one be certain of the facts that one man's son and the other's nephew have heard and yet tell so differently?

31

The Grands

It made sense to think twice about anything that was going to make new demands on our time. As far as I was selfishly concerned, I couldn't have been happier, but what problems, I asked myself, would this create for D? "Thank God," were his words when I told him of Frances's call and her children's decision. "Bless their little hearts. We'll give it our best shot."

In February of 1948, a date stamped indelibly in our memory, the Grands (our grandchildren) came to make their home with us on the ranch. We have had many days, months, and years to be glad that they did. The peace of those quiet rooms was broken with banging doors and squeals of happy laughter. When we told them the ranch would be their home, they turned circles around the room. "For ever and ever?" Anne asked. They hugged each other. As they ran happily through the house, the children chanted, "This is our home now." When the exuberance subsided they settled down with books that had belonged to their mother, their mother's favorites.

Just to hear them splashing in the bath tub was music to me. At first they bathed in our bathroom so that I could take a look at ears, necks, and feet. At first they slept in my bedroom, Anne on a day bed in the bay, Burns on the couch. Through I was under nearly unbearable pressure, the children's coming satisfied my need for self-sacrifice and affection. I have long known that my happiness lies in what I can do for others.

The children swung into ranch living as if they had been at it all their lives. They almost had. Remember, they were just three and a half and five months old when we came here, and they had been right by our side as often as we could wangle their parent's permission. Rose-colored days they were, seeing the ranch through their eyes. The children enlivened our household with their healthy animality. Though we often had to curb their fun and mischief, the joy they brought to our days more than made up for the small troubles they caused us.

Their youthful exuberance was something to cope with. I'd never had two before at one time. What one didn't think of, the other would. They left a trail of Coke bottles, balls, bats, mitts, and discarded jackets behind them, bicycles to be stumbled over and roller skates all over the place, and they had bubble gum too.

I worried about snakes, horses, and broken bones. I was unhappy about the grammar they would pick up. I don't know why; there were five nationalities of families living on my father's farm.

Growing up on a West Texas ranch is a wonderful opportunity—knowing, playing, and working with your neighbors; watching things grow; enjoying, participating in, and benefiting from nature's marvels. The ranch is an endlessly fascinating place to children. They had an eager reach for fresh experiences. They begged to go and to help.

Now, to my daily duties, my already crowded schedule were added tooth brushings, baths, storytelling, constant supervision, all the joys and responsibilities of children. We were everlastingly picking up paste and crayons, pajamas, ropes, balls, funnies, caps, and sweaters. "The labor we delight in physics pain"—a labor of love.

We spoiled them in some ways, but on the whole we were pretty strict disciplinarians. Our children, like most others, wished there were no such word as discipline. Their friends did not have so many chores or so many rules, no yard work, no onerous household duties. There were yardmen, maids, and cooks at their homes. I pointed out that we had help at the ranch too, when we could get them. They had to be reminded of this. "Would you exchange the things you have for their life? Your horses, the creek, the ranch?" I asked. "No. No," the answer came quickly. "We just didn't think." They knew and realized the freedom they enjoyed by virtue of living on a ranch. Yet no lecture of mine on the laws of compensation could change their minds about certain yard work. To them, as to Mr. Hinch, chopping weeds was joyless drudgery. We hoped to teach them that beauty is also to be found in a day's work.

There was a generation between us. We think in our case the

generation gap was a handy thing. The children had been taught to love, respect, and mind us before they came to live on the ranch. They did not expect us to join in their rough-and-tumble games or to wait on them hand and foot, as most children are pampered nowadays. Though just six and nine, they understood that they would miss some things that young parents living in a small town could give: TV, circuses, picture shows, next-door playmates. But they had visited the ranch so often they knew the things it offered and loved every bit of it. It was a place of adventure. They looked to us without question for all the necessities of life. They knew that we would manage to afford anything that was for their improvement. They were exactly the things they wanted or were looking for. To this day they don't worry about things like generation gaps or Ph.D.'s, not that they would consider the latter an obstacle.

I got provoked with the children, of course, especially their habit of dallying. Anne always finished the chapter she was reading before she answered. Burns finished off the Indians, those imaginary Indians he was chasing with an imaginary weapon. But the creek was not imaginary and he had to drive the last redskin or cattle thief across that creek before he could give me his attention. And, of course, they felt horribly put upon when it was time to come in and bathe and dress for dinner. "I wish we could bathe in the creek or at the bunkhouse," Burns said. How they dawdled on the way in to "dress for dinner," as they called showering and putting on fresh Levi's and shirt. They soiled so many clothes, and it seemed they were always dirty and their heads needed shampooing. But they had such a grand time riding, wading the creek, following the boys, playing make-believe. They were always out of pocket at meal time. Most of the men had infinite patience with them. "Oh, we get along fine," Jim said. "They give me an ornery time," Jake replied.

We had some hassles, of course. Some of them were about eating. Most vegetables they relished, raw and cooked, but Burns made most unattractive noises about boiled okra. We insisted he eat just two small buds. He would have had me believe it just couldn't be kept down. Twice he got away with bringing it up. The third time I was waiting for him. Just as he started making the dangerously unpleasant sound, I dashed a glass of ice water in his face. To his infuriated surprise the okra went down easily. To this day okra is not his favorite dish, but he likes it fried and can tolerate it boiled.

When the children were visiting us I had been watchful and uneasy, but now our lives were made up of fear. Fear that Cuppie would fall from a horse or would tangle with a rattlesnake, that Burns would cut himself to ribbons on that tractor or saw. But at least we were without fear of sudden death from the traffic. I knew they were riding gentle old horses. Yet there is great danger of an old horse stumbling. I knew they had to learn to watch out for rattlers. I knew that hundreds of children lived on ranches and that few had ever been bitten by a rattler, but just the same the children kept me terrified the first few years.

We deplored the dangerous things they could think up to try out, like putting the horses over jumping bars and leaping them into the creek from a ten-foot bank, but delighted in the fact that they could entertain themselves and never complained "What's to do" or "There's nothing to do out here."

There were several ranch children for the Grands to play with from the start. As we built the bank near the house, they laughed and shrieked, ran and jumped into the loose, soft dirt sinking their bare legs to their knees, straddled up the steep bank, and slid down again. "Miss Dugan Adams, riding Salty Dog!" they'd announce as Dugan, riding a stick horse, avalanched into the moist, sweet-smelling earth. "Burnsey Boy on Baby Bay," his short, fat legs waddling. "Burnsey falled," as he sprawled full length. But Burnsey Boy didn't cry!

To use a cattle-range expression, the children were "loose-herded" as they grew up on the ranch. They were not confined to a few areas around the house. D said, "Don't hang around headquarters all the time. Get out and see what's going on. Keep your eyes open, so you can come back and tell us what's happening." They did. The children took the words as permission to explore the neighborhood or the entire ranch. They roamed the range, reporting on all they saw: a windmill that wasn't pumping, a calf in a watering tank, a sick or dead animal, a coyote or bobcat in a trap, poachers, prairie fires, a preacher who did not navigate a cattle guard, a car stuck in the mud or sand, a rattler, or a covey of quail. The life gave them a chance to express themselves, to enlarge their abilities, to use their ingenuity. It broadened their sympathies. Burns later wondered not so much how he would impress the girls or how he could hold his liquor or what kind of car he drove as how he could stand up in a branding pen or how long he'd last on a roundup.

Ranch children may not know a tadpole from a pompano, a crayfish from an eel, but they do know a rattlesnake's hiss and that you can't lead a horse facing him. I have seen grown women and men, too, looking a horse in the eye, begging or coaxing him to come on. They also know that you don't walk up and slap every horse on the rump, especially if he is asleep. One visitor on the Pitchfork learned that the hard way. The sleepy old horse kicked him four times before he could get out of the way.

From a cowboy's point of view, a ranch had sound advantages of a more mundane kind that a city does not provide, but useful if you insist on vacationing in the country. For instance, you need not worry about providing excuses for being lost, for being off your horse and letting it get away from you, or having to lead him in. A ranch child knows if he turns the horse loose or gives him his head, the horse will bring him back to the ranch. He doesn't have to get off his horse as a rule, but if he does get off, it is crucial that he make certain sure he can get back on.

What a useful and rare gift it was to have Coy, Tom, Ed, and Baba as teachers. The children were taught without pressure. When they asked a question, Jim, Barney, John, or one of the other men would stop and answer it. Tom taught the children to tie a fast knot that even a smart horse could not untie with his teeth. From Newt they learned that when there are many rabbits the coyotes flourish. Ed was full of stories. "Did ya ever hear o' a horse thief shoein' his horse backwards to keep from being trailed?" The children recounted this story with glee.

Animals, of course, are a big part of the rural child's life. Possums and coons came up from the creek for nightly forays. Hoot owls screeched and screamed. A first wolf hunt is a memorable experience for a boy. As often happens in the world of animals, the children had seen animals couple every hour of the day. They came running with any small animal or bird they found in need of help. The three of us often patched up a broken wing or leg.

There was much to be learned, and the men filled them in. The children observed the habits of many animals: buzzards circling overhead indicated a dead animal in the vicinity; hawks that flew along with us, hovering just above us, were waiting for our car to flush unwary quail, mice, or baby rabbits from the underbrush ahead. Even on their short visits to the ranch they had learned.

A small animal came to our lighted window one winter's night, touched his nose to the pane, and moseyed on. In the light fall of snow, we found his tracks, and D showed them to Anne and Burns the next morning. They looked like those of a baby. "It was a skunk!" the youngsters cried. They knew what animal had visited our chicken house during the night and knew what kind of trap it would take to catch him. They knew why a puppy grabs a hop toad only once and why the clever skunk rolls one around and around in the dirt until the toad's glands are drained of the last drop of its bitter fluid.

They were learning caution of rattlesnakes, horses' hooves, and cattle horns, and the art of reading signs. In fact, Burns was practically an authority. He would pass this knowledge on to Anne and me. Jeet taught Burns how to shoot treed squirrels. "Takes two to hunt squirrels proper," he allowed. "A squirrel will flat himself one side of a tree or lay along a limb or in a crotch till he sees the shooter, then he'll scat to the fur side, an' that's when tother man shoots him." Newt Bingham taught him about trapping. Burns knew when a mare was in foal and about reproduction in its various animal forms, but in one instance at least the old authority had failed to read the fine print. He and Coy were at the corral one day. Coy was teaching him to rope when a very large, rather misshapen woman came around the corner. Out of the clear sky came the question, "Who's she bred to, Coy?" The Pitchfork foreman almost missed his calf.

Nor is it every child who has the opportunity and excitement of seeing ranch operations firsthand, hauling wood, putting out salt blocks, choosing and cutting their own Christmas trees, making drives, eating at the chuck wagon. The children loved to go to the wagon to eat with the men. Vanilla would make two cakes or pies for the boys, or something that couldn't be prepared before a campfire. We would pile in the car and go rattling over the cattle guards, lurching over the rough roads, up and down canyons. The children were in an ecstasy of excitement. As we'd quietly approach the outfit, I'd seek out D's figure. Sometimes he'd be on Dally Welte, sometimes Blue Bull, but more often he rode Patches.

What they learned on this ranch, they could never learn in any classroom. Purists might argue it's not the place to raise children. They might contend they'd be exposed to some pretty rough stuff. This I won't deny. The children had some new and magic words. My own intractable mustangs picked up some earthy information. But it taught them the love of horses, cows, chickens, and how to care for them, and an awareness of nature. They will always have enough of the country in them. And they will have acquired a rich background for living that will add to their enjoyment all their lives. They have learned to evaluate people—and other good things.

Then there was the creek. The world of children who live on a creek is limitless in scope, especially if those children are blessed with imagination, and ours were. The creek was a broad river to them. The snakes and turtles were dangerous alligators. Sometimes the children were Texas Rangers defending their state or defending their ranch against rustlers. They drove them back across the stream. Yet they rode their horses right out to meet and repulse the Indians who tried to cross the stream to make a foray on our cattle. They were cowhands of Texas and were there to defend their vaunted, exciting state. They had hideaways from Indians and cattle thieves. They'd eat a fast sandwich and streak for the creek. Nearly forty years fell away as I watched them at their play. I was back on old Salt Creek, digging a throne out of the bank where I took turn-about with the little Mexicans, Bohemians, Germans, Negroes, and "American" children, being the queen.

D and I were brought up under strict rules of obedience, duty, and respect. We had been taught to work. It's harder and more time-consuming to teach your children how to cook, clean, manage a house, and work in the garden than it is to do it yourself, but we tried. It seemed to me we spent about twenty-four hours a day teaching manners and grammar and explaining why such and such was forbidden. "How can chewing gum be vulgar?" Cuppie asked.

Practically every speck of credit goes to D. He taught them to come to grips with life.. D belongs to the "hard work never hurt anybody" school. Knowing *how* was a must. We were determined the children should be raised the same as we were. D hammered away by his daily example of loyalty, fairness, hard work, and learning the three R's of the range: roping, riding, and reading signs. Seeing things done and actually helping with the doing is the grandest way in the world for a child to learn. When they have gone along on a wood haul or salt scattering job, or mastered a wire gap, it gives them a sense of accomplishment not found in bicycling or skating around the block.

D made them learn the right way. He would not tolerate for one instant a hand on the saddle horn or the reins in the wrong hand, and getting up on the wrong side is just too bad. Once when Anne crawled under Darkie, D threatened to scalp her, and I think he might have, had she repeated the offense. "Just because this old pony is gentle is no sign the next one will be," he roared. I think the only whipping D ever gave the children was for putting a snake in Gus's bed. It was only a grass snake, completely harmless, and it was dead. But so terrified was Guy of anything resembling a snake, he was almost in hysterics as he burst out of his house screaming and running all over the yard. It took D to quiet him and get him back to his quarters and a sizable tip to persuade him to remain on the ranch.

They had great respect for and pride in D, and they had consideration of me. They were always wanting me to go and see something they had discovered or were working on. Often I had to say, "I'm too busy or too tired to go right now." Burns asked, "Couldn't you go if you rested real hard for about an hour, Mamie?" Of course, D was the real hero. I have never learned to spin a top, ride a bike, tie the right kind of knot, or rope anything. The children looked down on me in consequence. But the most precious time of the day was mine, the saying of their prayers. Most often we prayed aloud.

One night Burns prayed, "Dear God, I'm sorry if I have done any bad thing today but I know you know all about it so I'll just tell you goodnight and thank you." They were never quizzed about these confidences. Burns found as many excuses as most children can to pop out of bed after the nightly story and lights were out, but he and a friend who was spending the night with him thought up the idea of adding codicils to their prayers. Crawling out of the bed and on their knees, they'd say, "God, I forgot," or "Oh God, let me tell You something." Finally Anne could bear it no longer. She came to the top of the stairs and called, "Mamie, I wish you'd come up here. It's positively sacroiliac the way Burns is talking to God."

The children thanked God for the Williamses, the Pitchfork, and "Thank you God, for making it rain on the ranch," and things like that. I can see their bowed heads now. This moment was always the best of the day, incredibly precious. "Dear God," Burns murmured softly one night, "lend me thine ears." A giggle came from Cups. "Well, Anne," he shouted, "that's the way you're s'posed to start talking a prayer." More laughter from Anne. "Mamie, some really dreadful thing may happen to Anne 'cause she's laughing at God." "I'm not laughing at God, Burns." In less time than it takes to say Roy Rogers they were slugging it out on the bedroom floor.

The Grands worked us to a fare-thee-well. They knew where our soft spots were. "Baba, may I go on the drive this morning?" Or "Mamie, we've cleaned our rooms, washed our socks, and got our lessons. Could we ride to the Nolans and stay for lunch?" Great treat. I used the same system on the Williams brothers. If it would make the place more attractive, more comfortable and convenient, or help out in producing more quail, I talked to Mr. Gates. If it would save money or time or water, I appealed to Mr. Eugene.

The children had their little jokes about me, all concerning my old-fashioned ideas such as thanking the telephone time service, hastening to empty the food from a metal can, saying that so-and-so has taken the country like crabgrass.

"Tell us a story, Mamie. And tell us one without a moral 'cause we're tired of those. And don't tell about Jesus. We know about Him. Tell us a really and truly story, Mamie, not one out of a book." "Once, when I was a little girl—," I began. "How old, Mamie?" "Oh, about ten or twelve." "Gollee!" little Burns dragged out, "that was a long time ago." And it was. ". . . President Roosevelt came to Houston." "Was Roosevelt president then, Mamie, when you were a little girl?" I never returned to the story of Teddy Roosevelt.

It was just as well. All that my childish mind recorded of that speech is that he made it clear that a man who will steal *for* you will steal *from* you, and that the word we pronounced "prah-cess," he called "proh-cess" and "prah-gress" was "proh-gress."

It was D's stories they really enjoyed. A magic moment when, lying in the screened porch, they wheedled D into relating his childhood in Cuero, Texas, of boys playing on the Guadalupe River naked as jays, or of riding with his father. But they liked best the stories that D's Grandmother Cardwell told him and the neighborhood playmates. They learned their Texas history at her knees. She lived that history: Santa Anna, Goliad, Sam Houston. "I wish I could have been with them," Burns said. It was a solemn and hushed time when D finished with the siege of the Alamo, that brief but all-out battle that will live forever in history, and he quoted, "Thermopylae had her messenger of defeat, the Alamo had none."

Meantime, the children learned to ride horses and bicycles, to play baseball and croquet, to skate, and even to do a few useful things like chop weeds, stack wood into the fireplace woodbox, take out the ashes, and build fires. They also swept the walks and terraces. When we were without household help, they cleaned bathrooms, ran sweepers, and dusted. It finally became Anne's duty to train new maids in setting the table and serving and also to count laundry going out and coming in. Burns washed the car, the porches, and the walks.

They also learned to ask questions. Anne one evening quizzed, "Mamie, are we the ruling class or upper class or middle class or working class?" I said, "We would not be considered leisure class." "But definitely not steerage," D put in. "Anne, I don't think they know what class we are," Burns decided. Burns could ask the most dumbfounding questions. "How much nickels is three, Mamie?" or "What's a melting pot?" We had become somewhat of a melting pot ourselves. "Animal, vegetable, or antique?" they asked.

"Them young'uns," Mandy was fond of saying, "is hummers." We left the children with Mandy sometimes on weekends. "You won't be your own man fer a spell." Mandy would make them put on everything they owned when they made a drive on cold days. "Gollee, union suits!" Burns said, disgustedly.

Except to go to Guthrie, where the post office in the 6666 supply house was located, the children had to be dragged off the Pitchfork. They seemed to have swallowed the ranch whole and to have no room left in their hearts, minds, and bodies for any other place. In their prejudiced opinion, other ranches were just shirt-tail outfits. When they did go, there was the problem of getting them out of those Levi's. "Well, gollee, Mamie, what will people think? That we're sissies, that's what they'll think," Burns answered himself. "Well, it's true," Anne backed him up. "A man at Guthrie asked us where we lived when we had on those white camp shorts. He didn't believe we lived on the Pitchfork Ranch. He said we looked like city children." "We spit on his tires when he drove off," Burns said. The memory of their elegant manner of getting back at him threw them into gales of laughter and squeals of giggling.

Our greatest pleasure came from the love and appreciation they showed us. Seldom a day passed without some expression of their joy in living here. Burns said one day very thoughtfully, "I guess I'm the luckiest little boy in the world to live on the Pitchfork." I guess he was, too. This ranch would be heaven to any normal boy, and especially to Burns, for ranching was his passion and cowboys were his idols. He unconsciously imitated their poses, especially Coy's. We watched him at the wagon one day standing solemnly beside Coy, setting his feet wide apart as Coy's were set, holding his hands behind him to the campfire. Since one could have anything at all for the wishing, Burnsey wished he had feathers on him like Coy. He searched his chest to see if any were sprouting.

Burns was all eyes, big, blue eyes, with the longest lashes I have ever seen. He was not a big boy, but was endowed with great strength, a teeth-grinding determination, and an unshakable confidence in his ability to do absolutely anything. He lived dangerously. The cowboys said he had guts.

He was a sight to see walking down the middle of the road whistling between his teeth. Burnsey practiced tirelessly to rope, he haunted the bunkhouse, studied the cowboys mannerisms, copied their speech, and did his best to imitate Coy. He tried to stand tall, which was not very easy. All outdoors beckoned him. He learned early the joy of fishing and hunting, and he loved every sport—

baseball, football, tennis, golf. He was a natural athlete. He had a whip-like throwing arm and could climb—how he could climb!

Burns had a knack for looking and listening, for tuning in and soaking up. He was one big question mark, but every person on the ranch seemed to delight in answering and explaining to him. "Is Burns ever been a baby?" John Moreland asked of me. "Well, he shore asks mannish questions." "He sho do," Lola concurred.

D felt that hours spent on a horse riding with a knowledgeable cowboy would teach him more than he could learn anywhere else. Burns, using the smallest saddle and the shortest sweat leathers we could find, cut a manly figure with his fat legs standing straight out inches above the stirrups.

Even as a small child Burns's quickness with words was amazing and sometimes the words were astonishing. "Mamie, the grass is so juicy this morning." Or his "Look Mamie, the little calves are eating their wienies." There was the morning he sauntered in to tell me, "I'm just going to truckle down the path to the creek." He explained about his horse with, "He was nabbling some grass on the highway, and he's not above nabbling you if you don't watch him." And his joy with the beauty of the day, "This is a bird-singing day." The first time he realized he was seeing the caprock when approaching Lubbock, a frown clouded his face. "I thought it would be a big rock with a sort of cap on it." Burns muttered in stark wonder.

One day Burns complained to me of his teacher. "Yesterday she said two and two were four, and today she said three and one were four. I don't think she's very smart." But Aunt Lizzie was smart and said there were good bugs and bad bugs. One must learn the difference, but one must never kill a frog or a toad. Burns once saved a horned frog from a workman's hoe. "He's a good guy," screamed Burns.

Going with the men was the pinnacle of maturity to Burns. He'd come back using some words of Coy's or some he had coined. "We were just snailin' along." "I guess Jake's the strongest man in the whole world. He points with an iron bar." D said, "He could point with a bull." Burns was deeply impressed. He considered the remark several moments before asking, "Baba, which end of the bull would he hold in his hand?"

When he was bored with the subject matter, like where his suede jacket was, he'd spread his palms upward at the same time and shrug, raising his shoulders and his eyebrows as high as he could, as if to say he didn't know and didn't care a lot.

Burns would tell his friends some enchanting stories. "In the 1870's deer, buffalo, and cattle drank from this creek at the same time. Ed's father told him, and Ed told me."

Sometimes Burns had a philosophical turn. "We know things they don't, and they know things we don't," Burns explained to D. "Exactly," D answered. Or perhaps he wished to show his knowledge of ranching. "It takes a lot of acres to keep a cow in grass," Burns would say. Burns voiced his deep thinking with, "I love you but your face is so limber." With a heartless snicker D hid behind his newspaper. He managed to keep a straight face long enough to say, "I think Mamie's pretty."

It came my duty one day to ask him, "Burns, why didn't you tell me you had broken out the store window?" The soul of consideration, Burns fell back to his last line of defense. "Well, Mamie, I thought it would worry you." It sometimes took real effort to assume a scowl of disapproval. We did show our disapproval, however, when he decided he needed to increase his vocabulary. After several trys and our negative reactions, Burns asked, "When will I be big enough to cuss?" He handled "Gee whiz," "Gosh," and "Gollee" in a manner that left no doubt of his intentions. Finally he decided he was old enough, and I could see Burns's eyes dance with delight at the exciting new word. "Damn," he said, testing the word to see if it sounded as virile on his lips. "God damn." "You're not old enough." I was on ticklish ground now because Burns felt that he had heard the cowboys say this and thought he might even have heard Baba use it. "When will I be old enough? Mamie, gee whiz, gosh, gollee, you won't let me use any slang at all."

Burns definitely had a ranch slant on life, having spent most of his days on one. He was learning every aspect of the roundup work. Burns thought being a cowman was a family trait, and he wanted a ranch job either as cowboy or owner, but not as manager. He doubted if managers have so much fun. To be a cowman you must dress the part, and Burns was concerned with his image. He came in one day and asked me how to get blue jeans properly faded.

There followed several washings, throwing them over lawn furniture to dry in the hot sun. Next day we'd repeat the process with the other side to the sun. If this didn't fade them properly, only time could do it.

Miss Prissy, drinking a cup of tea, said, "Life on a ranch is just the dreamiest—" Burns, twirling a rope, thought it was the zowiest, until D put a hoe in his hand and told him to cut those weeds. This was the most humiliating thing that could happen to a cowboy. He hadn't noticed Coy or Jim or even Baba, who would stoop to any task, cutting weeds. He confided to Mandy that he just might not take it; he might just run away. "Leave us know when you're goin'," Mandy told him, "so's we can pack you a lunch."

Burns came flying into the room. "Mamie," he panted. When he had caught his breath, "I can chin myself," and was gone before I could exclaim over his achievement. Burns went through a stage of chinning himself whenever a projection of any kind made this possible. He also had his burping period. He was making the most unusual noises. Anne said he'd been taking belching lessons from Tom Dowdy. She said, "He's been doing it about a year. You should hear him over at the chuck house when you're not there." To Burns's disgust, Anne was growing up. "And now, Mamie, it's not proper for me to go into her room without knocking."

With the other ranch children, Anne and Burns created plays beneath the trees. Anne was being Cleopatra; she clasped her hand to her heart, stretched out on the grass, and died. "Phooey," said Burns sweetly and cracked her on the head with his gun. Sometimes he died too, but only from a gunshot or poison arrow. They often laid flowers on a quiet little grave on the hillside. To them it was a revered shrine. Burns would lope up to say, "We're going over to decorate Sally Bragg's grave." One hand full of daffodils and purple irises, they raced across the creek. "Off like a shirt button," Ed said, "and they don't keer if the river raises or rises." The little grave was the first place they took their friends.

Getting to visit on a ranch at any age is a real feat. A ranch is a busy place. There is no slack season. D made it clear to our two that they and their guests were not to cause extra work for anyone. They would not only care for their own horses and riding gear, they must remove boots at the door if it was wet. City children departed with a lively admiration for the things the ranch youngsters could do, the type of entertainment they furnished, their play. And some couldn't bring themselves to leave.

The rain couldn't have fallen better. "We may get some more," the ranch people exulted next morning. Eying the skies, the children hoped the sun would make up its mind to shine, which it did, and they took off with a picnic lunch to show their friends their places. They knew to be back at the ranch by three so that they could put up their horses and riding gear, shower, and be ready to leave in time to reach Lubbock before dark. But when we were packing the car, we discovered that Susan and her bag were not with us. Very soon the suitcase was located in her room, but no amount of looking, calling, or honking the usual long and three shorts on the car horn could bring forth Susan. "Are you sure she rode in with you?" "Yes," came from several throats. "I remember seeing her unsaddling in the corral." This thought started the lot of us running in that direction, and finally Susan was discovered hiding in the harness room, hoping we'd go back to Lubbock without her. So much did she love horses and a ranch.

An Englishman who was visiting for a day or two at the ranch had brought his small son with him. Since they were about the same age, Burns and the English boy hit it off at once.

"What is a cowboy?" the little Englishman asked. "Gollee!" Burns considered. He looked at his playmate to see if by chance his leg was being pulled, but the innocent expression he saw brought forth an explanation, bored but patient. "Cowboys are men who ride horses and rope cows and things,"—his eyes lighted on his gun—"when they aren't killing people," he finished happily.

"Gollee!" said the little Englishman. "Do you have a horse of your own?" he questioned further. "Yep," Burns exulted. "To ride when you wish?" "Sure," Burns replied. The little Englishman threw a curve of his own. "Flat out?" he asked. Burns shrugged expressively, which meant that he could say more if he cared to, but didn't choose to say anything.

Later the same day the two boys, Peter and Burns, joined some other children to play locomotive. Using a wheelbarrow for the engine and some dining room chairs placed outside for waxing and drying, they had soon assembled a train by coupling the chairs with a rope. Dugan, Dickey, Cups, Burns, and Peter were passengers. Billy Myers was the conductor. "I'm for Charing Cross," the small Britisher called out lustily. "I'm for A&M," Burnsey responded without a moment's hesitation, drowning out the conductor's "All aboard!"

No one can live on a ranch and not know how to ride a horse, so riding lessons began when the Grands were young. Jake was giving the children a riding lesson. "Now you allus git up on the horse's left side," Jake reminded.

Cups immediately started crawling on, but Burnsey, not quite four, got mixed up and was making for the side nearest him. "That's th' right side, Burns," Jake said. "I know it," beamed Burnsey, pleased at being approved. "I say that's the *right* side! That's the *wrong* side!" Jake shouted, "Git away from thet horse; he'll kick th' tar outta you!" Burns dropped his reins and came to the porch spluttering complaints. "Mamie, I wish you or Baba would teach me to ride. Jake doesn't know a thing about a horse's sides," he said indignantly. "And, Mamie, I wasn't eating that tar this morning, I was just playing with it." Jake was a knowledgeable critic of horsemanship, but things had become too involved for Burns ever to wholly trust him again.

It seemed no time at all from those first riding lessons until they both were expert horsemen. Then the day came Burns had dreamed of. The day he could ride with the men. You became a man, the cowboys said, when you could do a man's work. It was a proud day in Burns's life when he was allowed to go on a cattle drive.

Coy said, "Be on time at the chuck house. You've got to have something under your belt to ride with this outfit." He was. And D had not had to call him. "Up an' out there saddling his horse," D reported to me proudly. He could see Burns under the glare of the outside office light. It was pitch dark elsewhere.

I seldom made the 5 A.M. meals at the chuck house, but I was sitting at the table when Burns came striding in with the men. He sat beside Coy and did not look my way. He ate a strapping breakfast and was the first one out on his horse. His Stetson, at just cowboy-angle, pulled down almost over his eyes, gave his face the sternness he desired, and his Levi's were a very tight fit. He lifted his hand coolly, imperceptibly, just enough that I might see, but the boys might not, his leave-taking of me. Burns, dressed to his enormous satisfaction exactly like Coy, was making his first drive.

Coy never babied Burns when he was at the wagon with the men, not noticeably, that is. "Crawl under that wagon where it's cool and stretch out a few minutes," he'd say. That patch of shade made by the wagon was often the only one to be found at the camp site. Coy said Burns would hit the ground before he'd finished talking and be asleep by the time he'd put his hat over his eyes. A few winks in the middle of a twelve-hour day helped a nine-year-old cowboy.

While Burns had his heart set on being a cowman, Anne's heart and soul were captured by horses. One would never have suspected it, however, the day D first lifted her onto the back of Baby Bay. Cuppie, to whom riding was to become as natural as breathing, trembled, held on to Baba, and begged to get off. Her pinafore had lost its starched perfection. But it was not long before she would swing into her saddle and ride and jump just as Jake and Barney and Jim Mills had taught her.

Blue jeans were her uniform, and she was most at home astride a horse. She truly loved her horses, and Darkie was an early favorite. Only once was her deep affection for him strained. "I'm mad at Darkie, and we'll never be friends again." This came after her pony had run away while she and I were out riding. "No, darling, no. You are not angry with Darkie. Something frightened him, and he didn't know it was Mamie coming fast after you." D was white when he came in after hearing of the runaway. Mandy observed to Cuppie, "First time I'se seen you scairt."

But this in no way turned her heart from horses. The first pictures she ever drew were of a horse. Anne had a consuming ambition to be a horsewoman. She was going to raise horses. She got an A in story writing. "It was about a horse," she told Mandy. "You could a knocked me over with a saddle blanket," Mandy said and winked at me.

At nine she lived, breathed, and thought horses. I took her to the doctor. "She's been limping around for a day or so." "Where does it hurt, Anne?" the doctor asked. "In my flank," she answered and placed her hand on the spot.

Could this passionate interest in horses be a forecast of her life? "I certainly don't want a rodeo queen in the family," D complained. "I wish you would buy her some pretty little dresses." She had some pretty little dresses; getting her to wear them was my problem.

When the children were not playing at the creek, riding the range, or staging plays, they wanted to help me with my chores. The beauty of the morning and the sheer winningness of the children, Dugan, Dickie, and Cuppie, made me almost forget my disappointment in the carpenter's failure to show. Lonita (Dugan) Adams, a flaxen-haired little girl whose every wish was to please, was just enough older than Cups and Dickie to be worthy of their emulation. She kept them entertained and out of trouble. They danced about, asking, "May we help?" "May I dig the holes?" "May I cover them up?" "May I use the hose?" A real help they were, bringing tools and pushing the wheelbarrow.

In rapture or in distress, Anne would detail all that she saw on the ranch. One morning she came running into the house, her eyes big with wonder, fear, and compassion. "Come quick, Mamie, and see out the window. What are they doing to that horse?" "They're breaking that horse, darling, so it will be gentle, so it can be used, and you can ride him. See? That's the way they break a horse." Later she was back. "Mamie, that horse just standed and falled down and breaked himself." And in truth it had. The poor, frightened, quivering thing had reared, fallen backward, and broken its neck.

Cuppie was a Sarah Bernhardt when it came to play acting. There was the day that Cups held the funeral services. I could see them out the window. They were gazing at her sadly. There were tears in Burns's eyes. Cups was saying, "She's your cousin, Burns, your own little cousin and you'll never see her again, on this earth," she added dramatically. A tear rolled down Burns's cheek, and the other attendants mourned appropriately.

To live on a ranch was great fun, but it was even greater fun to Burns and Anne to get to show it to others on conducted tours. It gave them a sense of great importance to tell the stories. They felt pride to play the "courier," a superior being who lived there or had been there before. It was no doubt this instinct, as well as the desire to give them pleasure, that made us decide to take the Grands to their first stock show, even though I would have to leave my chickens, including some just a few days old, to the care of someone I wasn't altogether sure would look after them properly.

Having chickens very much on our minds, we started our trip to the Fort Worth Stock Show. At dinner we read our fortunes from Chinese cookies. Mine said, "Your efforts shall be rewarded." Burns looked at it a long time, then said seriously, "I think it means, Mamie, that not all of your chickens will be dead when we get back." "Do you believe in fortunes, Mamie?" Anne came in. "Absolutely," I responded. The children had drawn the same prophecy, "You are going to have more freedom to do as you like." "Maybe I am going to get to stay up an hour later at night," she hoped. "Oh, boy," said Burns, "maybe I won't have to bathe every night."

Anne had a way with words, too. Such as the day I was chastising her and pounding my hand on the table for emphasis when she said, "Careful, Mamie, you'll knock yourself out." And she also thought deeply and had questions. "Mamie, which would you and Baba rather do, go to Heaven or stay on the ranch? I'd rather stay on the ranch," she vouchsafed. "Me, too," Burnsey caroled. It was the one thing on which they had ever agreed. I was trying to phrase my preference for the Pearly Gates, without disappointing them too much. Waiting for my answer, D smiled at me over his paper. "You're going to be sorta lonesome up there, honey." His vote was a hundred to one for the ranch.

Even though there are still times I think of her as Cuppie, Anne recognized school as a time of change and growing. Frances told us that Cuppie, on her second day of school, came home with the request to be called Anne. "It will be all right if Mamie and Baba call me Cuppie. I don't think Baba would say anything else." It was D who told her that since she was in school now, he thought we should call her Anne. "Unless we forget," he added. A proud little smile crossed her face, "Thank you," she said.

Anne at thirteen was as omnivorous a reader as were her grandparents. It was not unusual to find her bent raptly over a book from my shelves, nor were they always horse stories. A visitor, coming through my bedroom to join a group at the living-room fireplace, had seen her there. "Do you know your granddaughter is reading

Gone with the Wind?" "She will love it," I said. "What about the Belle Watling bit?" she inquired. "Oh, that," I answered quickly, "Anne will get everything of interest and beauty it has to offer. Anything else will pass completely over her head." I knew it would; I'd seen it happen before. "I hope," our guest reposted. Thirty minutes must have passed before Anne opened the door from our quarters, stood holding her book, waiting for a lull in our conversation. "Excuse me," she said; then, "Mamie, what is a whore?" She emphasized the *w* in pronouncing the word. The room became still and quiet. My throat became dry, my mind went blank, then I heard a voice from somewhere within me answering, "An indelicate woman, darling." "That's what I thought," Anne said and closed the door. I think she might have done well to have stuck with horse books a while longer. She might have understood the subject matter better.

A dancing class seemed a good method of getting Anne into some pretty little dresses and diversifying her activities from horses. The other class members may have been more delighted to have Anne join than she was to join. The visitors, when they arrived at the ranch, included not only the thirty-two members of the dancing class, but also almost two dozen little brothers and sisters between the ages of two and twelve and about the same number of parents. I was so flabbergasted by the extras that I fled to my bedroom and remained temporarily incommunicado, trying to decide what and how I would feed them. The sandwiches, lemonade, and cookies would be just about enough for one-third of the crowd. This is the way visitors feel about coming to a ranch.

Burns and Anne loved school in Lubbock, the music lessons, and dancing class, but the ranch held their hearts. Scarcely an hour passed without some mention of horses from Anne. She spent most of her waking hours, and many of her sleeping ones, thinking about horses. "I dreamed last night that I had an Arabian horse, a little Arabian colt."

We had a little place in Lubbock for during the week. We called it the Little House. But rain or shine we always returned to the ranch and the Big House on the weekend. Trying to make my allowance pay our expenses at Little House, I was chronically hard up. We could go for hamburgers only once a week, no table to be cleared, no dishes to wash up. When Aunt Willie came to Lubbock to shop she always took us out for a treat. That's how she became the "zowiest!" Always she had the wonderful faculty of doing the thing that made you the happiest. If you were ill, she could find the way to make you the most comfortable. If your heart was heavy, she would find the words to ease the hurt, and her Christmas gifts were beyond description.

Burns and Anne knew I was there to have the costumes ready when they needed them, to haul them and their friends to the base-ball and football games, to arrange to chaperone all their parties. I explained and they understood why they must help out at Little House, and they did it, not without complaint on occasion, but they did it.

On Thursday we usually treated ourselves to hamburgers at the drive-in. One Thursday I announced, "Children, we have food in the refrigerator. I'm running a little short of money until the first (day after tomorrow), so we can't have our little treat this week. I will do the dishes after we eat." Anne said, "Mamie, here is some money I have saved, I will give you half of it." In a moment of typi-cal generosity Burns said, "Mamie, here is all of mine."

They could expect me to be at home when they arrived from school. They knew there would be good food three times a day, that their friends would always be welcome, that I could be counted on to provide the cookies, sandwiches, or whatever for PTA. How well I remember a Sunday afternoon, after a particularly busy weekend, when I was trying to corral the children for our ride back to Lub-bock. Anne came running to the car, "Oh, Mamie, I forgot to tell you I pledged six dressed, cooked hens for you to donate to PTA tomorrow. Some of the other mothers will make them into chicken salad sandwiches." The children helped catch six plump hens, I wrung their necks, and while I was dressing those chickens Anne and I had a serious conversation. It was after ten o'clock that night before we reached Lubbock and got those chickens cooking in two huge pots I'd borrowed from the ranch. I waited for them to start boiling, turned them on low, set the alarm for four when I had to be up to finish the job.

We wanted to give Anne the education for a life of leisure if she married into such a situation (from where I stood the idea seemed very appealing), or for earning her own living if need be. Anne thought all of this planning very boring, definitely silly, and beside the point. She was going to raise horses. All her allowance went for horse books. She was never going to marry, unless, of course, she met a horse lover, she decided a few years later.

Then they reached the age of "dig talk" and the stage of education when naturally was "natch," fabulous was "fab," "def" was definitely, the movies were "flicks," girls were "birds" or "pigeons," boys were "strongs"—"teddibly, teddibly strong"—and TV's became "tubes." And every so often one of the "birds" would ask a "strong," "Isn't it all confusing?" Then there was just one answer, "Wonderful." Later, of course, they reached the "what's-it-all-about" period. "Who am I anyway?" As they sipped buttered rum, they exchanged profound ideas. Everything was "far out."

The wish I carried in my heart was that some man could make life for Anne what D had made life for me. It was Tom who announced Anne's engagement after helping unload the car when Dave brought her home from the University of Texas in May. "Little Anne is wearing a diamond as big as home plate," he said solemnly to the chuck-house group, and supper was almost forgotten as they expressed their several different opinions. "Anne ain't old enough to marry." They agreed until somebody said, "Oh, yes, she is. She's nineteen—be twenty in October."

D and I had known about the engagement. Dave had given her the ring when she had visited his parents in Scottsdale at Easter time. Anne adored the Shulers.

"Have a simple wedding," D said. Oh, the cost of simplicity. When Mr. Eugene wired Anne that he would be at the wedding, she burst into tears. "Oh, Mamie, I couldn't be happier. Uncle Gene is coming." It was the first time I had really seen anyone cry for joy.

After that "simple wedding" Tom said, "Some of 'em was wearin' a lot of money but none of 'em coulda bought me when little Anne retch out and put her arms around me like she allus done."

If it appears a large portion of this book is given to the Grands, that is because they were central to our lives. We cared deeply about our Grands—their education, their manners, their hearts, their future, their friends, and the way they got along with people. It was a big order, knowing how to make them kind, yet tough enough to meet the world, humble and courageous at the same time. We wanted to help them avoid blind alleys, but we knew that essentially we had to give them practice in learning things on their own, in making their own decisions. We hoped to build up self-confidence in them and to teach them respect for the rights of others. We hoped to instill the conviction that certain things and certain values are worthy of esteem or reverence and need to be preserved at all costs. We wanted to give them a code to live by, to make them fair; to help them to know what they wanted to do with it; and to know the joy and wonder of the country and to develop hardiness. I believe Anne and Burns will know honesty, will know love, will know how to work, and they will know beauty for the rest of their lives.

They learned of good and evil. It was on the ranch that Anne and Burns were first awakened to the worth of honest and genuine people. We hope they feel a reverence for nature and that they see God's image in each thing and place. We hope they learned that happiness doesn't have to be bought and paid for with dollars and cents. Our children were used to creating their entertainment rather than paying for it.

I wanted Anne and Burns to float on their backs in salt water, climb the mountains, tramp the hills, fish the streams, learn the love of music and books.

Those years on the ranch gave direction and meaning to their lives. The Pitchfork was a combination of the twentieth century and the wild West. Picking up a flint point made by some prehistoric hand while a jet airplane roared overhead was not unusual.

We hoped they would take from the ranch the things it had to offer. We've had so many lovely things to share. The Grands will have them for all of their lives, the doings of the ranch, the memories. I hope Anne and Burns will tell their children.

"Last Rites for D Burns"

We are assembled for the last rites for our friend, D Burns. D is for Douglas. The change came about in this way. A & M College, where he went in 1912, had a military organization. Students fell out early every morning for reveille at which there was roll call. Two Burns boys, Douglas and Edward, no kin, were in the same company. The company clerk for brevity called them D Burns and E Burns. Both students and faculty did the same. In four years the first names were forgotten. Even the families took up the new designations. When he was out of college, D assumed the shorter version as his official name.

D was proud of his family, and he had an appreciation of history. His great-grandfather, Arthur Burns, Sr., came to Texas in 1826 and acquired a league and a *labor* of land in DeWitts Colony, seven miles south of present-day Cuero. His son, Columbus, was the first white child born in the colony. Columbus grew up in the area and became a stock farmer. He married Lois De Moss from Austin's Colony, and they had ten children. The second of these was Arthur, who married Mary Cardwell. To this union five children were born; the fifth was Douglas, who was to become D.

D's maternal grandfather was Crocket Cardwell, who came to Texas in 1833 and settled in the new village of Gonzales. He married Ann Eliza White, who became the mother of Mary Cardwell and the grandmother of D.

The Crockett Cardwells purchased a stage stand and store four miles north of where Cuero was later located. They also operated a plantation, post office, and engaged in the cattle business. Later, Crockett Cardwell established other stores at Port Lavaca and Halletsville, creating the first chain-store system in Texas.

Crockett Cardwell was an enterprising citizen. In the spring of 1866, when the state was in the throes of economic stagnation, he put together 1,800 big, five-year-old longhorn steers for the first drive after the Civil War to the northern market. The steers were

selected for traveling ability as well as for beef conformation. Cardwell selected Thornton Chisholm for trail boss. The cattle were cut
into two herds of 900 each. In all, there were thirty cowhands.
Later it was found that only fifteen men were required to drive three
times that number of cattle, but this herd was the first to cross Indian Territory, and Crockett Cardwell was taking no chances. This
drive blazed a trail later known as the Chisholm Trail.

Only last year I asked D Burns which of all the things he had
not done would he most like to have done. He replied, "I would
like to have lived 110 years ago and gone on that first trail drive."

D was born in Cuero on July 8, 1895. He finished public school
in Cuero and in the fall of 1912 went to A & M College. He started
to major in architectural engineering but found he was far more interested in land and cattle. He switched to animal husbandry and
graduated in 1916 with a bachelor's degree.

When he was twenty-one, he and his family acquired a ranch
in the east side of Dawson County. They had scarcely got it stocked
when the disastrous drouth of 1917–1918 ravaged the western part
of the state. With no prospect of wintering the cattle on the ranch,
D drove the herd of six hundred cows north two hundred miles to
Tule Canyon where some grass was leased. A one-room shack was
available with the grass land. In this, D camped for the winter. All
went well until January 18, 1918. It began with a pleasant morning.
D started a long ride to keep the cattle headed back toward the canyon. He was miles away when a fast-moving blizzard swept in from
the north. In minutes visibility dropped almost to zero and so did
the temperature. On the open prairie with no landmarks, he lost all
sense of direction. He soon realized that his only chance to keep
from freezing to death was to give his horse the reins and hope he
would go home. This he did. After what seemed an eternity, but
was only an hour or two, the horse stopped. D's eyes had frozen shut
and he could not see, but he noticed he was out of the wind. He
managed to dismount, feel around, and discovered he was on the
lee side of his shack. In the shack was a tiny little cook stove. Being
a methodical person, he had a supply of wood and corn cobs stacked
behind the stove. He got a fire going and for three days and nights
sat with his feet in the oven and his bedding wrapped around him,
never moving except to put more wood in the stove.

Cattle losses were enormous. Those which took refuge in the canyons survived. Those on the open prairie drifted south to the fence and froze to death.

This loss had not been overcome when the depression of 1920 set in. Price of cattle dropped from twenty to five cents almost over night, bankrupting at least half the cattlemen. D managed to hold on until the stock market crash in 1929, when he liquidated and started looking for a job.

In the meanwhile he married Mamie Sypert of Lamesa in 1924. They had a son, James Douglas, who died when he was six months old. They also had a daughter, Frances.

D had fought the elements and an unstable economy for thirteen years. In 1929 he started using his education in a less hazardous career. He took a job with the Texas Cottonseed Crushers Association in Dallas. He held that job for six years and learned the cattle-feeding business. In 1935 he went with the West Texas Cotton Oil Company in Abilene, becoming their salesman for all the states west of the Mississippi River. He stayed with this position for seven years. This experience was probably worth more than his college career, but his college training was a prerequisite for the position. He got acquainted with thousands of users of cottonseed meal, cake, and hulls. With his remarkable memory, he could meet these people year after year and always call them by name. He attended university short courses and kept abreast of new feeding techniques. He learned from others and at the same time passed on the new innovations to ranchers who had never heard of them.

By 1942 D Burns was one of the best-informed men in the land in every phase of the ranching industry. First, his training was academic, second it was the school of hard knocks and bitter reality, and third it was rounded out by travel and observation at first hand.

In 1942 Rudolph Swenson, manager of the Pitchfork Land and Cattle Company, was killed in an accident. The owners of the Pitchfork employed D Burns. He held the position of manager until he retired in 1965. These were wonderfully productive years for D and for the company. D's knowledge of the industry and his ability to handle men enabled the company to greatly expand the ranch and make a goodly profit at a time when other sizable ranches in the region were breaking up. Supported to the hilt by his employers, he inaugurated a number of diversified innovations. Commercial herds of saddle horses, sheep, and hogs were started. Four thousand acres of good land were put into cultivation, and a feed mill and feeding lots were constructed. A feeding program was implemented. The period of preparing a calf for market was reduced by eight months. While doing all this D was successfully fighting the mesquite menace, fencing, and improving the water supply with more tanks and windmills.

The successes and innovations attracted national attention. Illustrated articles appeared in national publications. Distinguished visitors came from many states and foreign countries to inspect and buy cattle and horses. With Mamie, gracious lady that she is, as hostess, hospitality at the Pitchfork rivaled that of the plantations of the Old South before the Civil War. Among the visitors were the owners, who loved it.

The first time we were ever at the Pitchfork headquarters, we experienced the Burns's typical hospitality. The Women's Council of the Museum Association organized a busload of museum members to go to Fort Worth for some kind of cultural event. Mamie heard that we were going and invited the group to stop by for a rest break. We did, and were amazed at the orderly layout of the buildings, far more extensive than appears from the road: an enormous bunkhouse, barns, shops, machinery sheds, neat cottages for married hands, a commodious chuck house, and other structures. The manager's house would have done credit to the owners had it been erected in Saint Louis, elegant and designed for entertaining. In the dining room, the table was so abundantly laden with delicious and varied food, we could have had a working hand's meal. Mamie, the charming hostess, made each feel he or she was a very special guest.

Activity all about the headquarters was like a beehive. A Caterpillar was clearing mesquite brush nearby. Hands were scurrying in all directions. D took off and came to the house. Tall, lean, straight as an arrow, he greeted the guests with genuine affability. We asked him to give us a brief history of the ranch. This he did, standing in the wide opening between the large living room and dining room. Gary Cooper could not have done better.

The group went on to Fort Worth, where we were entertained

in the art museums and the homes of the elite. To this day, twenty years later, if you should ask any individual who made that trip what he or she remembers most vividly about it, invariably the answer is the stopover at the Pitchfork Ranch. Many of that group had never been on a working ranch before, and here they saw one at its best.

When D retired at the age of seventy, Mamie called me one day with considerable anxiety, asking if I could get D interested in the Museum at Texas Tech University. Still vigorous, he was like a caged lion after moving from the ranch to Lubbock. He needed something to challenge his brilliant mind and physical energy. He was historically minded, and that was the kind of volunteer we needed. A short time later, Texas Tech University President Grover Murray appointed a committee to ascertain if it was feasible to obtain and restore an authentic ranch headquarters as an outdoor exhibit for the museum. D accepted a place on that committee, and this was the beginning of a new epoch in his life. What a valuable person he was! This project became almost as dear to him as the Pitchfork Ranch. We traveled tens of thousands of miles together, searching for the various units that were to eventuate in the Ranching Heritage Center.

D was a vital factor in selecting, obtaining, moving, and restoring the El Capote Cabin, the Martin Hedwig's Hill Double Log Cabin, the Matador Dugout, the Matador office, and the Slaughter Box and Strip House. He was solely responsible for the Matador Office and the Pitchfork Corrals. In regard to the latter, the materials were delivered on the grounds by Tom Simmons and Jim Humphreys. The construction was done by D Burns, then in his eighty-first year, with two hands as helpers, in the hottest days of June, 1976. It was a job by a master builder, and the corral will endure for a hundred years.

The last eleven years, until he became ill, were among the happiest of D's life.

Let us engage for a moment in a bit of fantasy. We can imagine D in Glory today, hunkering by a mesquite campfire, drinking coffee, and surrounded by people he has loved and idolized: his brother John, whom he adored, his grandfather Columbus, his other grandfather Crockett Cardwell, his mother and father, and Dan Gardner,

Clifford Jones, Dick Arnett, Coy Drennan, Joe B. Matthews, Howard Hampton, Frank Ford, and on and on. His friends were many. What a glorious roundup that could be!

(The following prepared to give at the cemetery in Lamesa, Texas)

Several years ago while traveling across country, D and I were talking about some of the serious aspects of life. He summed up his life in one sentence: "I was born in the ranching business, grew up in it, went broke in it, and now am back in it."

The matter of death was mentioned. D said that it held no qualms for him. When his time came, he wanted it to be without fluster or confusion.

As to his going, a few lines by that great English poet, Lord Tennyson, could have been penned especially for him. You have heard them before.

> Sunset and evening star,
>   And one clear call for me!
> And may there be no moaning of the bar,
>   When I put out to sea.

> But such a tide as moving seems asleep,
>   Too full for sound and foam,
> When that which drew from out the boundless deep
>   Turns again home.

That's the way D did it. He just slipped away. Without fear, remorse, or regret.

Now we commit him to the earth and the land he loved, beside the two children whom he held dear.

To him we must now say: Farewell, good-bye, adios, and, hopefully, *hasta la vista,* which in English means "until we meet again."

Curry Holden
October 11, 1977

Afterwords

Being reared on a large West Texas cattle ranch like the one I knew is a thing of the past. Today trucks and helicopters have replaced cattle drives, horses, and men. Taking two thousand yearlings cross-country twenty miles to the railroad, which I did as a twelve-year-old, is something I'll never see again and never forget.

My grandparents, D and Mamie Burns, will also never be forgotten. You'll never find a man with more honesty, integrity, or a larger love of the land than my granddad. There is no telling how many cattle he has sold over the phone. When the bulls, heifers, or steers showed up, you had exactly what you ordered. What more can you ask of a cowman?

Mamie too gave us values that we will live with forever. She wanted me to be as rugged as a cowboy but have the manners of a lamb and the vocabulary of a scholar. She taught me to appreciate birds, flowers, and all the things nature can provide. I hope I have retained some portion of these traits and can pass them on to my children.

Mamie spent some thirty years and at least as many typists compiling these stories about the Pitchfork. Any napkin, match-book, or scrap of toilet tissue in the Big House might carry a sentence, a word, or a thought that she would jot down as she went through her daily routine. Her bed would be covered with these scraps, plus index cards and papers she had written, rewritten, torn up, and written again. Only a small corner of the bed stacked with pillows and Mamie herself could be seen. No one dared touch a scrap of that paper lest her filing system be completely destroyed.

Mamie's fascination with both people and words gave her a special ability to tell an interesting story. Many a colorful character came through those Pitchfork gates, and Mamie tagged them one by one. From the men who helped with the chickens to the owner of the largest ranch, she had a story about them. If she didn't, no problem. She could take a particular characteristic and just make a

story up. I can't think of another person who better fits the old saying, "She never let the truth get in the way of a good story."

Many special people on the Forks made the characters in these
stories possible, made West Texas a better place to live, and made
my life better for knowing them. I can name here just a few: first of
all, Baba and Mamie. Their epitaph reads, "They never left a herd
on a dark night," and they lived this saying wholeheartedly. I owe
thanks to the Gates and Eugene Williams families, whose support
and kindness offered Anne and me a great place to live and grow
up, and to Jim and Bernice, who were there as long as I can remember. And I thank all these others, who helped us in every way: Coy
and Bessie, the Vinsons, Billy George and Charlene, "Slug" Mayo,
Tom Thornton, Chalma Reid, "Prairie Dog" Martin, Jack Gocher,
"Suckerod" Osborne, "Colonel" Merrick, the Tommie Smith family, Bill and Bobby Allen, the Olivers, John and Mabel, the Austins, and the Myerses. Baba, Mamie, Anne, and I will always remember you. I'll close with something I wrote about Mamie.

Mamie at the Pearly Gates

Can you see Mamie's entrance in Heaven
With a Pitchfork in her hand?
Not the kind with the pointed spikes,
But the kind the boys use when they brand.

They'll all be gathered to greet her.
There'll be Mommie and Gagoo and Gang;
There'll be Baba, Unkie, and Old Mister, too.
She'll arrive with her usual bang.

She'll be dancing like days long forgotten,
Arthritis a problem no more;
With everyone present, a can-can or two,
The envy of all on the floor.

Then Jesus will make his appearance,
Hands held low with an olive branch.
She'll bow down and say in her most solemn tone,
"Mrs. D Burns, of the Pitchfork Ranch."

Burns Hamilton
September, 1985

Anyone who has ever known Mamie knows she was a "larger-than-life" personality, the kind of person you always remember, even on casual acquaintance. My grandfather Baba, in his quieter way, was the same. They would top any list of unforgettable characters.

Life with Mamie was interesting, exciting, sometimes tempestuous, but never dull. The thing I cherish most about her was her great love for and loyalty to me. She always stood by me, right or wrong. Baba was my rock. He was always there when I needed him. The word that comes to mind when I think of him is respect; he was a man of his word. Together, they made quite a mark on the lives of many, and if their lives can be measured by the caliber of their friends, theirs was truly a success.

I am happy that Mamie could write their story, for it should be captured for posterity, and only Mamie could have done it so well. She wouldn't have approved of anyone else's version, anyway!

Mamie and Baba left us with a sense of values and a sense of love. Perhaps the best summation of their lives are the words inscribed on their shared gravestone, "They never left a herd on a dark night."

I write this with love and many happy memories.

Anne Hamilton Fabian
September, 1985